BISON
BOOKS

Portrait of Yellow Smoke (Shu'denazi), taken in 1883 when he was 75 years old. Photograph by Roland Bonaparte, courtesy of the Smithsonian Institution National Anthropological Archives.

Blessing for a Long Time

The Sacred Pole of the Omaha Tribe

ROBIN RIDINGTON, *text*

and

DENNIS HASTINGS (IN'ASKA),

illustrations and documentation

University of Nebraska Press

Lincoln and London

∞

First Bison Books printing: 2000
Most recent printing indicated
by the last digit below:
10 9 8 7 6 5 4 3 2 1
Library of Congress Cataloging-
in-Publication Data
Ridington, Robin
Blessing for a long time:
the sacred pole of the Omaha Tribe /
Robin Ridington and Dennis Hastings.
p.   cm.
Includes bibliographical
references and index.
ISBN 0-8032-3925-4 (cl: alk. paper)
ISBN 0-8032-8981-2 (pa: alk. paper)
1. Sacred Pole (Omaha rite)
2. Omaha Indians—Religion.
3. Omaha Indians—History.
4. Omaha Indians—Material culture.
I. Hastings, Dennis.   II. Title.
E99.04R53   1997
299'.74—dc21   97-6558   CIP

And this thing ain't no plaything here
It's blessed.
When you come in this arena
come in the right mind.
None of this other stuff in you—
trying to say something.
You come in with the right mind
and you're going to get blessing
for a long time to come.

From an interview with Clifford Wolfe Sr.
155th Annual Tribal Pow-wow
Macy, Nebraska
August 28–September 1, 1985
(Recorded by Robin and Jillian Ridington)

Contents

Illustrations

Foreword

In the middle of the last century, Onba'hebe (Half-Day), known later by the anglicized name of Solomon Grant, admonished his fellow Omahas to continue their prayers of gratitude to Wakon'da for their then bountiful existence, to hold in reverence and awe their unique tribal organization of clans, societies, and ceremonies, and to remember with wisdom and respect those events, both good and otherwise, which had shaped their religion and culture. Interestingly enough, this kindly orator of another time was not a chief, or a headman of a clan or society, or a religious leader of any consequence. Rather, this son-in-law of the renowned Big Elk who lived to be over ninety years of age was the historian of the Omaha tribe until his death in June 1886.

How fitting that a century later the Omaha people again have produced, in Dennis Hastings, an individual whose personal labors on behalf of his people have earned him an honored place among those who have served the Omaha tribe through the years. In the face of massive indifference and often open hostility, Dennis Hastings has initiated and accomplished so much for so many with so little recognition for himself. In this connection, receiving little or no commendation represents his usual style, inasmuch as he has worked with and consistently promoted others to the forefront in a myriad of Omaha Historical Projects that have as their goals the preservation or the actual renaissance of various elements of the Omaha culture.

I believe it appropriate and just that Dennis Hastings, whose family comes from the Washa'be itazhi subdivision of the Tha'tada clan, receives the acclaim that is due him as a consequence of his monumental efforts on behalf of the Omaha Tribe of Nebraska and its present and future membership. Rarely has one individual made such a difference, and I call attention to and publicly applaud that difference.

Paul E. Brill

Acknowledgments: All My Relations

In many contemporary Native American communities, it is a sign of respect to mark one's movement in and out of a ceremonial space with the phrase "All My Relations." Saying these words is a way of recognizing that you are supported by a circle of friends and helpers. Writing a book about the Sacred Pole of the Omaha tribe requires the utmost respect. Bringing this book into being has also required a circle of friends and helpers, both within and outside of the Omaha tribe. As a sign of my appreciation and respect, I begin this book with an acknowledgment of the people who helped me tell the story and end it with a tribute to the generations who will continue to share their lives with the Sacred Pole of the Omaha tribe.

First of all, I could not have begun to do this work without the inspiration and animation of my Omaha brother, Dennis Hastings. Dennis and I together wish to thank and honor Umon'hon'ti himself, the Venerable Man of the Omaha tribe, whose wisdom extends beyond the vision of a single generation. Among the Omahas of this generation, we particularly want to thank Doran and Vivian Morris, Edward Cline, members of the tribal council, and directors of the Omaha Tribal Historical Project. Elsie Morris, who translated Omaha prayers into English, her daughters, Wynema and Pri, and Wynema's son, Neil Benalli, also gave us support and good Omaha hospitality during the times Jillian Ridington and I were on the reservation. We also owe thanks to Pauline Tindall for telling us about the Blue Spot women, to Mabel Hamilton, and to Marguerite La Flesche for introducing us to Maggie Johnson and Helen Grant Walker. Thanks especially to Genevieve P. Robinson for making available the compilation of information from thirty-nine Omaha elders that her husband, the late Victor V. Robinson Sr., wrote in 1982. James (Quanah) Parker and Clifford Wolfe Jr. gave us support and encouragement as the manuscript neared completion. Tribal elders who contributed their wisdom to our project, but have since passed away, include Clifford Wolfe Sr. and Lawrence Gilpin, familiar voices at the annual tribal pow-wow, and Alfred Gilpin, "Uncle Buddy," whose remarkable prayers and invocations will long be part of Omaha oral history.

We thank the following non-Omahas who helped make this book possible: Roger Welsch, for his long devotion to Omaha ways; Alice Fletcher's biographer, Joan Mark; former Peabody Museum curator Ian Brown (now director of the Alabama Museum of Natural History); archivist Anne Diffendal; photographer Ilka Hartmann; ethnomusicologist Dorothy Sara Lee; University of Nebraska State Museum curator Tom Myers; John Wunder, director of the Center for Great Plains Studies; and Hugh Genoways, former director of the University of Nebraska State Museum. Thanks to the late Gary Galante for recognizing the Sacred White Buffalo Hide among the holdings of the Heye Museum of the American Indian and for bringing together documents leading to her repatriation. His information revealed to Dennis and me the tale of mystery and intrigue we tell in chapter 7. His knowledge of and devotion to Plains Indian spiritual traditions will long be remembered. Thanks to Regna Darnell and Larry Zimmerman for their careful reading of the manuscript and for their support of its approach to Native American poetics. Thanks also to Jarold Ramsey and Michael Elliott for bringing to my attention some unpublished texts by Francis La Flesche. We join with the entire Omaha tribe in thanking genealogist Paul Brill for his tireless and comprehensive documentation of Omaha family names and histories.

I want to thank Jillian Ridington who has been my partner in discovering the wisdom and generosity of the Omaha tribe and a supportive friend to my brother, Dennis Hastings. She read the book as it emerged, edited and reedited it with an eye to grace as well as grammar, and saw an entirety where I saw only bits and pieces. Thanks also to Dr. Zogo and Ms. Nyckeija for their contributions to the conversation. During the time I worked on this book, I lost both my parents. I particularly appreciate the fact that my mother, Edith Farr Ridington, took an intelligent interest in my work with the Omahas in the last summers of her life, those of 1990 and 1991, when Jillian and I went back and forth from being with her to being with the Omahas. Finally, I am eternally grateful to the Social Sciences and Humanities Research Council of Canada for understanding the importance of this project and making it possible for Dennis and me to document these important events in Native American history. A release-time grant from my teaching position at the University of British Columbia in 1990–91 allowed me to maintain contact with the Omahas during the time that the Sacred Pole and White Buffalo Hide came back to the tribe. A subsequent SSHRC research grant has supported the work Dennis Hastings is doing to further research on Omaha tribal history. Without this generous SSHRC support, it would have been impossible to document the events that we describe in the book. Dennis also wishes to thank Ms. Glenn C. Fuller, whose generosity at a critical moment was important to the success of his work with the Omaha Tribal Historical Project. Thanks also to the National Anthropological Archives, the National Museum of the American Indian, the Peabody Museum, and the Nebraska State Historical Society for permission to use photographs and documents in their possession.

It has been a privilege to know Umon'hon'ti and, through him, the Omaha tribe. It has been a particular privilege to work with such a steadfast and remarkable servant of Omaha tradition as Dennis Hastings. Dennis credits his grandmother Mary Burt Hastings with starting him on the path of discovering what it is to be Omaha. Throughout the difficult years of separation from his people in government school and during service with the U.S. Marine Corps, Dennis held onto a sense of purpose. He came back to Indian ways as a public affairs representative for the liberation of Alcatraz in 1970. Following that experience, he returned to the reservation in Macy, Nebraska, to begin work as a tribal historian.

When people ask me what Dennis does, I say he is an "animateur." He gets things done and he makes sure that others fulfill the roles they are capable of performing. His calling is very much like that of his Bear clan ancestors, who acted as servers and prompters in ceremonies conducted by priests of the Hon'ga or Leader clan. Thanks, brother, for calling me in 1984 and telling me that in order to write about the Omaha tribe I should be there in person. That admonition was also a generous invitation. The rest, as they say, is history.

Robin Ridington

Introduction: A Circle of Stories

Aho Inshta'thunda, Hon'gashenu ti agathon kahon.

Ho Inshta'thunda, Sky people; Hon'gashenu, Earth people, I greet
you as both sides of a single house joined here together as one people.

This book is a circle of stories from the life of Umon'hon'ti, the "Real
Omaha," and his companion, Tethon'ha, the Sacred White Buffalo Hide. In
English Umon'hon'ti is known as the Sacred Pole of the Omaha tribe. In
times past he was called the "Venerable Man." He is a physical object, a cottonwood pole—but he is also a person with a life of his own. His life centered
the lives of the Omahas after they moved from a homeland in the Ohio Valley
to their present location on the Missouri River several hundred years ago. He
served to symbolize the tribe's unity at a time when they were moving from
one place to another. He continued to stand for their tribal identity during
the good times when they controlled the trade up and down the Missouri
River. He was with the Omahas through years of war and epidemic disease.
He accompanied them on the great tribal buffalo hunts of the eighteenth and
nineteenth centuries. For a century, he was cared for by the Peabody Museum of Harvard University. In 1989 he returned to tribal hands. *Blessing for
a Long Time* tells the braided stories of his life as an emblem of Omaha identity.

Indian stories do not begin and end like the lines of words that make up a
book. Rather, they start and stop at meaningful points within a circle. Stories, songs, and ceremonies constitute a body of tribal literature, passed
down from generation to generation. Omaha tribal historian Dennis Hastings and I are writing a book, but we are also telling a story that connects to
the tribe's body of knowledge. We will try to stop at meaningful points in the
story and start again as one story suggests another. Each story suggests every
other story. Each story contains an essence shared by all. Each story is both a
fragment and an entirety. Indian stories are like holographic images—break

1. *Circle of tipis surrounding a lodge at Macy, Nebraska, in 1917. Photograph by Anna Sloan, courtesy of the Smithsonian Institution National Anthropological Archives.*

them apart, and each piece still expresses the whole of which it is a part; walk around one and you will see how it appears to change but actually remains the same. You may learn from such an experience. It is you who have changed, not the object you saw from different points of view. Like a moment of experience within the story of a person's life, a story in the life of an Indian people is constantly taking on new meanings, as the context within which you understand it widens. The stories Indian people learn as children take on new and different meanings as they experience them in the wider context of vision quests and ceremonies. It may take a lifetime to put all the stories together. There is no beginning and there is no end, but there is a common center.

When the Omahas were forced to abandon their buffalo-hunting way of life in the 1870s, elders of the tribe were uncertain about how they could continue to honor Umon'hon'ti. They were told that, to avoid being forcibly removed to "Indian Territory," they would have to adopt the ways of the Americans under whose laws and jurisdiction they now found themselves. They were under extraordinary pressure to abandon their old religious traditions in favor of Christianity and to give up tribal ownership of land for allotments to individual families.

In 1888 a young Omaha man named Francis La Flesche approached the Sacred Pole's last keeper, Shu'denazi (Robert Morris, Smoked Yellow, or Yellow Smoke), with a proposal. The name Shu'denazi is actually a title; it refers to the keeper as being smoked with age like the Pole himself. Victor V. Robinson Sr. gives Yellow Smoke's Hon'ga (Leader) clan name as Mon'cho'non'be, "Two Grizzlies" (Robinson 1982, 84). La Flesche was the son of an Omaha woman, Ton'inthin (Tainne or Elizabeth Esau), and In-shta'maza (Iron Eye or Joseph La Flesche), himself the son of a French-Canadian trader and a Ponca woman. Iron Eye had been adopted into the We'zhinshte (Elk) clan, which allowed Francis to use the name Zhongaxe (Woodworker). Francis was one of the first Native Americans to become a professional ethnographer. He began his ethnographic work as a translator for linguist James Owen Dorsey between 1878 and 1880. Later he collaborated in producing written descriptions of Omaha culture with Alice Cunningham Fletcher, a researcher and writer from Harvard's Peabody Museum. By 1911, when their great work *The Omaha Tribe* appeared as the Twenty-Seventh Annual Report of the Bureau of American Ethnology, he had become Fletcher's coauthor. La Flesche reports his conversation with Yellow Smoke as follows:

"Why don't you send the 'Venerable Man' to some eastern city where he could dwell in a great brick house instead of a ragged tent?" A smile crept over the face of the chieftain as he softly whistled a tune and tapped the ground with his pipe stick before he replied, while I sat breathlessly awaiting the answer, for I greatly desired the preservation of this ancient and unique relic. The pipe had cooled and he proceeded to clean it. He blew through it now and then as he gave me this answer: "My son, I have thought about this myself but no one whom I could trust has hitherto approached me upon this subject. I shall think about it, and will give you a definite answer when I see you again." The next time I was at his house he conducted me to the Sacred Tent and delivered to me the Pole and its belongings. This was the first time that it was purposely touched by anyone outside of its hereditary keepers. (Fletcher and La Flesche 1911, 248–49)

So it was that in 1888, Umon'hon'ti came into the care and keeping of the Peabody Museum. In 1988, a century later, Omaha hands once again touched their Sacred Pole. Omaha Tribal Chairman Doran Morris (Tehu'xthabi), who is Yellow Smoke's great-great-grandson according to the Omaha system of reckoning kinship, and Edward Cline, a former tribal chairman, wept as they held Umon'hon'ti and prayed over him in a little courtyard outside the Peabody Museum. They wept because of the break in ceremonial order caused by his long absence from his people. They wept as Yellow Smoke had wept more than a century before when a boy named Francis La Flesche nearly ran down the Pole with his father's horses. They wept for the Pole's century of confinement. They wept for joy at his release. And they wept to see him refreshed by sun and wind after so many years within the walls of the "great brick house." The following year, they brought him back to the Omaha tribal pow-wow arena in Macy, Nebraska. They brought him back in the hope that his return to the tribal circle would bring all his relations a "blessing for a long time to come."

Generations of white colonizers and their descendants have predicted that Native Americans were a "vanishing race." Alice Fletcher not only believed that Omaha culture was vanishing; she actively campaigned to replace it with what she considered to be a superior Christian "civilization." But as the five hundredth anniversary of the Columbus voyage recedes into history, aboriginal people are still a vital presence in this land. They survive as communities of relations. They survive in ceremonies and prayers. They survive in the gifts they give to honor one another. They survive as dancers and singers. They survive in the stories they tell of one another's lives. They survive when they conclude a sweat or ceremony by saying, "All my relations." They survive in cities and on reservations. They survive as nations. They survive.

In writing about Omaha ceremonies and oratory, I have tried to adopt some of the genre conventions that characterize Native American poetics. One such feature is studied repetition, an adaptation of which may be seen in the preceding paragraph. Similarly, when Omaha elder Lawrence Gilpin prayed to honor the return of Umon'hon'ti, he punctuated his message with the repeated phrase Dadeho, Wakon'da Xube, "Father, Most Holy Spirit Above." When Wakon'monthin, the Sacred White Buffalo Hide's last keeper, sang the Hide's narrative ritual of nineteen songs, he repeated lines within songs and sang many of the songs four times over, as the ritual order prescribed. Other songs in the narrative were repetitions of ones that had gone before, thus taking on additional meanings through their return to a different place in the story. Songs, prayers, and ceremonies often repeat key words and phrases to create a feeling of renewal and to suggest the return of something familiar in a new setting. Important texts in the story of Umon'hon'ti's life will return in a similar way as you read this book.

Native American ceremonial language embodies what anthropologist Edward Hall called "high context messages." By this he meant that understanding a particular text depends on the listener's already knowing a good deal of what it means from the context of shared knowledge and experience. The nineteen songs that make up the ritual of the White Buffalo Hide, for instance, make sense to traditional Omaha listeners who share the common experience of having just participated in the annual buffalo hunt. Repetition thus serves to emphasize key elements and bring them into focus. Rather than being redundant, a repeated song line or story episode creates additional meaning. In writing about Omaha ceremonial traditions, I have sometimes chosen to repeat key passages from Omaha ethnography in more than one context in order to create a sense of familiarity with the characters and their stories. Encountering the same passages more than once may help the reader realize a sense of shared authorship.

Native American narratives do not simply begin in one place and move toward a definitive ending. Rather, they take up positions in an ongoing circle of creation and recreation. Each time an important text or image appears in a different context, it marks a new beginning. The new context has a reflexive relationship to the original text. Its original meaning is enhanced by its renewed appearance elsewhere. Particularly when presenting information from the personal narratives or key translations of Francis La Flesche, I have brought back passages into successive episodes of the story to serve as keynotes. I have presented as a personal narrative some of what I know about Omaha history in the context of how I came to know it.

Like *The Omaha Tribe*, *Blessing for a Long Time* is also the result of collaboration between an Omaha ethnographer and an outsider. I am privileged to share the task of documenting the return of Umon'hon'ti with Dennis Hastings, an Omaha who is an anthropologist and historian. Dennis's Omaha name is In'aska, which refers to the white substance that is left on a holy fireplace after its use in ceremony. Dennis currently directs the Omaha Tribal Historical Project, a nonprofit body that coordinates research in support of Omaha language, culture, and history. With Dennis's assistance, I have been able to document speeches, conversations, prayers, letters, and recollections that tell the story of Umon'hon'ti's return. Many of these texts are reproduced here in their entirety so that the reader may follow the story in the actual words of those who made it happen.

LANGUAGE, VOICE, AND ETHNOGRAPHIC AUTHORITY

In parts of this book I have chosen to give the information published by Dorsey or Fletcher and La Flesche in a narrative form so as to make the tribe's past more easily available to outsiders, as well as to the generation of Omahas who are experiencing the Sacred Pole and his traditions for the first time. In describing the buffalo hunt and the Pole's renewal ceremony, for instance, I use the present tense to give the reader a sense of the immediacy and vitality these events had for the people who experienced them. I have been much assisted in this task by the immediacy and vitality of the Sacred Pole himself. From the first moment I set eyes on Umon'hon'ti in the Peabody Museum in

1962, my experience of him directed me to look for ways of touching the events of his past life. As a physical presence from days gone by, he invited me to read the old ethnography as a description of events that really happened. He invited me to think about the Omaha tribe and its history. He invited me to touch the life that continues from those distant times into our own and beyond.

Wherever possible, I have passed on the words of contemporary Omahas from recorded speeches and interviews. The Sacred Pole has chosen to come back to Omahas living a century later than the ones he last knew. Omahas continue to be articulate, although not yet of one voice, in their response to him. He has come back to them as an elder who has been away for a long time. Like their ancestors who held varying opinions about the events they were experiencing, this generation has responded to the Pole's return to the life of the tribe in a variety of ways. Like Dorsey before me, I discovered denial as well as affirmation of information in the written record. I have tried to do justice to the complexity of Omaha opinion.

In the 1880s there were differences of opinion among Omahas who spoke to the first anthropologists. Dorsey's publications are famous for the honesty with which he presents the conflicting perspectives of different informants. The books are full of statements like "Two Crows denies this," "Frank La Flesche denied this," or "These were disputed by La Flesche and Two Crows." However, such inconsistencies are found in documenting any living tradition. Where Dorsey freely reports differences of opinion about tribal organization, Fletcher and La Flesche sometimes present an unrealistic homogeneity of opinion. Differences of opinion continue to be heard among the present generation of Omahas. Now as then each family and clan passes on information about the tribe's past from its own perspective. Each one looks toward a common center from its own particular direction.

When the tribe camped together in their camp circle, the *hu'thuga*, each clan had its assigned place in the circle. Each one viewed the tents of the Sacred Pole and the White Buffalo Hide from that position. Each was assigned a special place in the ceremonies that pertained to the tribe as a whole. Indeed, the fundamental idea that defines the Omahas as a tribe is the union of different but complementary points of view. In a speech to the tribe in 1988, I quoted Fletcher and La Flesche, who said, "When an orator addressed the people of the tribe he did not say *Ho! Omaha!* but *Ho! Inshta'thunda, Hon'gashenu ti agathon kahon!*," which means "Ho! Sky people, Earth people, both sides of the house" (1911, 138).

All contemporary Omahas revere the Sacred Pole and look to him with awe and respect, but some are concerned that the traditional ceremonies for keeping him are no longer known. Some contemporary Omahas feel that the

Pole should not have been returned at all in the absence of knowledge about the ancient songs and ceremonies. Others trust that the Pole will not blame them for a situation that is beyond their control. They are convinced that to have allowed him to remain in the Peabody much longer would have been disrespectful. Some people remember old factional disputes within the tribe and reject the information that was recorded by Fletcher and La Flesche because of their role in imposing allotment of reservation land upon an unwilling majority. Others say that La Flesche was not an Omaha because his father was adopted rather than born into the Elk clan, thus making Francis only an adopted member of the tribe. Because Omaha clan membership passes through the father's line, the fact that his mother was a full-blooded Omaha would not have any bearing on his clan. Some have internalized the reformers' teachings and believe that bringing back the Sacred Pole is a return to paganism.

Despite all of these qualifications, the fact remains that the Pole has come home and the information Dorsey and Fletcher and La Flesche recorded is often all that the present generation retains regarding songs and ceremonies long since abandoned. Certainly, what Fletcher and La Flesche say should be approached with a critical intelligence, but it makes no sense to reject their information out of hand. They were clear in stating their points of view. They generalized to emphasize the principle of complementarity. They saw male balanced by female, day by night, sky by earth. They read these relationships from the particulars of Omaha myth, ceremony, and social organization that are accepted without dispute by Omahas of all generations.

Perhaps there is also a complementarity in the striking contrast between the cultural experiences of Fletcher and La Flesche themselves. That complementarity energized their collaboration. Fletcher, whose name means "puts feathers on arrows," worked to transform Indians into Americans. La Flesche, whose name means "the feather," worked to explain the integrity of Indian culture so that Americans would change their opinion of them. Like the male Sacred Pole and the female White Buffalo Hide, Fletcher and La Flesche also brought together complementary male and female perspectives. The legacy that La Flesche has left us is an enduring and unparalleled collection of Omaha and Osage texts that document the intricacy of a Native American language of ritual and ceremony. Whatever personal compromise he may have made in order to be both an Indian and an anthropologist in his time, the texts remain.

Dennis and I have reconstructed an account of nineteenth-century Omaha ceremony from stories that Omaha elders told ethnographers of the past century and from the descriptions these ethnographers gave of their own experience. *The Omaha Tribe* contains a wealth of information, so much that it sometimes overwhelms the real story it tries to tell. In reading Fletcher and La Flesche, I tried to discover how the information they convey fits together into a circle of stories. I also looked at the language they used to represent Omaha customs and ceremonies of the nineteenth century. I found a language of description and interpretation in their work that continues to make sense in the world we inhabit now. With Dennis's guidance, I attempted to find what Fletcher and La Flesche called "a point of view as from the center," from which to understand the Venerable Man, who has returned to his people after a century in the care and keeping of anthropologists.

Anthropologists kept the Sacred Pole in one of their museums. Anthropologists kept information about Omaha ceremonies in one of their books. Now that anthropologists have returned Umon'hon'ti to his home in Nebraska, it is appropriate for them to acknowledge the blessing that the information still in their keeping bestows. Dr. Ian Brown spoke on behalf of the Peabody Museum upon the occasion of the Pole's return to the tribe in 1989. He told of the blessing his institution had received from the Venerable Man:

> In the 1880s many sacred materials of the Omaha came to the "great brick house" in the East which I represent today. The Sacred Pole was one of those items. Since 1888 it has rested in the Peabody Museum, protected from the ravages of time, studied by several generations of anthropologists, but certainly, certainly not revered. Its sacred nature continued, however, because the Omaha themselves continued. Fletcher was wrong. The missionaries were wrong. And the government bureaucrats were dead wrong.

Ian Brown's remarks indicate that anthropologists have now come to realize that it is impossible to study a living object like the Sacred Pole without revering it. If the study is to continue, reverence must return. Dennis and I share the reverence and respect that Ian indicated had been missing in the way anthropologists have viewed the Sacred Pole. This book is our way of acknowledging the blessing we have received from thinking about the meaning of Omaha sacred symbols. It is our reading of a circle of stories.

Umon'hon'ti was central to the language of Omaha ceremony for hundreds of years. He was away for over a century, during which time Omahas turned to other ritual orders such as those of the Native American Church. His place in contemporary Omaha life may not emerge immediately. He is used to taking his time. While he and the tribe rest and get to know one another, it seems appropriate that Dennis and I tell the stories that are relevant to understanding what has happened so far. As Yellow Smoke told Fletcher and La Flesche, "'And the people thought' is the preamble to every change; every new acquirement, every arrangement devised to foster tribal unity and to promote tribal strength, was the outcome of thought." *Blessing for a Long Time* is our contribution to that process of thought.

Dennis has been particularly successful in tracking down a wealth of historic drawings and photographs. These comprise an incomplete but nonetheless vivid visual record of Omaha life prior to and during the years when Umon'hon'ti was in the care and keeping of anthropologists. Photographs and drawings can give us glimpses into the Omaha world during the tribe's buffalo-hunting days. They show how a photographer or artist saw things at a particular time and place. Images particularize; words generalize. Visual images have an unusual capacity to represent the past, but they are not the past. They are its artifacts, moved by time and circumstance from one world into another. They represent what was real to an artist or photographer; what that person made of his or her experience. They carry information from one time and place and deposit it elsewhere and elsewhen. Images, like tape-recorded sounds, may be thought of as actualities. They actualize both what people saw and what they looked like. A physical object like the Sacred Pole also represents the lives of people from a different era and carries information between generations. In and of themselves, though, images and physical objects actualize only what people saw in their world, not how people saw from within that world. For this kind of inner meaning, this insight, we need the subtle testimony of words.

Words are what Omaha elders gave the ethnographers who came among them in the nineteenth century. They gave them words in the Omaha language. Dorsey understood that "It is very important to attempt to settle the exact meanings of certain native words and phrases" (1894, 365). Fletcher tried "to make as far as possible the native his own interpreter" (1911, 30). Francis La Flesche was a speaker of both Omaha and English. He translated spoken Omaha into written English. With the assistance of Alice Fletcher, he found an anthropological style of writing into which to translate what he knew of the Omaha world. Now, almost a century later, the Omaha tribe has asked me to take these words and breathe them back to the place where Omaha people are living.

Fletcher and La Flesche wrote about the Omahas in an ethnographic style that came out of nineteenth-century experimentation, even though their book did not appear until 1911. They wrote as members of a pioneering generation for whom there was no established canon dictating the "correct" method of documenting Native American ways or representing them to outsiders. They allowed themselves to be guided by Omaha categories rather than by those of an emergent academic discipline. They were educated by the task at hand rather than by an academic institution. The generation that followed them reversed their focus from the Indian world to that of the academy. Many of them valued the university programs they were founding above an abiding personal interest in the lives of Native Americans.

In the years immediately following the publication of the Twenty-seventh Annual Report, anthropology experienced a radical reorganization in thought and practice. University training came to be an essential prerequisite for fieldwork. Anthropologists began to search for the scientific "objectivity" that they envied in the physical sciences. As they began to train students and grant graduate degrees in anthropology, they rejected the philosophically sensitive work of authors like Fletcher and La Flesche as "subjective" and "unprofessional." *The Omaha Tribe* appeared at a time when a generation of newly self-important professional anthropologists was already prepared to reject it as old-fashioned. According to Joan Mark, Alice Fletcher's biographer, Fletcher "found herself facing an unsympathetic generation of younger anthropologists, many of them connected with Columbia University, who were eager to assert themselves and disavow the mistakes of their elders" (1988, 337). A highly negative review of their book by Robert Lowie, for instance, "criticized them for classifying the material in accord with 'aboriginal' rather than 'scientific' logic" (1988, 338).

Anthropologists have now come full circle; once again we appreciate the language and interpretation of nineteenth-century ethnography. We have become aware that anthropological representation requires more than the repetition of ethnographic facts. We know that the information we place upon the page is constructed and contextualized jointly by ourselves and by the people who are our sources. Ethnographic description is generally recognized now as being inherently interpretive. We have come to realize that the ultimate ethnographic instrument is human, not mechanical. True objectivity requires understanding and interpretation. An ethnography that denies its own interpretive instrumentality risks becoming, itself, uncritically subjective.

As I took some of the words and interpretations of Fletcher and La Flesche from the pages of the Twenty-seventh Annual Report of the Bureau of American Ethnology and placed them between the covers of the book you are reading, I came to realize that the world of anthropology has changed as dramatically in the last hundred years as has the world of the Omahas. The world of literate communication has also changed. Educated people probably now read and write less (or at least less well) than they did a century ago. Certainly they read and write differently from their ancestors. To the best of my ability, I will use the writing of Fletcher and La Flesche and their predecessors in a way that is true to the Indian way of telling a circle of stories.

In order to make the story of Umon'hon'ti complete, I will tell about the tribe's survival during the difficult years following the buffalo's disappearance. I will tell about the spirit of renewal that is strong among Omahas of the present generation. Contemporary Omahas are thinking about ceremonies and institutions that existed only in memory or on the pages of dusty books for nearly a century. Despite the repeated predictions by generations of non-Indians that the Omahas were a vanishing tribe, they continue to be strong in their ways. Umon'hon'ti has chosen to be among his people once again. He has already brought about blessings to the tribe, not the least of which is their cooperation with the University of Nebraska to study and then rebury the remains of more than a hundred Omahas from the village of Ton'wontonga; the university had been holding the remains for fifty years. Dennis and I have been honored to witness and support the Pole's return, the return of the Sacred White Buffalo Hide, and the reburial of these ancient ones. We are witnesses and we are also scribes. Dennis has been a faithful servant of the process, following the traditional work done by the Bear clan, of which he is a member. This book is a record of what we have learned.

Information about traditional Omaha ceremonies has not changed in the years since 1884 or 1911, but North American culture has changed considerably. The world in which the Omahas now live is quite different from the world of buffalo hunting and fur trading that passed out of existence more than a century ago. Then, the Omahas were concerned about keeping themselves together as a tribe during the course of their travels from place to place. Now, their concern is staying together as they travel through time. Dennis and I will tell the story of their responses to both these challenges. We will tell it in words and also in visual images, drawings, and photographs.

We greet you as both sides of a single house joined here together as one people.

CHAPTER ONE

They Come Back to See Us

The presence of the Pole was regarded at all times as of vital importance. "It held the tribe together; without it the people might scatter," was the common expression as to the purpose and needed presence of the Pole.

Fletcher and La Flesche (1911, 229)

The presence of these articles was regarded at all times as of vital importance, it held the tribe together. Without it the people might scatter. Hence, the United States Government broke the backs of the people by carrying away illegally the Omaha Tribe's sacred articles.

Victor V. Robinson Sr. (1982, 84)

The sacred objects that gave their ancestors strength and guidance for so many years have now returned to Omahas of the late twentieth century. The Sacred Pole, the White Buffalo Hide, and their beautiful catlinite pipes are once again reunited. Now the tribe is seeking to recover the spirit of unity that was so deeply wounded during years of oppression at the hands of a government bent on Americanizing Indians by eliminating every vestige of Indianness. Omahas are looking for ways to rediscover their old traditions and make them relevant to present-day experience. To assist in these efforts, Dennis Hastings and I have studied written and visual accounts of the tribe's past.

In particular, we have sought to understand the great ceremonies that held the clans together during the eighteenth and nineteenth centuries, when Omahas were adapting to changing conditions. We have also participated in and documented the tribe's recent repatriation of its sacred objects. This book is a report of our studies and our experiences. We have tried to communicate the insight we have gained from our reading of the old texts as well as to understand the meaning of contemporary events. The book is also our re-

2. *Doran L. Morris and Edward Cline receiving Umon'hon'ti from Joseph Johns at the Peabody Museum of Harvard University, June 27, 1988. Photograph by Hillel Burger, courtesy of the Peabody Museum, Harvard University.*

2

sponse to a request from tribal leaders to present information about the past in a way that will help Omahas today understand their peoples' history. We hope that it will also give those who have not had direct contact with Native American traditions a chance to experience some of their richness and beauty.

The Omahas are fortunate among Native Americans in being connected to physical objects that have survived, as the people have survived, from the distant past. Most important among these are Umon'hon'ti, the Sacred Pole of the Omaha tribe, and his companion tribal emblem Tethon'ha, the Sacred White Buffalo Hide. Each is accompanied by a distinctive catlinite pipe. In times of tribal ceremony the two sacred objects and their pipes occupied sacred tents at the center of the camp circle, the *hu'thuga*. Following the return of Umon'hon'ti in June 1989, the Omahas began negotiating with the National Museum of the American Indian for the return of his companion, Tethon'ha. In the summer of 1991 the Hide, too, came back into Omaha hands. With that transfer, a chapter in the tribe's history came full circle.

The life of Umon'hon'ti spans many generations. He knew the Omahas who first came west to the Missouri River. He was with them when the Poncas and Omahas were still one people. He knew the earth-lodge villages they made along the Missouri river's fertile bottom lands. He knew their camp circle, the *hu'thuga*. He knew the buffalo who gave them life. He sorrowed with the Omahas when they experienced epidemic diseases and raids from enemies. He was with them during those times, and he continued to be a presence in their thoughts during the time he rested in the keeping of anthropologists at the Peabody Museum of Harvard University.

Along the way, Umon'hon'ti entered the stories of many people's lives. The Reverend James Owen Dorsey wrote about him in 1884 and 1894 in the Third and Eleventh Annual Reports of the Bureau of Ethnology (later renamed the Bureau of American Ethnology and known by readers of its classic ethnographies as "the BAE"). Alice Cunningham Fletcher and Francis La Flesche wrote down stories they knew about him from their own experience and from the accounts of tribal elders. They published a wealth of information in another BAE volume, the Twenty-seventh Annual Report. They called this book *The Omaha Tribe*.

TO SAVE THE INDIAN FROM HIMSELF

The last two decades of the nineteenth century were very difficult times for the Omahas, as they were for most Native American tribes. In 1882 Interior Secretary Henry M. Teller wrote to the commissioner of Indian affairs authorizing him to institute "courts of Indian offenses" designed to eradicate all indigenous cultural practices that he felt would hinder the process of Americanizing the Indians. He wrote, "If it is the purpose of the Government to civilize the Indians, they must be compelled to desist from the savage and barbarous practices that are calculated to continue them in savagery, no matter what exterior influences are brought to bear on them" (Prucha 1973, 295–96). In particular, Teller singled out "the old heathenish dances, such as the sun-dance, scalp-dance" for eradication. The Sacred Pole, of course, not only stood for the unity of a clan-based form of government, but was also adorned with a scalplock, suggesting to men like Teller a "heathenish hindrance to civilization."

On the secretary's orders in 1883, the commissioner of Indian affairs directed his agents to set up a system of tribal courts and judges to rule upon all questions presented to it for consideration by the agent. "Specific jurisdiction was granted over the dances objected to by Teller, polygamous marriages, interference of the medicine men with the civilization program, thefts and destruction of property, intoxication and the liquor traffic, and misdemeanors" (Prucha 1976, 209). The courts were specifically designed to promote "civilization" and suppress aboriginal religion and government. In 1892 the rules were strengthened to require "that if an Indian refuses or neglects to adopt the habits of industry, or to engage in civilized pursuits of employments, but habitually spends his time in idleness and loafing, he shall be deemed a vagrant and guilty of a misdemeanor" (Morgan 1892, 30, cited in Prucha 1976, 211). As Indian Commissioner Merrill E. Gates loftily put it in 1885, "Indian chiefs are never law-makers, seldom even in the rudest sense law-enforcers. The councils where the chief is chosen are too often blast-furnaces of anarchy, liquefying whatever forms of order may have established themselves under a predecessor" (Gates 1885, cited in Prucha 1973, 46–47). The institutions of tribal organization and the collective holding of reservation land, he wrote, "must go if we would save the Indian from himself."

Omaha keepers of sacred objects must have been particularly distressed at the government's direct assault on the traditions they considered to be most holy. Removing the sacred objects from Omaha hands was part of a deliberate attempt by non-Indians to destroy the tribal unity they represented, and to replace it with Christianity and nineteenth-century American individualism. Some of the sacred objects, such as the pipes kept by particular clans and families, were simply kept hidden from the police. Those associated with public tribal ceremonies, though, were exposed and more vulnerable. While it is probable that La Flesche consulted Yellow Smoke about removing the Pole from his "ragged tent" to a "great brick house in the East," the context of that conversation was clearly oppressive.

Omahas today consistently maintain that La Flesche took the Sacred Pole without permission. Fletcher and La Flesche themselves admit that "influences were brought to bear on the chiefs and their keepers" (1911, 222) to

4

prevent the keepers from taking their sacred objects with them to their graves. Removing sacred objects from the reservation and redefining them as objects of scientific inquiry supported an overall government program designed to take away the power they continued to have as representations of Omaha identity. Fletcher and La Flesche were clearly instruments of the Indian commissioner's plan to "save the Indian from himself," but La Flesche must have experienced enormous inner conflict at being an Indian while "saving the Indian" through removing the tribe's most sacred symbols from the control of their legitimate keepers. He, and other Indians who had received a "Christian education," were often held up as examples of Indians who had been successfully, if forcibly, "saved" from their own cultures and traditions.

However conflicted La Flesche may have been about his position as a redeemed Indian, the work he did during the darkest days of assimilationist pressure has given contemporary Omahas information about the tribe's ceremonial life that would otherwise have been lost. Most of what has been written about the ceremonies that once honored Umon'hon'ti comes from what knowledgeable people in the 1880s told J. Owen Dorsey, Alice Fletcher, and Francis La Flesche. La Flesche, himself, was witness as a young man to the Pole's renewal ceremony. The elders told as much of what they knew as they thought proper to make known to outsiders. They told Francis La Flesche what an Omaha boy taking part in the buffalo hunt needed to know. Later they spoke to him in his role as Omaha ethnographer. They told Dorsey, a missionary turned linguist, the meaning of words relating to their sacred traditions. They told Alice Fletcher what she needed to know to discover what she termed "a point of view as from the center" from which to understand the tribe's ceremonies. Elders told anthropologists the information that they thought should be written down for the coming generations.

More recently (around 1980), the late Victor V. Robinson, of the Hon'ga clan, interviewed thirty-nine Omaha elders in order to preserve their knowledge about clans in relation to traditional Omaha government. He began his book, *The Hu'thuga* (Tribal Circle), with a lament for the loss of family and clan traditions caused by enforced assimilation:

> In the late 1800s the United States Government came up with a solution to civilize the Omahas by sending the young Indian members off to school for an education. These young members were sent away without the consent of their families. During that time the family really had no choice but to go along with the Government. Some children were kept away for as long as twelve years. While in school they were forbidden to speak the Omaha language or to practice the responsibility of their Clans. From then on the Omahas continued to urge

and send their children away for an education without realizing the neglect they were creating in not preserving Omaha history and passing it on to the upcoming generations. (Robinson 1982, 1–2)

Robinson goes on to describe how the government "appointed new tribal leaders called 'Paper Chiefs,' whose only purpose was to cede lands to the United States Government." These Paper Chiefs, he said, "did not represent the Clans nor the people of the Omaha tribe." The real government was a council of clan leaders who came together as "the outcome of prayer, visions and visitation." Each of the clan leaders belonged to a family that was *nini'baton*, that is, authorized to possess a pipe. "Among the Omaha tribe the pipe was regarded as a medium by which the breath of a man ascended to Wakon'da" (Robinson 1982, 12). None of the elders Robinson interviewed, however, had been alive when the Sacred Pole was still among the people. The information he presents about the Pole is taken directly from Fletcher and La Flesche.

People today still tell stories about how Umon'hon'ti was taken from them. Old stories are being rediscovered. New ones are being created. The Venerable Man, as he is sometimes called, continues to lead a truly storied life. Omahas today are thinking once again about the symbols and ceremonies that enriched the lives of their ancestors. Like their ancestors of a hundred years ago, they are collaborating with scholars and scholarly institutions to care for and interpret the treasures of their past. This book is the result of one such collaboration.

AN AGE OF DISCOVERY

In 1879 the Smithsonian Institution established the Bureau of Ethnology to collect information about the languages, arts, and cultures of Native Americans, then believed by non-Native Americans to be disappearing as distinct cultural entities. The bureau's founder and first director was Major John Wesley Powell. He knew that the Reverend James Owen Dorsey had done missionary work with the Poncas between 1871 and 1873 and had learned to speak Ponca, a Siouan language very closely related to Omaha. When illness forced Dorsey to return east in 1873, Powell signed him on as an employee of the new bureau. Although Dorsey never said so in as many words, his contact with Ponca language and thought subtly shifted his focus from teaching Christianity to being a student of Indian religion. When Powell asked him to conduct linguistic and ethnographic work with the Omahas in 1878, Dorsey leaped at the opportunity. A flavor of his respect for Native American language and religion may be seen in his comparison of the words that the English and Ponca languages use to categorize the supernatural.

In considering the subject from an Indian's point of view, one must avoid speaking of the supernatural as distinguished from the natural. It is safer to divide phenomena as they appear to the Indian mind into the human and the superhuman, as many, if not most, natural phenomena are mysterious to the Indian. Nay, even man himself may become mysterious by fasting, prayer, and vision. One fruitful source of error has been a misunderstanding of Indian terms and phrases. It is very important to attempt to settle the exact meanings of certain native words and phrases ere we proceed further with consideration of the subject. (1894, 365)

While native people today would probably choose to describe nature as powerful and worthy of respect rather than "mysterious," as Dorsey did, his respect for native spiritual traditions places him beyond the chauvinism and racism that dominated the views held by many of his contemporaries. Dorsey lived on the Omaha reservation from 1878 to 1880. In describing his field-work technique, Dorsey later wrote that he had "learned by experience that it is safer to let the Indian tell his own story in his own words than to endeavor to question him in such a manner as to reveal what answers are desired or expected" (1894, 365). He obtained much of his information with the assistance of Frank (Francis) La Flesche, then a young man.

Francis had been educated in English at the Presbyterian Mission School on the reservation. He described his experiences there in a 1900 autobiographical book, *The Middle Five*. He had also experienced the tribe's last buffalo hunts and had once been sent out as a runner to locate the herd. He was also given the ceremonial role of *hunga*, or sacred child, in the great peace ceremony of Wa'wan. Being literate in English and fluent in Omaha, La Flesche was a perfect guide for Dorsey in his study of Omaha language, culture, and philosophy. The work La Flesche did with Dorsey also proved to be an ideal apprenticeship in what was to be his life's work as an ethnographer. Dorsey found in La Flesche a skilled and sensitive interpreter of Omaha terms and concepts. He wrote, "I have had many opportunities of testing his skill as an interpreter, and I did not find him wanting" (Dorsey 1890, 2). Dorsey's most important reports on Omaha culture were *Omaha Sociology* (1884) and *A Study of Siouan Cults* (1894). In both of these publications, Dorsey drew extensively from information provided by Omaha informants. Like other good ethnographies, the books are as much his informants' as they are his. Dorsey left the Omaha reservation in 1880, but continued his work through correspondence and meetings with Omahas in Washington until his death in 1895 at the age of forty-seven (Barnes 1984, 11).

Alice Fletcher met Francis La Flesche briefly in 1879 when he and his sister Susette (Bright Eyes) accompanied Chief Standing Bear of the Poncas

7

and the journalist Thomas Henry Tibbles on an eastern lecture tour to pro-
test the government's forcible removal of the Poncas from Dakota Territory
to Indian Territory, now the state of Oklahoma (Mark 1988, 38). Eastern reformers took up the cause of the Poncas, but looked to assimilation and the
individual allotment of reservation land as the best means of avoiding removal. Francis probably made little impression on Fletcher during that trip.
His role was largely that of translator and chaperon to his sister. For Fletcher,
meeting Standing Bear and the Omahas turned out to be a pivotal event that
would change her life. She determined then that she would "go and live
among the Indians" to learn about "Indian family life, the role of women,
and the relation between the sexes" (Mark 1988, 39, 65). Two years later she
convinced Tibbles and Susette La Flesche, who had married, to take her to
the Omahas, and then beyond to the Rosebud Sioux reservation.

The trip east with Standing Bear was equally pivotal for young Francis.
He was introduced to Senator Samuel J. Kirkwood of Iowa, who in 1881, as
secretary of the interior, offered him a position as clerk in the Indian Bureau
(Barnes 1984, 17). Kirkwood was then advocating that Congress pass a bill
that would break up collectively held reservation land and allot it to individual Indians. Whatever he may have thought of the idea, Francis was obviously beholden to the senator for his employment and was obliged to carry
out the bureau's policies that were increasingly aimed at assimilating Indians
into the American melting pot through education. At the age of twenty-four,
La Flesche moved from the Omaha reservation to Washington. His next
meeting with Fletcher took place there, following her return from an amazing and arduous expedition to the Rosebud Sioux reservation and a subsequent winter among the Omahas. During the spring of 1882 they met frequently, often with other ethnographers of the new Bureau of Ethnology.
Joan Mark, Fletcher's biographer, points out that their work as an ethnographic team really began that winter in Washington (1988, 78).

During the spring of 1882, Fletcher's work turned from ethnography to politics. With the support of Francis's father, Joseph La Flesche (Inshta'maza),
(who represented a minority opinion among the Omahas), Fletcher began to
lobby Congress in favor of Senator Kirkwood's proposed legislation that would
break up reservation land into individual allotments, an objective she honestly
but mistakenly thought would benefit individual Omahas by removing them
from what she considered to be a "primitive" tribalism. She was aware that there
were two parties in the tribe, "one desirous of civilization, one that clings to the
past." In her opinion, those of the first group were "the true leaders among the
people" (Mark 1988, 70). Thus, she worked hard to support the group she considered to be the "progressives."

8

3. Alice C. Fletcher in her garden. Photograph courtesy of the Smithsonian Institution National Anthropological Archives.

Her efforts on behalf of the progressives resulted in the Omaha Severalty Act of 1882, which provided "that each Omaha man, woman, and child was to be given a portion of the tribal land" (Mark 1988, 76). Her work on Omaha allotment was later instrumental in bringing about the General Allotment Act of 1887 (known more generally as the Dawes Act for its sponsor, Senator Henry L. Dawes of Massachusetts). In fact, Fletcher played a key part in discussions that led to the act and was one of its strongest advocates. The Dawes Act directed Congress away from its previous policy of removing whole tribes to Indian Territory and toward a policy of assimilation and "privatization" of Indian lands on a national scale. She consulted with La Flesche often during the "long, and for a time single-handed campaign" in the spring of 1882 (Mark 1988, 75).

The following year, 1883, the commissioner of Indian affairs appointed Fletcher as a special agent to carry out the Omaha allotment. He assigned Francis La Flesche to be her interpreter. Fletcher arrived at the Omaha reservation in May of that year. Their difficult and often unhappy allotment work required going against the wishes of the well-organized "Council Fire" group, which wished to retain tribal land ownership as set out in a treaty the tribe had signed in 1854. At first Francis worked as Fletcher's clerk and interpreter, but their relationship deepened when she became seriously ill and he nursed her back to health.

Along with their allotment work, Fletcher and La Flesche began to collaborate in collecting information about the tribe's history and ceremonies. Together, they began to invent a style of ethnography based on an uneasy combination of documenting traditional culture and enforcing its replacement by what Fletcher, at least, considered to be the inevitable and progressive blessings of Western "civilization." Omahas today look back on Fletcher's allotment work as an instrument of oppression and loss. They remember the 1880s as a time when the Tent of War, the Sacred Pole, the White Buffalo Hide, and other religious objects and their ceremonies were stolen from them. They are correct in identifying Fletcher and La Flesche as being responsible for these objects leaving tribal control. In documenting Omaha tradition, Fletcher and La Flesche also worked to suppress it. A key to their work was the transformation of sacred objects into ethnological specimens.

In June 1884 Fletcher wrote to Peabody Museum Director F. W. Putnam regarding their first acquisition of sacred objects from the tribe, the contents of the Omaha Tent of War:

> My Dear Prof. Putnam,
> It is with peculiar pleasure that I convey to you the intelligence of the presentation to the Peabody Museum for preservation the entire belongings of one of the sacred tents of the Omaha Tribe. These articles are yielded to you by the descendants of the hereditary chief of the tribe, the Elk family, and presented through Mr. Frank La Flesche and myself.
> The articles were the peculiar care of the We-jin-ste gens, the family of the hereditary chief—always of that gens—having charge of them. These possessions indicated the family's rank so to speak and the articles were used to confer honors for valiant deeds. They were never absent from the tribe and when the people moved out on the yearly round were carried with peculiar rites and care. In their presence warriors passed through certain ceremonies before leaving for war and when the tribe was pressed to defensive warfare, and the chief must lead, these articles were taken with him to battle.

The sacred shell, the two ceremonial war pipes, the staffs and other articles, some of them as yet unknown to me, are included in this presentation. As far as I know it is the first time a people have parted peaceably with such peculiar sacred symbolic signs of authority. The peculiar position of the people toward their past growing of the loss of the sacred ritual together with the growth of a progressive spirit foretold by their changed environment, have contributed to make this unique action possible and I would that it might find its meeting place in history. The act marks a firmness in stepping forth toward an unknown and inevitable future, wherein the Indian must be merged in the American, that indicates a people of more than ordinary gifts of character.

To us these relics may appear strange and some of them forbidding. But are they really more so than other relics which speak of warfare? They show another aspect of war as yet unidentified. The Indian warrior prepared for death. His traditions and his honor forbade his doing other than death to another or himself. The chances were generally even, and thinking of that and of the inner meaning of the ancient rites so far as yet revealed, one looks with more than antiquarian interest upon these articles, and in contemplating their removal from the family of the hereditary chief of the tribe, one feels respect for the historical significance of the transfer.

Today, as the old man has carefully guarded in a place set apart these articles during the recent years of change, one cannot but wish that his aspect, his tone, his word, might linger about this ancient trust. In a low voice he said:

These sacred things have been in my family for many generations. No one knows how long. My sons have chosen a different path from that of their fathers. I had thought to have these things buried with me but if you desire to care for them and place them where my children may look upon them when they wish to think of the past way their fathers walked, you can do so.

Should there come a time when I crave to look once more on that which has been with my fathers, I would like to be permitted to do so. I know that the members of my family are willing I should do this thing and no others have a right to question my action, though there are men in the tribe who will say hard things to me because of this act.

It was late in the afternoon when we reached his lodge. The sun had set. The old man was sitting alone outside. He had gathered the articles and was taking a last look at them in the fading light. On our arrival he led the way to where he had placed them and lifted them into the wagon with quick haste. "They are all there!" he said and turned away bereft of his life trust. We too turned left, as the round moon rose with a sudden surprise over the valley.

Sincerely yours,

A. C. Fletcher

(Fletcher to Putnam, June 6, 1884, Peabody Museum Papers)

In their 1911 ethnography, Fletcher and La Flesche repeated the keeper's words as Fletcher gave them to Putnam in 1884. They went on to say, "This act of Mon'hinthinge (Fredwin Tyndall) drew a sharp line that marked the close of a chapter in Omaha history. It is fitting that the name of one who was brave enough to draw that line should be remembered with honor and sympathy for his courageous act" (454).

Omahas today insist that their sacred objects were stolen and treated with disrespect. "Men in the tribe" continue to "say hard things . . . because of this act." It is true that the Peabody Museum opened the sacred bundles and put them on public display. In this, they violated the trust Mon'hinthinge placed in them. But Fletcher's letter documenting the transfer also gives room to suppose that a complex negotiation was taking place. While there is no question that she exercised authority as a government agent, her letters to Putnam indicate a respect for the "inner meaning" of ceremonies such as those related to the Tent of War. Considering the virulent opposition by whites at the time to anything having to do with Indian warfare, Fletcher chose to question whether these objects are really more forbidding "than other relics which speak of warfare." Now that the sacred objects have come back into Omaha hands, the words of Mon'hinthinge take on heightened meaning. Because of the transfer, it is possible for his descendants to "look upon them when they wish to think of the past way their fathers walked."

The environment in which Fletcher and La Flesche worked was charged with an inherent contradiction. Reformers in the 1880s admired Native American culture as it had existed in the past, yet worked tirelessly to suppress it in the present. It is hard for many of us today to imagine the unquestioning certitude that white Americans had in the superiority of Christianity, western civilization and "progress." While superficially well-meaning and benevolent, the reformers had no qualms about using coercion to impose their notion of progress on aboriginal people. Prucha described their policy aims as "Americanization of the Indians":

> [The] main lines of Indian policy reform converged in one ultimate goal: the total Americanization of the Indians. All were aimed at destroying Indianness, in whatever form it persisted. The aim was to do away with tribalism, with communal ownership of land, with the con-

centration of Indians on reservations, with the segregation of the Indians from association with good white citizens, with Indian cultural patterns, with native languages, with Indian religious rites and practices—in short, with anything that deviated from the norms of civilization practiced and proclaimed by the white reformers themselves. (Prucha 1973, 7–8)

In 1875 the Board of Indian Commissioners reported that "the true policy in dealing with the Indian race, as with every other, for the purpose of elevating them to the social and moral conditions of Christian civilization, consists not so much in feeding or governing the *adults* as in educating the *children*" (Prucha 1976, 269). In 1883 Congress set up "Courts of Indian Offenses" which eventually included "dances etc., plural or polygamous marriages, practices of medicine men, destroying property of other Indians, immorality, intoxication, and a variety of misdemeanors" (Morgan 1892, 28–32, in Prucha 1973, 300–5).

Francis La Flesche had experienced both Omaha and Christian education directly. He was fluent in both traditions, but not entirely at home in either. Perhaps it was his very marginality that made him such a sensitive translator of philosophical concepts from one culture to another. His life's work may be understood as an attempt to bring the two worlds together. As Garrick Bailey points out in a book on La Flesche's later studies of Osage ritual texts, "He wanted his readers to see the world of the Osages for what it was in reality—not the world of simple 'children of nature' but a highly complex world reflecting an intellectual tradition as sophisticated and imaginative as any Old World people" (Bailey 1995, 3). La Flesche began *The Middle Five* with the following revealing statement:

> As the object of this book is to reveal the true nature and character of the Indian boy, I have chosen to write the story of my school-fellows rather than that of my other boy friends who knew only the aboriginal life. I have made this choice not because the influences of the school alter the qualities of the boys, but that they might appear under conditions and in an attire familiar to the reader. The paint, feathers, robes, and other articles that make up the dress of the Indian, are marks of savagery to the European, and he who wears them, however appropriate or significant they might be to himself, finds it difficult to lay claim to a share in common human nature. (La Flesche 1963, originally published in 1900, xv)

La Flesche devoted his life to documenting how aboriginal traditions can hold their own against those of white Americans. Perhaps his references to "a common human nature" were an attempt to bridge the gap between cultures.

Because his position as a bureau employee precluded any overt political resistance to western hegemony, he turned to the task of proving unequivocally that Indian traditions were as complex as those of any other people. His contribution to the book he and Alice Fletcher coauthored was critical to its success. He not only understood Omaha ceremonial traditions in their own terms; he was also able to translate them into terms that made sense to a reader in English. The book he and Fletcher produced together is graced with his detailed translations of ritual texts and the sensitive language of his interpretation.

FRIENDS OF THE INDIAN

While La Flesche worked to demonstrate that an Indian could be as good as a white man, Fletcher poured her energies into demonstrating that a woman could be as good as, if not better than, a man in the dual tasks of documenting aboriginal culture and replacing it with civilization. Fletcher's work as an agent of civilization can only be understood by reference to her involvement with a group of reformers known as "Friends of the Indian." Beginning in 1883, she began attending a series of conferences at which eastern cultural and political leaders interested in "the Indian question" met at a resort hotel in Lake Mohonk, New York, owned by Albert Smiley, a Quaker philanthropist (Mark 1988, 103; Prucha 1973, 5). (As a personal aside, I was amazed to learn during the course of writing this book that my Quaker grandfather Edward Lincoln Farr spent his honeymoon at Lake Mohonk in the summer of 1885.) There, Fletcher was praised for being different from Bureau of Ethnology scientists like John Wesley Powell and (later) James Mooney, whom the reformers suspected of encouraging Indian culture simply in order to study it. Philip C. Garrett spoke out passionately on her behalf, saying that with the "brilliant exception" of Alice Fletcher, "the scientific desire to preserve the Indian animal for study is . . . a further impediment to his civilization." In praising her, he said that "her philanthropy swallowed up her anthropology" (Garrett 1886, cited in Prucha 1973, 59).

What to the Lake Mohonk reformers was philanthropy, we would now describe as a well-intentioned, but hopelessly ethnocentric, form of cultural imperialism. It is important to remember, though, that our experience is so different from that of people in the late nineteenth century that it would be presumptuous to stigmatize their opinions and world view with our labels. We can appreciate, however, that Omahas remember the oppression of those times and continue to grieve for the culture that was stolen from them. It seems unlikely that Fletcher could have imagined that a hundred years after the Pole's going to the Peabody Museum, Omahas would once again be looking to their sacred objects with respect and the anticipation of renewed blessing. She could not have known that more than a century after her unhappy allotment work, "the Indian" would continue to resist being "merged in the American."

In the years leading up to the Pole's transfer to the Peabody Museum in 1888, Fletcher was increasingly determined that Indians should abandon traditional dwellings and establish themselves in single-family western-style frame houses. Indeed, Joseph La Flesche was already building such houses in a settlement his Omaha contemporaries called "the village of the make-believe whitemen" (Fletcher and La Flesche 1911, 633). Evidently, she felt that the Pole should make a similar change of residence. The traditional Omaha earth-lodge homes accommodated large extended families, some of which included polygynous marriages. Joseph La Flesche himself at one point had three wives. The first wife was Mary Gale, a mixed blood like himself. The second was Francis's mother, Tainne (Elizabeth Esau), an Omaha, and a third was a young Omaha woman with whom he had no children. La Flesche came under pressure for polygyny from Presbyterian missionaries, and in 1872, after the birth of Tainne's third child, Carrie, he removed Tainne and his third wife from his official family, thus repudiating his Indian side in favor of the part that was white.

Joseph's rejection of Tainne must have been very difficult for Francis, who was then in his midteens. Joan Mark suggests that "the removal had a powerful effect on his life" (1988, 151). While his father moved toward the white world, his mother was forced to fall back on her Omaha relatives for support. "Emotionally and defensively," Mark writes, "he was drawn to the old ways his mother represented." After Tainne died on April 24, 1883, his connection to the part of him that was Omaha became increasingly realized through his work as an ethnographer (1988, 149). At the same time, he began to accept Fletcher's wish that he look on her as a stepmother.

Fletcher seems to have supported Joseph's move toward monogamy, but she also struggled to understand the complexity of the Omaha extended family system. She commented in a letter to F. W. Putnam, her mentor and the director of the Peabody Museum, that "the family relation is very hard for a white person to understand without imposing his own heredity and trained thought upon it. I've worked hard at that and have some times succeeded in twisting [my] mind to the Indian view" (Mark 1988, 65–66). Whether or not she succeeded in so "twisting" her mind regarding Omaha family life, she had no doubt that the younger generation, like Francis, would have to adopt new ways.

Fletcher was convinced that "progress" could be achieved by sending Indian children to institutions such as Captain Richard Henry Pratt's recently established Carlisle Indian School in Pennsylvania. "The end to be gained,"

Pratt wrote Senator Henry Dawes, "is the complete civilization of the Indian . . . [and] the sooner all tribal relations are broken up; the sooner the Indian loses all his Indian ways, even his language, the better it will be" (Pratt 1964, 266). Omahas were reminded of Pratt's beliefs in 1991 when the National Museum of the American Indian returned the Sacred White Buffalo Hide to them. In speaking to the tribe, museum director Richard West, himself a Southern Cheyenne, reminded them that Pratt had even gone so far as to assert that "all the Indian there is in the race should be dead. Kill the Indian, save the man" (Pratt as cited by Richard West August 3, 1991). It was in this climate of opinion that Fletcher worked to ensure that Indian children (and by extension all her Omaha "children") adopted a Euro-American rather than an Indian way of life upon return from schools in the East. Joan Mark writes, "The message that Alice Fletcher preached was that the Omahas could completely change their way of life. They could be born again, as white people, if they put their minds to it and trusted God and Fletcher, who was at work for them in Washington. She urged a version of the Protestant ethic on the Omahas, like the motto of the Carlisle Indian School, 'God helps those who help themselves'" (Mark 1988, 124).

Fletcher proposed "that a fund be started for Indian home building" in order that returning students "would be an example of civilized living among their own people" (Mark 1988, 105). While the idea failed because the recipients of funds regarded them more often as gifts than as loans, Fletcher did not abandon the grand principle of assimilation around which all her activities turned. She even seems to have used Francis in an attempt to assimilate the Sacred Pole itself. It is startling to recall what Francis says he told Yellow Smoke in 1888, since the words sound so much like those of Fletcher: "Why don't you send the 'Venerable Man' to some eastern city where he could dwell in a great brick house instead of a ragged tent?" Like the returning students, the Sacred Pole should be assimilated by taking up residence in an American institution. The words reflect Fletcher's strange combination of respect for Indian culture and her missionary zeal to replace it. She wanted to confine and transform the Sacred Pole in her own institution, in the same way that the children of Omaha elders were to be transformed by attending schools in the East. Even the Sacred Pole, she seems to imply, could become a "make-believe white man," by becoming an ethnological specimen.

In 1888, the same year that the Sacred Pole left Yellow Smoke's hands, Fletcher published a 693-page special report for the U.S. Bureau of Education entitled *Indian Education and Civilization* (Dippie 1982, 170). It clearly reinforced the belief that only through a combination of education and the eradication of traditional culture could Indians be brought up to the lofty level of civilized white Americans. Following her attempt to establish housing for returning students, Fletcher directed her energies to the larger issue of land allotment, arguing that "under no circumstances should land be patented to a tribe. The principle is wrong." Joan Mark wryly comments that through Fletcher's efforts, "paternalism, or rather a fierce form of Victorian maternalism, came to hold sway in the United States Indian policy of the 1880s" (1988, 106).

Fletcher's commitment to using the power of government to force allotment seems to have caused her to place the Indians she knew as contemporaries in the 1880s into a different category from those she revered as having a complex and beautiful form of government. As Joan Mark puts it, "In their old way of life [Indians] were adults—they worked, they worshipped, they governed themselves—but in the new way of life which was unfamiliar to them they were children, not knowing what to do" (1988, 107). If Omahas were children, then Fletcher was more than willing to be the mother who knew better than they did what was best for them. The Omahas, of course, never thought of themselves as children or of Alice Fletcher as their mother. She clearly projected her fantasy on them, and they either resisted or simply ignored it.

Both Alice and Francis were very much products of their times, each one coming to the ethnographic work they undertook together by the energy of opposite and sometimes fiercely competing cultural forces. Their respective roles in removing the Sacred Pole may derive from equally different motivations. While Fletcher certainly believed that the sacred objects were an impediment to progress, La Flesche seems to have been more interested in preserving them in order to demonstrate that Indian religion was complex and beautiful and not the delusion of childlike savages. Perhaps it was in this spirit that La Flesche approached Yellow Smoke in 1888.

During the years when these influences were being brought to bear on the keepers of Omaha sacred tradition, the personal relationship between Fletcher and La Flesche also deepened. When the Omaha allotment was completed in 1884 and La Flesche returned to Washington, he moved into the same residential hotel as Fletcher. Gradually, their relationship shifted from collaboration to adoptive kinship. La Flesche began referring to Fletcher as "Mother," and in 1891 she informally adopted him as her son. For the next fifteen years, he shared a house in Washington with Alice and her companion, Jane Gay (Mark 1988).

The professional and personal relationship between Alice and Francis was complex. As their work together intensified, it became obvious, first to him and then to her, that he was a partner rather than simply a son, an interpreter, or an informant. The matter came to a head with her plans to publish a substantial paper entitled "A Study of Omaha Indian Music." Francis, himself an accomplished Omaha singer and the source of much of her information, managed to convince his adopted mother that his part in the work should be recognized in print. In 1892 she wrote to Putnam, "I find that Francis has a great deal of feeling concerning the recognition of his share in the work involved in this monograph . . . He wants his name to appear on the title page . . . 'aided by Francis La Flesche'" (Mark 1988, 216). By the time of their most comprehensive publication, *The Omaha Tribe*, in 1911, Francis had achieved the status of coauthor.

Francis was fluent in Omaha and Fletcher relied on him entirely for translations of Omaha texts. Some of their most sensitive insights appear in this context, and it is clear that the portrait they drew of Omaha philosophy relied entirely on his insider's knowledge. Through the material La Flesche contributed to their joint work he seems to have expressed his resistance to what might have been an oppressive situation. While the surface language may be that of Fletcher, the crucial language of translation comes from La Flesche. The quality of his insight can be seen in the extensive translations of Osage ceremonial texts he went on to do after Fletcher's death in 1923.

The book Fletcher and La Flesche produced is very much the result of their joint thinking about the meaning of Omaha philosophy, as well as the result of shared ethnographic work. It is 650 pages long. For the most part it has gathered dust on library shelves since it appeared in 1911, although the recent two-volume Bison edition makes it more readily available. The authors believed when they wrote the Twenty-seventh Annual Report that the Omaha tribe would soon disappear into the American melting pot. As a result, they attempted to document everything they knew about the tribe. They were wrong about the tribe's assimilation, but were correct in the careful documentation they undertook. Fletcher probably drafted a good deal of the actual text, but the book very much depends upon the insider's knowledge of Omaha language, culture, and thought that only La Flesche could supply. Fletcher addressed the question of shared authorship in the book's foreword. What she describes is a compelling example of what is now referred to as "shared ethnographic authority."

The following presentation of the customs, ceremonies, and beliefs of the Omaha is a joint work. For more than twenty-five years the writer has had as collaborator Mr. Francis La Flesche, the son of Joseph La Flesche, former principal chief of the tribe. In his boyhood Mr. La Flesche enjoyed the opportunity of witnessing some of the ceremonies herein described. Later these were explained to him by his father and by the old men who were the keepers of these ancient rites and rituals. Possessed of a good memory and having had awakened in his mind the desire to preserve in written form the history of his people as it was known to them, their music, the poetry of their rituals, and the meaning of their social and religious ceremonies, Mr. La Flesche early in his career determined to perfect himself in English and to gather the rapidly vanishing lore of the tribe, in order to carry out his cherished purpose.

This joint work embodies the results of unusual opportunities to get close to the thoughts that underlie the ceremonies and customs of the Omaha tribe, and to give a fairly truthful picture of the people as they were during the early part of the last century, when most of the men on whose information this work is based were active participants in the life here described—a life that has passed away, as have those who shared in it and made its history possible. (1911, 30)

Despite fine words such as those quoted above, most Omahas today are certain that Fletcher and La Flesche stole the Sacred Pole, or at least obtained it through coercion. The late Victor V. Robinson Sr. wrote in 1982, "The Omaha members who were interviewed say that they [the Sacred Pole, Tent of War, and White Buffalo Hide] were stolen along with some other sacred packs, and the family of the man who stole the sacred contents from the tribe received royalties, a reward from the United States government" (Robinson 1982, 84). Fletcher and La Flesche themselves write:

The disposition to be made of these sacred objects, which for generations had been essential in the tribal ceremonies and expressive of the authority of the chiefs, was a serious problem for the leading men of the tribe. To destroy these sacred relics was not to be thought of, and it was finally decided that they should be buried with their keepers.

The importance of securing the objects became more and more apparent, and *influences were brought to bear on the chiefs and their keepers* to prevent the carrying out of the plan for burial. After years of labor, for which great credit must be given to the late Inshta'maza (Joseph La Flesche), former principal chief of the tribe, the sacred articles were finally secured [emphasis added]. (1911, 222)

THE SACRED POLE IN MY LIFE: A PERSONAL STORY

I first came into contact with Umon'hon'ti in January 1962, when I began graduate studies in anthropology at Harvard University. There he stood, an object shadowed in mystery, within a glass case framed in dark wood next to the anthropology department office in the Peabody Museum. I remember distinctly the sense of shock I felt at seeing sacred bundles laid open on the floor of the case. It seemed an invasion to look at them, since at one time they had been opened only in ceremony. Instead, I focused on the Sacred Pole himself. I had no idea how to interpret or relate to this object that had obviously been sacred and alive to native people from another time and place. What impressed me most was simply the Pole's physical presence. Through him I knew with certainty that a world different from my own was native to the continent in which I was born. I was certain, from the first day we met, that the Sacred Pole was an object of great power. I knew that he would have stories to tell if only he could speak. During my preparation for examination in the area of North American ethnography, I was introduced to the Twenty-seventh Annual Report. I remember devouring it in wonder at the rich and beautiful culture it revealed. I still have the pages of notes I took on that first reading.

In 1984 I read *The Omaha Tribe* again after being away from it for many years. To clarify and consolidate my thoughts about the treasures Fletcher and La Flesche made available in their book, I wrote a paper about the Sacred Pole as a central symbol of tribal identity. I sent that paper, "Mottled As by Shadows: The Life and Death of a Sacred Symbol," to Omaha tribal historian Dennis Hastings. Until I learned about Dennis from Joan Mark, I knew nothing of contemporary Omahas and recalled that Margaret Mead had described them in her introduction to *The Changing Culture of an Indian Tribe* as a "broken culture" (Mead 1965, xiii). A few weeks later, I was surprised to pick up the phone and hear the voice of Dennis Hastings inviting me to visit the tribe in the summer of 1985. In good Omaha fashion, Dennis responded to my paper on the Sacred Pole by telling me that if I wanted to write about the Omahas, I should visit them in person.

Thanks to a small grant from the University of British Columbia, I was able to attend the Omaha pow-wow that summer. When Jillian Ridington and I went to the tribal building around noon of the day we arrived and asked for Dennis, the receptionist told us he was at home asleep. That seemed strange, but we took the advantage of being on our own to drive around the rolling hills of the reservation and get our bearings. We had lunch in the little town of Homer, the site of what we later learned was the nineteenth-century Omaha "Big Village" of Ton'wontonga. Back at the tribal building in Macy, we finally met Dennis, who told us he had been up before dawn with tribal elders to bless the pow-wow arena. Dennis showed us where to set up our tent and introduced us to the late Clifford Wolfe Sr., the pow-wow master of ceremonies, and "Uncle Buddy," the late Alfred Gilpin. Then he disappeared and left us to our own devices.

The next day Dennis showed up again and asked us to tell him whom we had met and what they had told us. Then he informed me that I should ask Clifford about when it would be appropriate to introduce myself to the tribe. I had not really expected to be asked to speak in public, and when the time arrived, I gave a very short talk in which I didn't say much more than thanks to the tribe for making me welcome at their pow-wow. When I had finished, Dennis came up to me and said, "That wasn't enough. You'll have to do it again." The Omahas, I then understood, expected me to explain how my story related to theirs. Why would a university professor from Canada want to know about their lives? What might he have to offer the tribe? I resolved to wait and listen in order to prepare myself for a more successful second attempt. As we were walking around Macy the following morning, we met Clifford Wolfe, and he gave me some encouragement. He began to speak about what the pow-wow means to contemporary Omahas:

> The way the weather keeps changing, bright and that, they say, "The spirit is here." Just like old people say, "They come back to see us again." You heard it out there yesterday afternoon, you probably heard it too, that loud thunder. Then they went around, and the old people say, "Oh, they come back to see us." We can't see them but they see us. So that's the way we been told. And this thing ain't no plaything. It's blessed. When you come in this arena, come in the right mind. None of this other stuff in you, them trying to say something in here. You come in the right mind and you going to get blessing out of it for a long time to come. You come in this way and walk that way. There's tobacco laying at the entrance way. We believe in that peace pipe, way back. Anytime you want anything, on top of these big hills, that Blackbird Hill or any big hill, they talk to him and sometime they fast up there, four days and four nights, asking something for our tribe, food, clothing.
>
> Seem like it happens, I guess. The buffalo probably come in a vision. They could see him and the hunt starts. That buffalo is everything— our home, he is clothing, he is food. And that eagle, pretty mighty. We use his clothing to represent ourselves, who we are. We use his clothing, we say, his feathers. (1985)

Clifford's words made me realize that the spirits of buffalo and eagle and thunder are still important in Omaha experience. They are still sources of power for those who seek them "in the right mind." The next day I felt ready to speak to the tribe again and asked Clifford to let me know an appropriate time. When he motioned me to come up to the platform, I took the microphone gratefully and tried to explain to the tribe why I had come among them. I said that although my trip from Vancouver to Macy had only taken a few hours by air, I had really been traveling toward the Omahas since I had been touched by encountering the Sacred Pole at Harvard twenty years before. I told them that in my reading of Fletcher and La Flesche I had discovered that the Pole's old name was Waxthe'xe, which the authors said refers to "the power of motion and the power of life, the power of Wakon'da." Fletcher and La Flesche wrote that it more literally means "mottled as by shadows." Then I said:

Mottled means like a balance of light and dark. And I thought about that as I was watching this pow-wow for the last few days and I noticed how the sky changes. Sometimes it's light and sometimes it's dark, and sometimes right here in the center of this arena, there was a balance of light and dark. And then I thought about—that name (*Waxthe'xe*) also refers to a balance of people that make up this tribe, the Omaha people. There's a balance of Earth people and Sky people. And so that name seems to me to refer to something that is the life at the heart of this tribe.

And then there's one other thing that book said Waxthe'xe means, and that is, "bringing that power into view to be seen by all the people," and that's what I've seen over here for the last few days. That in the center of this arena, there's that life, the power of motion that is being brought into view to be seen by all the people, by all the Omaha people, and by all their guests and visitors. And I really count myself privileged and fortunate to be among those guests and visitors and to see this.

I wrote in my notes later:

Today, the *hu'thuga* has been replaced by the pow-wow arena in Macy, Nebraska. It is a circle of oak trees, open to the east. The circle has been created by selective cutting over the years. A flagpole stands at its center, symbolic of the ancient Sacred Pole. In this consecrated place, the tribe gathers in ceremony once a year. On a bright day, the arena appears to be "mottled as by shadows." During the five days of the 1985 pow-wow, thunder clouds rumbled in circles around the arena but the dancing was never interrupted by rain. That is what Clifford Wolfe meant when he said, "The way the weather keeps changing, bright and that, they say, 'The spirit is here.' Just like old people say."

While I was speaking, Jillian found herself chatting to an Omaha woman who was sitting next to her in the stands. She introduced herself as Marguerite La Flesche, and she said she was a grandniece of Francis La Flesche. Jillian introduced her to me and to our great surprise, she told us that there were still women alive who bear the tattooed Blue Spot or Mark of Honor, whose name is also Xthexe' (mottled as by shadows), the same root as the ancient name for the Sacred Pole. She then introduced us to Helen Grant Walker and Maggie Johnson, two women who received the Mark of Honor in the early part of this century. Mrs. Walker expressed her pride and that of the tribe when she exclaimed, "My father, he's a great great chief. He gave it away for a hundred horses," referring to the traditional "count" of a hundred gifts to the tribe that a man offered prior to initiation into the Night Blessed Society. Such membership gave him the right to have his daughter tattooed with the Mark of Honor (see chapter 5 for a description of these ceremonies). Although we were not on the Omaha reservation long enough to understand all the details of how the contemporary culture relates to the past as described by Fletcher and La Flesche, our hosts made it clear that the Omaha people have neither vanished nor assimilated.

THE COUNT OF A HUNDRED YEARS

I continued to visit the tribe and write about its traditions as represented in the ethnographic record. Gradually, the ethnographic past and contemporary reality seemed to be converging. In the late 1980s the tribal council expressed a renewed interest in reestablishing contact with the sacred objects being held by the Peabody. On March 8, 1988, at the tribal chairman's suggestion, I wrote the following letter to Dr. Carl Lamberg-Karlovsky, director of the Peabody Museum.

Dear Dr. Lamberg-Karlovsky:

I am writing to ask if you can give me some information about the current location and status of the Sacred Pole of the Omaha tribe and the associated bundles from the Sacred Tent of the Pole and the Sacred Tent of War.

My interest in these sacred objects began when I first saw them as a graduate student in anthropology at the Peabody in 1962. More recently, I renewed my interest in the Pole and in the Omaha tribe and wrote a paper entitled, "Omaha Survival: A Vanishing Indian Tribe that Would Not Vanish" for *American Indian Quarterly*. I enclose a copy of the paper for your interest.

I understand that the Pole is no longer on public display but that it is still in the museum's keeping. I have been in touch with the Omaha tribal historian, Dennis Hastings, and with Doran Morris, chairman of the Omaha Tribal Council. Mr. Morris is a great-grandson of Yellow Smoke (Shu'denazi), the last keeper of the Pole, who gave it over to the keeping of Alice Fletcher and Francis La Flesche in 1888. Mr. Morris tells me that the tribe understands that Yellow Smoke was persuaded to transfer the Pole to the Peabody for safekeeping rather than support the alternative plan of having it buried with him. My own contacts with the tribe indicate clearly that the symbolic and sacred meanings associated with the Pole are still very much alive in their contemporary lives. Fletcher and La Flesche describe the transfer as follows:

The contents of two of the Sacred Tents of the Omaha tribe have been placed for safekeeping in the Peabody Museum of Harvard University—those of the Sacred Tent of War in 1884 and the Sacred Pole with its belongings, in 1888 (See p. 411.) All these relics are unique and of ethnologic value. The disposition to be made of these sacred objects, which for generations had been essential in the tribal ceremonies and expressive of the authority of the chiefs, was a serious problem for the leading men of the tribe. To destroy these sacred relics was not to be thought of, and it was finally decided that they should be buried with their keepers.

For many years the writers had been engaged in a serious study of the tribe and it seemed a grave misfortune that these venerable objects should be buried and the full story of the tribe be forever lost, for that story was as yet but imperfectly known, and until these sacred articles, so carefully hidden from inspection, could be examined it was impossible to gain a point of view whence to study, as from the center, the ceremonies connected with these articles and their relation to the autonomy of the tribe. The importance of securing the objects became more and more apparent, and influences were brought to bear on the chiefs and their keepers to prevent the carrying out of the plan for burial. After years of labor, for which great credit must be given to the late Inshta'maza (Joseph La Flesche, fig. 49), former principal chief of the tribe, the sacred articles were finally secured. (1911, 221–22)

It is now a century since the Pole made its journey from Yellow Smoke's cabin in Macy, Nebraska to "the great brick house" in Cambridge, Massachusetts. I think anthropologists have had sufficient time to gain "a point of view whence to study, as from the center, the ceremonies connected with these articles and their relation to the autonomy of the tribe." The Omaha tribe has not vanished, as Alice Fletcher thought it must. It is not the "broken" tribe that Margaret Mead described. It has continued ceremonies that have maintained "the autonomy of the tribe."

As Fletcher and La Flesche wrote in 1911, the Pole itself is meaningful only in relation to its Sacred Story. That story is now well known, both to anthropology and among members of the tribe. When I first visited the tribe in 1985 and described in a public speech my first contact with their Sacred Pole in 1962, a young singer came up to where my wife and I were camping and told me his version of the Sacred

Story. During that same visit to the tribe, we met women bearing the "Mark of Honor," a symbol deeply rooted in language and tradition to the tribal identity carried by the Pole itself.

The Sacred Pole has now resided in the Peabody Museum for a full century. I suggest that 1988 is an appropriate time to reconsider "the disposition to be made of these sacred objects, which for generations [have] been essential in the tribal ceremonies and expressive of the authority of the chiefs."

Could you please investigate any documentation you might have about the acquisition of the Pole and let me know its current status among the Peabody's holdings. Perhaps we could correspond further about "a point of view as from the center" to accommodate both Omaha interests and those of anthropology.

Sincerely yours,
Robin Ridington
Associate Professor, UBC
(Harvard Ph.D. '68)

Dr. Lamberg-Karlovsky did not answer my letter, perhaps hoping that the whole issue would go away. I wrote him again on May 2, 1988, and was more specific about the tribe's interest in the sacred objects:

> Because of my interest in recontextualizing traditional Omaha ethnographic information, representatives of the tribe have asked me to help bring about a dialogue with the Peabody Museum in order for them to renew contact with the Sacred objects that their predecessors gave to Alice Fletcher and Francis La Flesche for safe keeping in the Peabody.

At the end of that month, I drove to Macy and met with Dennis Hastings and Doran Morris. We phoned Joan Mark, Alice Fletcher's biographer and an associate of the Peabody, asking her to help arrange for an Omaha delegation to visit the museum. After some further calls and letters, it was arranged that Doran Morris and Edward Cline would journey to the "great brick house" in Cambridge, Massachusetts. It was there that they touched the Sacred Pole on June 27, 1988, in a little courtyard outside the museum.

That year, 1988, was important to the Omahas. It had been exactly one hundred years since Yellow Smoke handed over the Sacred Pole to Francis La Flesche for safekeeping. As former tribal chairman, Edward Cline had visited the Peabody Museum in the 1970s. At that time, the Pole was on public display in a glass case on the first floor of the building. Mr. Cline was disturbed at the lack of respect such public display implied. He spoke to the museum director, Dr. Stephen Williams, about his concern. As a result of their meeting, the museum agreed to remove the Pole from public display.

Doran Morris and Edward Cline came to the Peabody on behalf of the Omaha tribe. Mr. Joe Johns, a Creek Indian artist-in-residence at the Peabody, carried the Pole to where Mr. Morris and Mr. Cline were waiting outside the building. Museum director Carl Lamberg-Karlovsky, former director Stephen Williams, and curator Ian Brown spoke on behalf of the museum. Joan Mark, Jillian Ridington, and I were there as witness to this momentous event as members of the anthropological community. Other witnesses were Native American members of the Harvard community.

The meeting was arranged by phone and neither party knew quite what to expect of the other. The ceremony they were bringing about was without precedent. Mr. Morris and Mr. Cline had spoken of the possibility of burning cedar for the Pole as part of their communication with him. The museum officials did not know whether to expect the Omahas dressed in ceremonial regalia. They were prepared for any eventuality. As it turned out, the flight bringing Mr. Morris and Mr. Cline from Omaha was delayed. When they arrived, they were dressed in the ordinary clothes they normally wore on the Omaha reservation. They had come, in Mr. Cline's words, "as simple and humble people, not as a great leader or former leader or anything like that." Their decision to come dressed as ordinary people had been intentional. It was their way of giving honor to Umon'hon'ti, the Real Omaha. He was the Venerable Man. He was the great chief. He was Washa'begle, the silhouetted chief who stands out with distinction to be seen by all the people. They were elected officials and members of Omaha families, not pipe-bearing dark or *sha'be* chiefs.

The summer of 1988 was extraordinarily hot. Already by June 27, near the beginning of "the moon when the buffaloes bellow," cornfields on the Omaha reservation were withering in the relentless heat. It was hot in Cambridge, too, but a gentle breeze made it pleasant to be outside on that day. A small group of people including reporters, anthropologists, and American Indians from the Harvard community, waited with the two Omahas outside the north entrance of the Peabody. Museum officials were still with the Pole somewhere inside the cavernous building. Ian Brown later reported that something remarkable had been happening as we waited outside. When museum staff carried the Pole into the elevator to go from the basement to ground level, the elevator suddenly refused to respond to their commands and took them back and forth between the top and bottom of the building. "I never thought we were going to get out of the elevator," he later wrote. "We went up and down for no apparent reason, before it finally lighted on the first floor." When he told me about the incident he said simply, "I don't know how to explain it. Just add it to the story."

Finally, the door to the building opened and we could see a technician carrying something wrapped in pure white cloth. With great care and reverence, Mr. Johns lifted Umon'hon'ti from these wrappings and grasped him firmly with both hands. Holding him at an angle toward the heavens, he stood at the top of a small flight of stairs for a moment of silence, during which the people assembled below looked up to the Pole in awe. It was a memorable moment. I thought of the words Alice Fletcher wrote about the day a century earlier when Yellow Smoke told the Pole's Sacred Legend: "It was a memorable day. The harvest was ended, and tall sheafs of wheat cast their shadows over the stubble fields that were once covered with buffalo grass. The past was irrevocably gone" (1911, 224).

The past that once seemed irrevocably gone now had returned and was standing before us, "to be seen by all the people as something distinctive." Slowly, Mr. Johns came down the stairs toward the two Omahas. Tears began to stream down the face of Doran Morris as his hands touched the Pole that his great-great-grandfather, Yellow Smoke, had placed in the hands of Francis La Flesche a hundred years before.

Tears have always carried important messages for the Omahas. An old man standing in the presence of death told Fletcher and La Flesche:

> Tears were made by Wakon'da
> As a relief to our human nature.
> Wakon'da made joy
> And he also made tears!
> From my earliest years
> I remember the sound of weeping.
> I have heard it all my long life
> and shall hear it until I die.
> There will be partings
> As long as man lives on the earth.
> Wakon'da has willed it to be so.
> (598)

There will always be partings. There will also be moments of return and renewal. Omaha elders used to send their children out to the hills on solitary vision quests. They sent them "to cry to Wakon'da." They sent them out to the hills and they rejoiced upon their return. They told them:

> You shall go forth to cry to Wakon'da.
> When on the hills
> You shall not ask for any particular thing.

The answer may not come as you expect.
Whatever is good.
That may Wakon'da give.

Tears have always been an Omaha way of appealing to Wakon'da. Elders told Fletcher and La Flesche that the young person's vision quest replicates the people's first appeal to Wakon'da. The person who prays to Wakon'da stands "alone in the solitary place, with clay on his head, tears falling from his eyes, and his hands lifted in supplication" (130).

Four days upon the hills shall the youths pray, crying. When they stop, they shall wipe their tears with the palms of their hands and lift their wet hands to the sky, then lay them to the earth. This was the people's first appeal to Wakon'da. (128–29)

On June 27, 1988, Doran Morris and Edward Cline shed tears as they reached out across a century of separation to renew contact with the Sacred Pole. Doran later recalled:

You remember the day we brought the Sacred Pole out of the museum there that day in the courtyard. I felt that power. I always thought that as a man I never cried. I felt sad a lot of times but when they brought that Pole out, boy it just overwhelmed me. Shivers up my spine, and I just started crying. That's what happened. And that day, any other time that elevator worked, second floor, third floor, but when they was bringing him out, it went right on, past the third floor and back down to the basement.

Theirs were the first Omaha hands to touch the Venerable Man in exactly a hundred years. Doran Morris wept as Edward Cline spoke to the people assembled in the little courtyard outside the museum:

I'm going to say a few words to Our Creator in our Omaha language and I hope that you might forgive us. We hope in a very short time, that we can take it [the Pole] home where it belongs—among the people. This is a living tree. This is a living person—as far as we're concerned. Maybe, to some of you, it's just an old piece of wood, but the teaching . . . it was there for the People to see, to become a part of, to touch, and to be tied to it—what kept the tribe together—that's the teaching. And so, we would like to have this at home—so that our People could have the opportunity to look upon it and to maybe even—to touch it. So, I'm going to say a few short words to Our Creator on behalf of our tribal chairman and this living tree that we look upon this day.

Mr. Cline's prayer was in Omaha, the language the Venerable Man had

lived with for centuries but had not heard for a hundred years. This is what
Mr. Cline said, as translated by Elsie Morris:

Aho! Wakon'da [Most Holy Spirit].
You have created everything good.
This Umon'hon'ti.
He is a living spirit [Umon'hon'ti Ni'kie].
He has a body, the wood.
Because of him I am offering a prayer.
Dadeho [Father].
This day the chiefs [the tribal council],
The head of the Leaders [the Hon'ga clan],
My grandson, are here.
As you see him, know him.
Pity him, whatever his thoughts.
This tree has been living, standing.
Whatever his thoughts, make them possible.
Make his good thoughts possible.
Dadeho Wakon'da [Father, Most Holy Spirit].
Hopefully, all the Omahas that see him
Will have good feelings.
That is what I am praying for,
What I am asking you, Father.
The white people have taken care of him
And this day the Omaha people have welcomed him home.
He is in the center of the Omaha people.
He was to stand in the center of the Omaha people.
That was probably his thought
And you will make it possible.
The tree that was living is a living being.
They have said that for the Omaha.
I pray that good things will come our way.
I pray that you will hear these words.
I pray with your name.
My grandson here depends on you.
I pray that you will listen to him.
I hope that you will listen to us.
I hope that you will see us and pity us.
I pray for people on the council.
I pray that you make life good for them.
That is what I pray to ask you with these humble words.
Plain humble prayer!

Words that I pray to you, Dadeho.
I pray that you will make all this possible.
I pray that you see us and that you will pity us.
Aho!

Then Dr. Stephen Williams, former director of the Peabody, spoke for the museum:

I just want to say that during the ten years I was Director of the Peabody Museum that—I certainly knew of the Omaha Pole and was concerned for its preservation. Indeed, Mr. Cline was here with a group of Omaha about fifteen years ago—looked at the Pole, looked at our care of it, made some suggestions. We had it on display but removed from display because of its sacredness and respect for their concern for that. I think the trust that was placed in the Peabody Museum over a hundred years ago was what one must call an "ethical" and even almost a "sacred" trust that—it was given to us by the leadership of the Omaha tribe at that time. It was not a good time for Omahas or many Native Americans. They were concerned about whether there would be an Omaha tribe in the future. There was some suggestion that the Pole might be buried. But Francis La Flesche—Omaha—and his mentor, Alice Fletcher, asked the tribe and the keeper—if it could not be preserved—if it could not go to the museum where it would be preserved. And, Frederic Ward Putnam accepted that trust, and from the very beginning, the fact that it has been given to us in trust has been made very clear, as I pointed out to Mr. Cline and the other members of the Omaha tribe when they visited some fifteen years ago. Our concern has always been that when we relinquish that trust that we relinquish it to the right people, to the right group—and in a situation where it would, indeed, be preserved as we have preserved it for a hundred years. . . .

I—we're—I'm delighted that we have a representation from the tribe, Mr. Morris and Mr. Cline here, to discuss the possible return to the tribe, and—it's going to have to be a negotiated, or—a discussed—relationship of how it's going to go back, but I think we're anxious to enter into those negotiations with every expectation that the interest of the tribe will be served by our decision, which I trust will be that which the tribe wishes.

I hope that this kind of relationship with Native American groups around America can be continued to be interacted with by the museums who should, I think, be seen as, in many cases, the trustees of the heritage of all groups—all anthropological groups, and that—as we have a trust—we want to carry forward that trust in a good way, preserving the materials. Professor Lamberg-Karlovsky and the renovations that he's carried out during his administration has seen that the materials are properly taken care of under the proper conditions, and that the heritage of a hundred years in this old red building, as the Omaha referred to it, is that what you are asking may, indeed, come to pass—because of the Peabody Museum, and we're delighted to take part in it. Thank you.

Next, Dr. Ian Brown, Associate Curator of North American Collections, spoke about the trust relationship that anthropology has to the Pole. In the year that followed, it was Dr. Brown and Dennis Hastings who steered the museum and the tribe through what proved to be delicate, even precarious negotiations (see chapter 7).

Today is truly an honorable day. It has been over a hundred years since proper respect has been paid to the Venerable Man, the Sacred Pole of the Omaha. No object embodies so much of the soul of the Omaha. It represents the authority of their leaders, the unity between man and woman, and the binding element that has held the Omaha people together for so many centuries. Many hundreds of years ago, the Sacred Pole came to the Omaha. The layers of paint encrusted on its surface are testimony to the respect offered yearly to the Venerable Man. The last time this event occurred was in 1875—a very long time ago, but a short episode in the rich history and promising future of the Omaha. Since 1888, the Sacred Pole has rested in the Peabody, protected from the ravages of time, studied by several generations of anthropologists, but certainly not revered. Over this past century, it has failed to play the role it was meant to serve among the Omaha, but it should be emphasized that the sacred symbol of the Omaha has still survived. It is our hope that the ceremony which has occurred here today will, once again, be an annual event, and that someday, in the not-too-distant future, the ceremony will be held where it should be held— among the Omaha themselves. Thank you for coming.

When the Pole had returned to his place of repose in the museum basement, the Omahas met with museum officials in the museum's Bowditch Room for refreshments. Mr. Cline spoke again:

We come as humble people, and in comparison to us, the significance of the Pole, we don't even rate consideration with the Pole—as people. You know we look up to it and, our people at home, hopefully, will have the opportunity to regain their ties, to revitalize [the tribe].

Maybe this Pole will inspire us, will get us together so that we can talk as one person, think and do as one group of people. We have high hopes for it. . . . Doran said, "Maybe that Pole will give us strength. Maybe it will bring something to us. . . ."

The teaching is that they put food for that living person—the old ways. And, I'm sure that if you take a microscope and shave some of it off, you'll find the remains of food on there yet, that they fed that person, wanting him to continue to live. So, we feel good. We feel humble in front of it and the significance of the meaning. A hundred years it's been here and we prayed for this building. We prayed for all the other things that you have here that belong to other people that saw fit to bring them in and put them here for safekeeping. We prayed that way today. We prayed for the people who work here in this building, so we had that opportunity so we took advantage of it, and said those things to God and it makes us feel good. We can go home and tell—the chairman will report to the people that the reaction was good here, and that they support the ideas that the chairman has for the people—so we'll leave you with a good feeling in our hearts—and I just wanted to say thank you, all of you.

Mr. Cline then addressed me directly:

> Well, Dr. Ridington, you visited with us and we had a visit up at Dennis's place, and we talked about this—coming here. And you indicated that, and appreciated that the approach to the Pole would be with a sincere heart and mind, and I guess that's—as Indians—that's the way we are. Regardless of what kind of day-to-day people we are, we have a very strong feeling about the things that were meaningful to the tribe—some of the culture that still exists—very meaningful to us, and I guess the Sacred Pole, you indicated—and I hope that we've satisfied your thoughts along those lines.
>
> Before we came, we went and visited with my sister [Emily Parker], as the keeper of the good things that belong to the families and the tribe—and she was, and we—the chairman and I, and her—we sat and cried. We talked about the Pole—and you see the reaction of the chairman out there—and I hope that, as an interested person, as a trained person along the lines that we're looking at here, we're hopefully returning to our village—you've seen our village—very humble, very small, insignificant in comparison to some of the tribes across this country. But, to us, it, it was a way of life—the Pole. It was a living tree. And they went even further, and said it was a living person, according to the people that made up our tribe. They held onto it, and they done

32

things together. And I've heard our chairman say it's not that way now—we're going this way and that way. I know my sister said that to us down there.

And so, we come as simple and humble people, not as a great leader or former leader or anything like that. We come as humble people, and in comparison to us, the significance of the Pole, we don't even—we don't even rate consideration with the Pole—as people. You know, we only we look up, we look up to it and, our people at home, hopefully, will have the opportunity to regain their ties, to revitalize what was once a great group of people. . . . I think that we have, as the chairman said, many problems, and maybe this Pole will inspire us—will get us together—so that we can talk as one person. Think and do as one group of people. We have high hopes for it. The chairman does. He has great reliability on what it can do for us, and so I hope that we can realize that.

The return of our lands, he said we went to—our grandfather's town—Washington—that's what the Omaha say—grandfather's town—and we're going to talk about something that we can see and feel once again—land—that the white people have that belong to us—rightfully, and legally—our land. We've been in a federal lawsuit for fifteen years, you know, and that's not very long in comparison with some of the tribes, you know, but we've been in an active lawsuit for fifteen years, and Doran said, "Maybe that Pole will give us strength. Maybe it will bring something to us. . . ." I'm sure he's talking about land.

So, we appreciate your reaction, your interest, and on behalf of our people at home, we thank you. Each of you had some thought, some—done all of the work getting this together. We appreciate that. We couldn't, we wouldn't have been able to do anything, and so our thanks to you on behalf of the people at home. And, we have—we're anxious for this to happen. We're anxious—to send someone to take that home. And, hopefully, it will reside in the center—be the centerpiece again of our tribe—to bring good things to them. We look at the youngsters. We want them to have a good way of life. We look at the old people. We want them to have a good ending to their lives. Hopefully those all-in-between will have something good and this, this I pray someday—maybe this will help us—so, we feel good. So we say thank you on behalf of the chairman—he talk better than I can. I'm older so he expects that I will say these things. With all our hearts we thank you for being here, you know—for your participation. I know that Dr. Ridington there has very much interest in what we saw today.

I replied:

> You know, when they—when the people renewed the Pole in the old days, they selected—the seven chiefs selected a reed from a bundle of reeds that represented every man of the tribe, and then they—those people who were selected—they sent them back into each of the lodges that was in the camp circle when they were on the buffalo hunt—and the person who'd been selected would go and touch one of the poles—in one of the lodge poles—and touch it as counting coup on it—touch it, he would touch it. And that pole would then be brought by, by members of your clan to the center where they'd make a sacred lodge, and that was the beginning of the Renewal Ceremony—that's where it took place. And I see the two of you here today, as being like members of your tribe whose, whose sticks have been chosen—and you're going to go back and you're going to be touching the lodge poles of other people back home—all of the Omaha people who are interested in this—and, this is the beginning of building another sacred lodge—a sacred lodge where the tribe will continue to renew itself.

Then Doran Morris spoke:

> Well . . . I was telling the gentleman here that every three years council was elected, and I've got another year left and I've been thinking about this a long time—and, interestingly, you know . . . because my great-great grandfather was the last keeper, Yellow Smoke. I think in that way, you know, with the election coming up—the interest is going to be lost in this, you know—so, I'm going to do this within the year—take it home where it belongs—otherwise, we'll have to wait another nine years.

I replied with a story about having seen the tops of thunder clouds on the flight to Cambridge:

> When we were flying up here, we flew up from Cincinnati—via Cincinnati—and it was very, very hot, and we flew at 41,000 feet, and we flew up along a line of thunderheads, and we could see them even above us. They were even higher than 41,000 feet, and we were looking off to the side and the sun was setting on one side and the moon was almost full—a waxing moon getting bigger, but right towards full—above them, and so there was this golden glow on the clouds, and then, looking down at the bases of all the clouds, we could see they were connected to one another by these dark storm masses. And then, as it got dark, we could see that—that lightning was flashing between all the clouds. And, I've just never seen anything like that before.

34

It made me think, "Well, I'm seeing something in a very elevated and spiritual way," but it also reminded me that in the story of the Pole, the boy who found it saw it as something that was—was spiritually endowed, that was glowing, as if it was on fire, but it wasn't consumed. And when he told that story—took that story back to the chiefs, they told him, "That's the Thunder birds. That's the place where the Thunders come to rest, and they come from the four directions, and all of the animals come together at that place as well." And so I thought, that was a very good sign—to be able to look across to those Thunder Beings, when what was in my mind was the Pole and this meeting that was going to be taking place.

I gather from the ethnography—the book by Fletcher and La Flesche—that the Renewal Ceremony took place in the moon that would be the one following this full moon. It was the moon "when the buffaloes bellowe." I don't know how you say that in Omaha, but I think that would be the one that we're just coming into after this full moon.

Following the speeches, we left the Peabody and went to a Mexican restaurant with Doran, Eddie, Dr. Bette Haskins, director of Harvard's American Indian Program, and Emma Featherman-Sam, volunteer coordinator with the Job Corp's Women in Community Service program. Because the Omahas had been delayed in getting to Cambridge, they had not made hotel reservations. It turned out that accommodation in Cambridge was very expensive and almost unobtainable on short notice. Finally, Jillian noticed a listing in the yellow pages that said, "Reasonable accommodation for transients." It gave an address within walking distance. Six of us, four Indians and two white people, walked the few blocks to what looked like a haunted house on Kirkland Street. Yes, they had a room, not in this house but in another, a block away. It would be forty-five dollars a night plus a key deposit of five dollars. When we finally found the place, it turned out to be humble indeed. The lodging was a clean but otherwise bare room, a glorified flophouse. Doran and Eddie were tired and happy to have a place to lay their heads before going on to testify before Senator Daniel Inouye's committee on Indian affairs in Washington.

A few weeks after Jillian and I had returned to Vancouver, I got a call from Doran. He asked if I could give him the proper titles and addresses of Dr. Haskins and Emma Featherman-Sam. I had the information and gave it to him. Then I reminded him of the speech Eddie Cline had given after touching the Pole. I reminded him that Eddie had said they had "come as simple and humble people—not as a great leader or former leader or anything like that. We come as humble people, and in comparison to us, the significance of

the Pole, we don't even—we don't even rate consideration with the Pole."
"Maybe," I told Doran, "the Great Spirit was listening to what Eddie said.
That is why he sent you that flophouse to stay in." Doran laughed. Then he
came to the main point of his call. "We would like to invite you, Dr. Ridington, to speak to the tribe at our pow-wow in August, about what you
have learned of the traditions relating to the Pole."

So it was that on August 13, 1988, I found myself once again speaking in
the sacred circle of oak trees that is the Omaha pow-wow arena in Macy, Nebraska. I found myself giving breath to words that had long been locked between the covers of a book. I found myself breathing the words of a story that
Doran's great-great-grandfather told Alice Fletcher a century earlier. Some
said that Yellow Smoke was buried on the little hill just overlooking the
arena. This is how I introduced myself to the tribe for the second time, at the
184th annual tribal pow-wow on August 13, 1988:

> I feel very honored and very humble at being given the opportunity
> to speak in this sacred arena here today, and I pray that the words that I
> say will receive the blessing of this circle. Your arena is open to the east
> like a single lodge. It's open to the east like the great camp circle, the
> *hu'thuga* in which your elders used to come together for ceremonies of
> renewal during their annual buffalo hunt. And it's open to the east like
> the earth altar of long ago—a place called Uzhin'eti—where long ago
> they offered meat and buffalo fat to feed your Sacred Pole. So I will be-
> gin my words of greeting to you in the manner of these elders as they
> used to say long ago (I hope my pronunciation is reasonably good),
> *"Aho Inshta'thunda, Hon'gashenu ti agathon kahon."* That means,
> "Hello Inshta'thunda, Sky people; Hon'gashenu, Earth people, I greet
> you as both sides of a single house joined here together as one peo-
> ple"—one tribe in the sacred arena, just as they did, long ago, in the
> *hu'thuga*—the camp circle.
>
> You may wonder, as I sometimes do myself, what business I have, a
> non-Indian, speaking to you, a great nation that is native in this land to
> which my ancestors came as strangers not so many years ago. And the
> answer I will try to give you in the form of a story, and in the form of a
> teaching. My story is simple. The teaching, from your tradition, is
> more complex—and I hope that you will bear with me as I try to con-
> vey what I have learned of your traditions and I hope those of you
> among you who know a great deal more than I do will come forward to
> me, as time goes on, and give me the benefit of your wisdom and your
> understanding.
>
> The story goes like this. In January 1962 I began to study anthro-
> pology at the Peabody Museum of Harvard University in Cambridge,

Massachusetts. And there, your Sacred Pole (whose name I later learned is Waxthe'xe, or Washa'begle) was on public display. At first, I didn't know what this stood for; I didn't know what it meant. I didn't even know whether the Omaha people were still together on their lands. But I did know, even then, that the Pole must have represented a power of life, and a power of motion—a power of unity—for the people who once carried it with them from place to place. I knew also that the Pole had touched and moved my own life.

I'll give you an example of this. Nearly every day that I studied in the Peabody Museum library I did what student scholars usually do—you get bored, you get restless, you get tired, you want to go for a walk— and somehow I got drawn toward that Venerable Man—the Sacred Pole. When I was on my little walks away from the library, I would go up to the Pole and I'd stand by it and look at it. It was on public display at that time. And I'd just contemplate it. I'd think about the times that this Pole represented, even though I didn't know very much about it at the time. Being close to your Venerable Man—to your Sacred Pole— has turned out to be as important to my education as the courses I took in anthropology at Harvard University. So that's the story of how my life came into contact with your sacred symbols.

In what I referred to as a teaching, I went on to talk about what I had learned about the tribe's sacred traditions. I had discovered, as I told the tribe that day, that in Omaha philosophy there is no such thing as abstract and disembodied thought. By visiting the Pole in 1962 and writing about him in 1984, I made a connection with the living energy that is the Pole's enduring presence. I referred to a passage from Fletcher and La Flesche that was particularly relevant to my situation:

> The Omaha estimate of the value of thought is strongly brought out in their Sacred Legend which briefly recounts their experiences from the time when they "opened their eyes and beheld the day" down to the adoption of the Sacred Pole as an emblem of governmental authority. Every acquisition that bettered the condition of the people was the result of the exercise of the mind. "And the people thought" is the preamble to every change; every new acquirement, every arrangement devised to foster tribal unity and to promote tribal strength, was the outcome of thought. The regulation of the annual tribal hunt, wherein the individual was forced to give way for the good of the whole people; the punishment of murder as a social offense; the efforts to curb the disintegrating war spirit, to bring it under control, to make it conserve rather than disrupt the unity of the tribe—all were the result of

"thought." So, too, was the tribal organization itself, which was based on certain ideas evolved from thinking over natural processes that were ever before their observation. The Sacred Legend speaks truly when it says, "And the people thought." (1911, 608–9)

Once I began thinking about the Sacred Pole in 1962 and writing about him twenty years later, I became drawn into the story as a participant rather than a distant observer. When Dennis phoned me in 1984 I began to realize that my initial paper about the Sacred Pole was only one episode of a story in which Dennis and I would both become actors. It felt as though I had discovered another chapter in the book that Fletcher and La Flesche began in 1911. Dennis and I had, it seemed, taken over where Fletcher and La Flesche left off. The Pole's story did not end when he entered the great brick house in 1888. The story continues and we have played a part in it. A century later, Umon'hon'ti has returned as a presence in the life of the tribe. This book is our way of responding to the challenge of placing contemporary Omahas as well as ourselves in the story.

Dennis carries on a tradition of Omaha tribal ethnography that Francis La Flesche began a century ago. He is also a member of the Bear clan, or Watha'be itazhi, a subclan of the Tha'tada clan. One division of the Bear clan, the Xu'ka, traditionally acted as prompters for the Hon'ga, or Leader clan, during the singing of rituals pertaining to the White Buffalo Hide and the Sacred Pole (1911, 160). The word *Xu'ka* means "teacher or instructor in mystic rites." Throughout the process of repatriation, Dennis has worked tirelessly to support tribal chairman Doran Morris, a member of the Hon'ga and a descendent of Yellow Smoke. Thus, both men have respectfully carried on in the spirit of work traditionally done by their clans.

My collaboration with Dennis has also grown into friendship and kinship. In 1991 we agreed to look after one another as brothers. In that same spirit, we accept a sense of shared responsibility for the story in which we have become actors. The tribal council has asked me to work with Dennis in telling the story of Umon'hon'ti's return. They asked us to tell what we have learned and thought about traditional Omaha symbols and ceremonies in a language that reflects both an Indian way of story telling and a way of learning based on written documents. They particularly want people to remember the difficult times during which they lost control of their sacred objects. I agreed to do my best to interpret and explain the information that the early ethnographers left for us. Dennis agreed to help me with information and to locate historic photographs that complement the written text.

Omahas today know about the works of Dorsey and Fletcher and La Flesche, but they want to know how anthropologists familiar with the Omaha tribe today would make sense of these books. Dennis and I have done our best to carry the information they contain back to the people. We also wish to pass on this information to interested outsiders. Omahas have always welcomed non-Indians to their pow-wows. Their history is closely connected to that of traders and explorers. They have a long and distinguished tradition of producing lawyers, educators, scholars, and medical professionals. Omahas value education, but have never wished it to be thrust upon them. Similarly, they are happy to collaborate with institutions like universities and museums, provided that the relationship is mutually respectful. In a spirit of cooperation, they welcome outsiders to share in the story that is unfolding.

CHAPTER TWO

An Invisible and Continuous Life

Wakon'da

An invisible and continuous life
permeates all things, seen and unseen.
(Fletcher and La Flesche (1911, 134)

History, to the Omahas, is more than a list of events and dates. It is the story of their life as a people. Omaha history reveals the presence of a spiritual will and purpose beyond the events of the physical world. Omaha oral traditions provide detailed information about the tribe's movements since they left an original homeland in the Ohio Valley, but their real history is about the meaning of these events. James Dorsey, Alice Fletcher, and Francis La Flesche were aware that Omaha history is religious and philosophical as well as factual. Fletcher and La Flesche introduce their description of Omaha ceremonies and institutions with an account of the religious and philosophical ideas on which they are based. These ideas, they say, suffuse every aspect of Omaha life: "The tribal organization of the Omaha was based on certain fundamental religious ideas, cosmic in significance; these had reference to conceptions as to how the visible universe came into being and how it is maintained" (134).

Omahas view their history as the expression of a universal life force or power they know as Wakon'da. This power is present as "an invisible and continuous life" that "permeates all things, seen and seen." In a particularly beautiful passage that I have rendered here in poetic form, Fletcher and La Flesche describe the qualities of Wakon'da. These words reflect the profound understanding La Flesche had for the traditions into which he was born.

An invisible and continuous life
Permeates all things, seen and unseen.
This life manifests itself in two ways.
First, by causing to move:

All motion, all actions of mind or body,
Are because of this invisible life.
Second, by causing permanency
Of structure and form:
As in the rock, the physical features
Of the landscape, mountains, plains, streams,
Rivers, lakes, the animals and man.
This invisible life
Is similar to the will power
Of which man is conscious
Within himself.
A power by which things are brought to pass.
Through this mysterious life and power
All things are related to one another
And to man.
The seen to the unseen,
The dead to the living,
A fragment of anything
To its entirety.
This invisible life and power
Was called Wakon'da.
(adapted from Fletcher and La Flesche 1911, 134)

Wakon'da is the spirit of life in the universe, "the mysterious life power permeating all natural forms and forces and all phases of man's conscious life" (597), but it is not a spirit, even a "Great Spirit," removed from human experience. Wakon'da is within and around the conscious life of the universe, not separate from it. Wakon'da "causes day to follow night without variation and summer to follow winter." Wakon'da animates all motion and dwells within all fixed forms. It may be seen in the world's changes and in its structures. It may be seen in the changes a person experiences in his or her life and in the continuity that carries life on from one generation to another. Wakon'da is the spirit of physical bodies in motion and the spirit that animates thought. It shows itself in the permanent structures of a physical landscape; "the rocks mountains, plains, streams, rivers, lakes, the animals and man." It shows itself in the moving winds and resounding Thunders. It shows itself in the sun's path across the daytime sky, and in his momentary passage through the zenith point to become aligned with the earth's center. It shows itself in the fixed star of the night sky, the star around which all others turn. It shows itself in the wanderings of the planets. It shows itself in the structure of thought and in the mind's quick changes of mood. It shows itself in the cosmic union

4. *Nom-ba-mon-nee, the Double Walker. Painting by George Catlin (#116). Courtesy of the Smithsonian Institution.*

of male and female principles, each one giving to the other in order to create a completed whole. It shows itself in the camp circle, the *hu'thuga*.

Wakon'da is a comprehensive indwelling spirit of life and of thought. The lives of humans and animals alike "are animated by a life force emanating from the mysterious Wakon'da." In Omaha thought, "man is viewed as no longer the master but as one of many manifestations of life, all of which are endowed with kindred powers, physical and psychical" (599). Omahas told Fletcher and La Flesche that they view the world's physical forms as points where Wakon'da has stopped. Wakon'da is an intelligence, an "integrity of the universe, of which man is a part." As such, Wakon'da has the authority of cause and effect. The person who fails to keep sacred vows, the person who lies, and the person who fails in pity and compassion will each be touched by Wakon'da in the same way that the forces of nature come back upon a person who ignores them. Wakon'da is both compassionate to people and a reflection of the compassion that exists within them:

> Not only were the events in a person's life decreed and controlled by Wakon'da, but man's emotions were attributed to the same source. An old man said: "Tears were made by Wakon'da as a relief to our human nature; Wakon'da made joy and he also made tears!" An aged man, standing in the presence of death, said: "From my earliest years I remember the sound of weeping; I have heard it all my long life and shall hear it until I die. There will be partings as long as man lives on the earth; Wakon'da has willed it to be so!" (1911, 598)

In 1889 Omaha elder George Miller told Dorsey about a ceremony for offering tobacco to Wakon'da. Whenever Omahas traveled, he said, they extended the pipe's mouthpiece toward the sun and said the following words:

> Wakon'da Ho!
> You who are the Sun!
> Here is tobacco!
> I wish to follow your course.
> Grant that it may be so!
> Cause me to meet whatever is good
> And give a wide berth to anything
> That may be to my injury or disadvantage.
> Throughout this island (the world)
> You regulate everything that moves,
> Including human beings.
> When you decide for one
> That his last day on earth has come
> It is so. It can not be delayed.
> Therefore, O Wakon'da, I ask a favor of you.
> (adapted from Dorsey 1894, 377–8)

Wakon'da is the power of feeling as well as the power of intelligence. The expression of emotion is important to the events of history as Omahas experience them. Omahas have known times of great pride as well as times of suffering and despair. In days gone by, the keeper of a particular ceremony wept whenever there was a break in the ritual order for which he was responsible. He wept because he trusted that the compassion of Wakon'da would always send someone to wipe away the tears. In the 1870s the keeper of the Sacred Pole wept to "wash away the anger of the Venerable Man" when a boy named Francis La Flesche nearly knocked him over with his father's unruly horses. In 1988 the chairman of the Omaha tribe wept when he touched the Sacred Pole after this "Venerable Man" had been in the Peabody Museum for a hundred years. Many Omahas wept when their Venerable Man returned to them in the sacred arena of Macy, Nebraska, in the summer of 1989.

Omaha people pray to Wakon'da in times of need. "A man would take a pipe and go alone to the hills; there he would silently offer smoke and utter the call, Wakon'da Ho! . . . Women did not use the pipe when praying; their appeals were made directly, without any intermediary" (1911, 599). Like their ancestors, Omahas today continue to pray to Wakon'da. They prayed for the blessing of their Sacred Pole's return in 1988. As Edward Cline said when he and Doran Morris began the process of negotiating for the Pole's return, Omahas pray now as they did in centuries past "that we can talk as one person; think and do as one group of people." Lawrence Gilpin prayed with tears of thanks to Wakon'da when the Sacred Pole came back to the tribe in 1989. He addressed Umon'hon'ti and Wakon'da together:

> Aho! Umon'hon'ti
> Umon'hon'ti!
> We're humble people the Omaha village
> That you have come home to.
> Today you have come home.
> There's a few words I want to say to Wakon'da.
> Umon'hon'ti,
> You have come back to the Omaha camp.
> I am very happy that you have come home.
> Umon'hon'ti,
> I am very happy that you have come home today
> To our poor, humble reservation.
> And towards Wakon'da, I'm going to say a few words.
> Aho! Dadeho (Aho! my father).
> Wakon'da, Most Holy Spirit above, you sit above us all.
> (translation by Elsie Morris)

UPSTREAM PEOPLE

Non-Omahas might call the Pole's origin story a "myth." To the Omahas, it is tribal history. It tells an essential truth about their existence as a people. Its

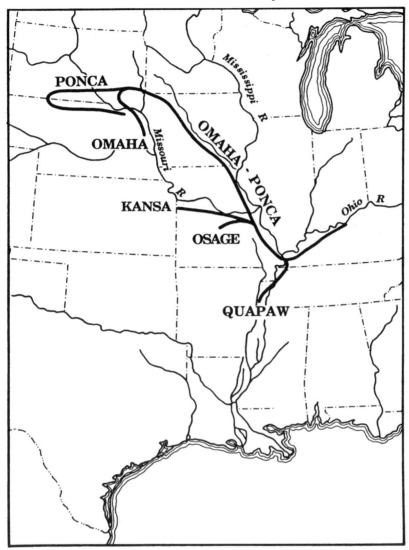

5. *Map of the migration of the five cognatic tribes. From Myers,* The Birth and Rebirth of the Omaha *(1992), figure 1. Courtesy of the University of Nebraska State Museum.*

events reflect universal patterns of relationship between the social and the natural order, as well as their particular experience as a tribe. It continues to be enacted in the tribe's ceremonies. So it was that Umon'hon'ti came to be an emblem of the Omaha tribe and an instrument of Omaha survival. Members of the Hon'ga clan kept the Pole and his ceremonies; they passed them from mind to mind, hand to hand, and generation to generation, for many years. He stood with the people through times of prosperity and through the suffering caused by epidemic diseases and raids from hostile neighbors.

More than four hundred years ago, ancestors of the Omahas were united in language and culture with people who later became the Ponca, Osage, Kansa, and Quapaw (see fig. 5). Over the past four hundred years the five tribes have developed separate but closely related languages of their common Siouan family. In recognition of that common origin, linguists refer to the five cognate tribes as the "Degiha Siouans." The Omaha word for tribe is *uki'te*, a nominal form of the Omaha verb meaning "to fight." Fletcher and La Flesche explain that "the verbal form signifies 'to fight' against external foes, to take part in conflicts in which honor and fame can be won . . . the word *uki'te* as 'tribe,' explains the common obligation felt by the Omaha to defend, as a unit, the community, the tribe" (1911, 36). The name Omaha refers to an event in the history of tribal migration. It comes from the Omaha word, *umon'hon*, which means "against the current" or "upstream." The name Quapaw comes from *uga'xpa*, "with the current" or "downstream." Omaha tradition describes how the two peoples separated when crossing the Ohio River at the southern border of what is now Indiana.

> The people were moving down the Uha'i ke (Ohio) River. When they came to a wide river they made skin boats in which to cross the river. As they were crossing, a storm came up. The Omaha and Iowa got safely across, but the Quapaw drifted down the stream and were never seen again until within the last century. When the Iowa made their landing they camped in a sandy place. The strong wind blew the sand over the people and gave them a grayish appearance. From this circumstance they called themselves Pa'xude, "grey head," and the Omaha have known them by that name ever since. The Iowa accompanied the Omaha up the Mississippi to a stream spoken of as "Raccoon river"—probably the Des Moines, and the people followed this river to its headwaters, which brought them into the region of the Pipestone quarry. (36)

Tradition says that after parting from the Quapaw, the Omaha and Ponca followed the Des Moines River to its headwaters in what is now northwestern Iowa, building several villages there prior to 1700 (1911, 73–74). O'Shea and Ludwickson suggest that "it is possible that one of these villages is known today as the Blood Run site" where "the Omahas may have met colonial Europeans for the first time" (1992, 17). The tribe then moved west to the Missouri River, where the French trader Le Sueur encountered them in

1695. They are depicted in a map drawn by Guillaume De l'Isle in 1703 as living on the Big Sioux River near the present location of Sioux City, Iowa. De l'Isle called the river, "R. des Maha," river of the Omahas (1911, 80). Omaha and Ponca oral histories describe how together they learned to make earth lodges from the Arikara, a non-Siouan tribe whom they displaced to further north along the Missouri:

> When the Missouri river was reached by the Omaha, they found the Arikara there, cultivating the maize and living in villages composed of earth lodges—evidently a peaceful, sedentary folk. Omaha war parties from the east side of the river harassed the Arikara, who were living on the west side. The Arikara sought to obtain peace through the influence of the Wa'wan ceremony, as already related, but Omaha war parties seem finally to have driven them away from their homes and to have forced them northward up the Missouri River. (1911, 75)

The Sacred Legend goes on to describe how each of the arts and industries known to the Omahas came about through their exercise of thought. The most recent technology the Legend speaks about is that related to horses and the hunting of buffalo. The legend also speaks about the system of government the Omahas developed to keep them together as a people in competition with other Plains Indian tribes. Fletcher and La Flesche quote an unnamed "old narrator" as saying:

> We made peace with the Cheyenne. At that time the Ponca were with us, and the Iowa and Oto joined in the peace. The Osage say they were with us, too; but it is not so told by our people. At this place [where peace with the Cheyenne had been made] we formed a government. The people said, "Let us appoint men who shall preserve order." Accordingly they selected men, the wisest, the most thoughtful, generous, and kind, and they consulted together and agreed upon a council of seven who should govern our people. (74)

A tribe on the move has an inherently more difficult problem keeping itself together than one that is settled on a common territory, particularly in the absence of a centralized governmental authority. The Omahas of protohistoric times probably governed themselves through a system of complementary clans and subclans distributed throughout a loose alliance of neighboring villages. Prior to that, some of their ancestors may have participated in the Mississippian system of chiefdoms which were "kin-based societies with strong clans that provided chiefs and subchiefs" (Conrad 1989, 93). Because of diseases that swept through Mississippian territory in early historic times, many of the former chiefdoms had become decentralized and held together by their clans rather than by hereditary chiefs. Later, at the height of Omaha control of the Missouri River trade, chiefs like Blackbird achieved great power within the sphere of trading. They did not, though, establish hereditary positions like those of the former Mississippians. Their power was personal rather than mandated by membership in a noble family.

THE TWO SACRED PIPES AND THE COUNCIL OF SEVEN

Fletcher and La Flesche record Omaha history relevant to the time when the tribe was moving toward the Missouri River. As a tribe on the move, Omahas faced the task of creating a decentralized form of government based on an existing system of clans that was probably of great antiquity. Like every other aspect of Omaha life in the early nineteenth century, Omaha government was adapted to the tribe's new life on the Missouri River. The traditions Fletcher and La Flesche describe tell how the tribe attempted to keep itself together by creating a council of seven religious and ceremonial chiefs, rather than giving authority to a single overall chief. The council, in turn, acted under the authority of two Sacred Tribal Pipes which stood for the two great divisions of the tribe, the Inshta'thunda (Sky people) and Hon'gashenu (Earth people). Dorsey reported in 1884 that the two Sacred Pipes were still in existence and kept by the Inke'sabe (Black Shoulder) clan. Probably because of their sacred or *wa'xube* nature of the pipes, neither Dorsey nor Fletcher and La Flesche were given permission to illustrate them in their reports. Dorsey says: "These pipes are called "Niniba waqube," Sacred Pipes, or "Niniba jide," Red Pipes. They are made of the red pipestone which is found in the famous red pipestone quarry. The stems are nearly flat and are worked near the mouthpiece with porcupine quills" (1884, 222).

The two Sacred Pipes were always kept together and never separated when used in ceremony. They suggest the tribe's identity as a union of its two halves. Fletcher and La Flesche provide additional information about their appearance and speculate about their relationship to the tribal division into Sky people and Earth people:

> Both had flat stems; one was ornamented with porcupine-quill work, and had fastened on it the head of a pileated woodpecker, with the upper mandible turned back over the crest of the bird. The stem of the other pipe was plain, but had bound in a row along its length seven woodpeckers' heads, the mandibles turned back as just described. It is not improbable that these pipes pertained to the fundamental ideas on which the two grand divisions of the tribe were based; but which pipe belonged to the Sky people and was masculine, and which to the Earth people and was feminine, the writers have been unable to learn. (135)

Fletcher and La Flesche describe the rites connected with the Sacred Tribal Pipes as "the medium between the chiefs and Wakon'da" (602). Smoking the pipes was a sacrament that empowered the chiefs when they met in council.

> After the members of the council were in their places the keeper of the Sacred Pipes laid them before the two principal chiefs, who called on the keeper of the ritual to prepare the Pipes for use. As he filled them with native tobacco he intoned in a low voice the ritual which belonged to that act. He had to be careful not to let either of the Pipes fall. Should this happen, that meeting of the council would be at an end, and the life of the keeper would be in danger from the supernatural powers. (208–9)

Francis La Flesche described one such incident to Dorsey:

> The sacred pipes are not shown to the common people. When my father was about to be installed as a head chief, Mahin-zi, whose duty it was to fill the pipes, let one of them fall to the ground, violating a law and so preventing the continuation of the ceremony. So my father was not fully initiated. When the later fall was partly gone Mahin-zi died.
>
> Wacuce, my father-in-law, was the Inke-sabe keeper of the pipes. When the Otos visited the Omahas (in the summer of 1878), the chiefs wished the pipes to be taken out of the coverings, so they ordered Wacuce to undo the bag. This was unlawful, as the ritual prescribed certain words to be said by the chiefs to the keeper of the pipes previous to the opening of the bag. But none of the seven chiefs know the formula. Wacuce was unwilling to break the law; but the chiefs insisted and he yielded. Then Two Crows told all the Omahas present not to smoke the small pipe. This he had a right to do, as he was a Hanga. Wacuce soon died, and in a short time he was followed by his daughter and his eldest son.
>
> It takes four days to make any one understand all about the laws of the sacred pipes; and it costs many horses. A bad man, i.e., one who is saucy, quarrelsome, stingy, etc., cannot be told such things. This was the reason why the seven chiefs did not know their part of the ritual. (Dorsey 1884, 224)

Dorsey describes how the Sacred Pipes were used on ceremonial occasions:

> When the chiefs assemble and wish to make a decision for the regulation of tribal affairs, Ictasanda fills both pipes and lays them down before the two head chiefs. Then the Inke'sabe keeper takes one and the Te'dait'aji keeper the other. Inke'sabe precedes, starting from the head

6. Inke'sabe tent decoration. From Dorsey, A Study of Siouan Cults *(1894), figure 185.*

chief sitting on the right and passing around half of the circle till he reaches an old man seated opposite the head chief. This old man (one of the Hon'ga wagea) and the head chief are the only ones who smoke the pipe; those sitting between them do not smoke it when Inke'sabe goes around. When the old man has finished smoking Inke'sabe takes the pipe again and continues around the circle to the starting point, but he gives it to each man to smoke. When he reaches the head chief on the left he gives it to him, and after receiving it from him he returns it to the place on the ground before the head chiefs. . . . In smoking they blew the smoke upwards, saying, "Here, Wakon'da, is the smoke." This was done because they say that Wakon'da gave them the pipes, and He rules over them. (1884, 223–24)

While neither Dorsey or Fletcher and La Flesche illustrated the tribal pipes directly, Dorsey does provide drawings of Inke'sabe tents on which are painted images of the pipes (see fig. 6). George Miller described to Dorsey the duties of the keepers:

Those persons who belong to the Inke'sabe sub-gens known as Keepers of the Pipes, paint their tent(s) with the pipe decoration. I do not know of any other persons, members of other gentes, using this decoration; I think that the Inke'sabe chief decorates his tent in this manner, and that he did not decorate it in any way he pleased. When the sacred pipes were made (on the tent) the pipestem was made flat, porcupine work was put around it, several heads of birds were fastened on it, and tufts of reddened horses' hair were tied to it at intervals. (Dorsey 1894, 408)

The tent Miller refers to (Dorsey's fig. 184) shows two pipes, painted horizontally, one on either side of the door. He went on to describe another tent (fig. 6) to Dorsey:

When, in my childhood, I saw the tents in which the people dwelt, they were of this sort (Fig. 185). I saw the tent decorated with the pipes having feathers attached to each pipe at right angles. I saw a tent of this sort when it was occupied by Waqaga of the Pipe sub-gens. Though these pipes closely resemble the peace pipes (*niniba waxube*), they are made with the feathers attached to the stems at right angles. These are the pipes used in the pipe dance. By means of the pipes the people made for themselves that which was equivalent to (or, lead to) the chieftainship. So they regarded the sacred pipes as of the greatest importance. Even when the people were very bad, even when different tribes continued to struggle with one another; even when they shot often at one another, when some persons came forth with the peace pipes, and bore them to a place between the opposing forces, carrying them all along the lines, they stopped shooting at one another. The Indians regarded the pipes as precious. (Dorsey 1894, 409)

The tribal pipes provided the basis for an authority vested in both halves of the tribe. During the He'dewachi, or harvest festival of the nineteenth century, the Omahas paid special honor to these two pipes because they stood for the tribe's "two grand divisions, one representing the Sky people, or the Inshta'thunda; the other, the Earth people, or the Hon'gashenu." The pipes were separate but always kept together. The way they were honored indicated the tribe's respect for "the fundamental ideas on which the two grand divisions of the tribe were based." The He'dewachi reminded people that the union of male and female cosmic forces was "necessary for the perpetuation of all living forms and to man's life by maintaining his food supply." Although there is no record of what happened to these pipes, the ceremony has evolved into the present day Omaha tribal pow-wow.

Fletcher and La Flesche talk about how the two Sacred Pipes are connected to the overall idea of tribal government:

The keeping of them belonged to the Inke'sabe clan of the southern (earth) side of the *hu'thuga*; the office of ceremonially filling the Pipes, making them ready for use, was vested in the Inshta'thunda clan of the northern (upper) realm of the *hu'thuga*, representative of the abode of the supernatural forces to which man must appeal for help. Through the ceremonies and use of the two Sacred Pipes the halves of the *hu'thuga* were welded, as it were, the Pipes thus becoming representative of the tribe as a whole. The prominence given to the Pipes, as the credential of the "old men," as their authority in the creation of chiefs and the governing council, seems to indicate that the institution of the Nini'baton [pipe-bearing subclan] and the establishment of the council, although a progressive movement, was a growth, a development of earlier forms, rather than an invention or arbitrary arrangement of the "old men." The retaining of the two Pipes as the supreme or confirmatory authority within the council rather than giving that power to a head chief was consonant with the fundamental idea embodied in the tribal organization. The number of the council (seven) probably had its origin in the significance of the number which represented the whole of man's environment—the four quarters where were the four paths down which the Above came to the Below, where stood man. The ancient ideas and beliefs of the people concerning man's relation to the cosmos were thus interwoven with their latest social achievement, the establishment of a representative governing body. (1911, 207)

Fletcher and La Flesche say that the idea of seven chiefs in council reflects fundamental Omaha philosophy about the way their world is structured. The number seven is sacred to the Omahas because it is made up of the four directions, the zenith, the nadir, and the place where all of these directions meet at the center. The Sacred Pole himself suggests the sacred number. He stands on earth and points toward the center of the night sky. Four trails converge upon him. He stands at a place where the four directions, the night sky, and the earth come together to a single point. He is the one who makes the number seven. He is an individual who stands for all the people, a singularity who stands for an entirety.

The authors' description of tribal government clearly embodies both Fletcher's belief in progressive social evolution and La Flesche's understanding of how symbolic and social structures reinforce one another. Fletcher and La Flesche tried to obtain the tribal pipes for safekeeping in the Peabody Museum along with the Sacred Pole but were unsuccessful in their attempt. Unlike the Sacred Pole, the pipes were still in active use. Despite the legal and social pressures to abandon aboriginal religion and government, the chiefs resisted. The authors reported that "all the other sacred articles used in tribal ceremonies have been turned over to the writers for safe-keeping, but no arguments could induce the leading men to part with the two Sacred Pipes. The answer was always, 'They must remain.' And they are still with the people" (1911, 209). There is no public record of what happened to the pipes after 1911 or whether the ceremonies connected with them continued into the twentieth century. In their wisdom, the Omahas have chosen not to make such information public.

Fletcher and La Flesche suggest that "it was prior to the cutting of the Sacred Pole that the Omaha organized themselves into their present order" (73). By this they mean that the system of complementary clans was already in existence when the son of a chief discovered "a tree that stands burning." It is also clear from both Omaha and Ponca tradition that the Pole came into their lives prior to the Ponca's becoming a separate tribe. According to Yellow Smoke's narrative, the men of the tribe first rushed upon the miraculous tree as they would have in the He'dewachi ceremony that must have been part of the heritage common to both tribes. "A Ponca was the first to reach the tree, and he struck it as he would an enemy" (218).

The earliest reference to the Ponca as a separate tribe is an unsigned French map of 1786 (Howard 1965, 24). As late as 1794 the French trader Jacques Clamorgan referred to the Omahas and Poncas as "really only one nation, since the Poncas are nothing but Mahas who have left the tribe" (Nasatir 1952, 206). A 1718 draft copy of De l'Isle's map shows "Les Mahas" on the Big Sioux and another group, "Les Mahas, Nation errante," far to the north and east of the Missouri. Howard identifies these "Wandering Omahas" as Poncas who had recently set out on their own, having previously been a clan of the Omahas. If the Omahas and Poncas separated in the early eighteenth century as these maps suggest, the Pole was most likely cut sometime in the late seventeenth century, making him at least a century old when the tribe moved to Ton'wontonga, two centuries old when he went to the "great brick house" in Cambridge and three centuries old when Joe Johns carried him back to the tribal arena in 1989.

Yellow Smoke said in his narrative that the tree that became Umon'hon'ti "stood near a lake" (1911, 218). Dorsey identifies the place as Lake Andes, just northeast of where the Missouri River crosses the Nebraska–South Dakota border:

> So at last the three tribes [Omahas, Poncas, and Iowas] went west and southwest to a lake near the head of Choteau Creek, Dakota Territory, now known as Lake Andes. There they cut the sacred pole, and assigned to each gens and subgens its peculiar customs, such as the sacred pipe, sacred tents, and the taboos. There were a great many gentes in each tribe at the time, far more than they have at the present; and these gentes were in existence long before they cut the sacred pole. (1884, 212)

Fletcher and La Flesche dispute Dorsey and report that "this identification has not been accepted by the best tribal authorities and traditions do not favor placing the act in the vicinity of this lake" (1911, 73). However, they do not provide an alternative identification of the place. Whatever the case may be, it is clear that finding the Sacred Pole provided the tribe with a powerful new symbol of Omaha identity. In 1895 La Flesche wrote a brief note on the Pole's origin as told to him by Wa-ke-de:

> At one time the seven bands were divided and each one wandered about independent of the other. Each one had a pipe, and a leader. It occurred to one of the Hunga gens that if that state continued, there would be feuds between the bands, so he said to his band; "Let us gather the bands together, so that all may live and move together, that there may be no danger of quarrels." He then took the idea of making a Wa-khu-be, around which the different bands may gather. He cut the tree out of which the Wa-ghdhe-ghe was made and called all the seven bands together. Then they all united, and have been so ever since. So that branch of the Hun-ga have care of the Pole. (La Flesche 1895)

The Pole was a symbol appropriate to the Omahas' recognition of their place in the rapidly changing flow of history. Rather than looking to a single chief to stand over them, the Omahas looked to the Pole to represent a common but movable center shared by all. The Pole's power within the tribe is concentric rather than hierarchical. He represents a center they share, not a ruler who stands over them. He stands for a spiritual rather than a temporal authority. According to the legend Yellow Smoke told Fletcher and La Flesche, "attention was called to the tree from which the Sacred Pole was shaped by the Thunder Birds coming to it from the four directions and the mysterious burning which followed, all of which caused the Sacred Pole to stand in the minds of the people as endowed with a supernatural power by the ancient Thunder gods" (229).

During their travels, the Omaha experienced many changes. Omaha leaders became particularly concerned about keeping the tribe together as they moved from one place to another and learned new ways of making a living. The divisive forces that led the Poncas to separate from them may have caused the chiefs great concern. Fletcher and La Flesche were told that following the tribe's departure from its original homeland, elders felt compelled to devise a new form of government:

> The Sacred Legend and other accounts tell the story of the way in which a central governing body was finally formed and all agree that it was devised for the purpose of "holding the people together." One ver-

sion speaks of seven old men who, while visitors to the tribe, inaugurated the governing council. The Sacred Legend declares that the council was the outcome of "thought" and "consultation among the wise old men," their purpose taking form in the plan to establish a Nini'baton [pipe-bearing] subdivision in some of the new gentes [clans], each subdivision to furnish one member to the council, which was to be the governing authority, exercising control over the people, maintaining peace in the tribe, but having no relation to offensive warfare. (201)

Seven of the Omaha clans possessed their own pipes in addition to the two Tribal Pipes. It was from these seven clans that the council of seven chiefs was derived. The subclan within each clan that possessed a pipe was known as Nini'baton, meaning that each of these had the right "to possess a pipe." The council may have been more of a ceremonial than a political form of government, although it carried considerable moral authority. Forming a council representing the seven pipe-bearing clans was an Omaha way of relating their ideas about cosmic structure to the ancient and organic system of clans. In theory, the seven tribal chiefs were selected by the seven pipe-owning lineages to represent their respective clans. Today, the tribal council is composed of seven elected members in recognition of the sacred and symbolic importance of the number seven, and the council room of the tribal building is enclosed within a circle of seven posts.

Dorsey describes a less elaborate system than do Fletcher and La Flesche. He says nothing about a council of seven chiefs, but does say that "the keepers of the sacred pipes are regarded as chiefs in some sense, though they are not allowed to speak in the tribal assembly." He seems to view their role as more religious than secular, making a distinction that may reflect his own culture's separation of sacred and secular institutions rather than an Omaha way of thinking. "The chiefs," he writes, "are religious officers during the buffalo hunt; they are always praying to Wakon'da, and showing the pipes to him" (1884, 357).

What Dorsey describes as a "tribal assembly," seems to be composed of all the people holding any degree of chiefly rank. Fletcher and La Flesche provide a detailed description of two orders of chiefs whose members make up this assembly. The lower chiefs, whose numbers are essentially unlimited, are referred to as Ni'kagahi xu'de, "Brown Chiefs." The name, they explain, "has reference to a uniform color, as of the brown earth, where all are practically alike, of one hue or rank" (202). A higher and more limited order of chiefs were known as Ni'kagahi sha'be, "Dark Chiefs." The word *sha'be*, they explain, "does not refer to color, but to the appearance of an object raised above the uniform level and seen against the horizon as a dark object" (202).

One of the names contemporary Omahas call the Sacred Pole is Washa'begle, a reference to one who stands above the others like the highest order of chiefs. Admission to the Ni'kagahi sha'be order of chiefs, Fletcher and La Flesche explain, "was through the performance of certain *wathin'ethe* . . . acts and gifts which do not directly add to the comfort and wealth of the actor or donor, but which have relation to the welfare of the tribe and promoting internal order and peace, by providing for the chiefs and keepers, by assuring friendly relations with other tribes" (202). There were seven grades of *wathin'ethe* leading to a man's entry into the order of Ni'kagahi sha'be. I have adapted Fletcher and La Flesche's description as follows:

First. Washa'be ga'xe (to make the *washa'be*). The first and most arduous grade required a man to procure the materials necessary for making the *washa'be*, the ornamented staff carried by the leader of the annual buffalo hunt. (see fig. 7 and description, chapter 4). These items consisted of a dressed buffalo skin, a crow, two eagles, a shell disk, sinew, a pipe with an ornamented stem, and a cooking vessel of pottery (or later copper).

Second. Bon'wakithe (I caused the herald to call). The second grade required making a feast for the keepers of the two Sacred Pipes and presenting these men with gifts.

Third. *U'gashkegthon* (to tether a horse). A man would make a feast for the dark chiefs and tether a horse bearing a new robe outside the tent as a gift.

Fourth. *Gathi'ge nonshton wakithe* (moving abreast, causing the people to halt). When the people were moving on the annual buffalo hunt a man would bring a horse and new robe up to where the Sacred Pole's keeper and the chiefs were leading the way. The herald would call out his name, the entire tribe would halt, and he would present the horse to the Sacred Pole.

Fifth. *Te thishke wakithe* (causing the Sacred White Buffalo Hide to be opened and shown). A man would call for the White Buffalo Hide to be shown and would present it with a shell disk to be cared for by the Hide's keeper.

Sixth. *Wa't'edonbe* (causing the dead to see things having power and purpose). This act consisted of taking gifts to the family of a chief who had died.

Seventh. *Wathin'ethe* (contributing gifts in order to maintain peace in the tribe). When a person had been killed accidentally or in anger, the chiefs took the Sacred Tribal Pipes to the kindred of the man, accompanied by gifts, in order to prevent an act of revenge.

When a man had completed a hundred of these acts, he was eligible to join the Hon'hewachi (the Night Blessed Society) by making a public count of the *wathin'ethe* he had accomplished. He also obtained the right to have Xthexe tattooed on the body of a young daughter. (See chapter 5 for a complete description of this ceremony.)

OMAHAS ON THE MISSOURI RIVER

When the Poncas finally took their own direction, they left the Omahas in possession of all the tribe's sacred objects, rituals, and ceremonies. Because of this, the Omahas came to refer to the Poncas as "orphans." One of the sacred objects the Omahas retained was Umon'hon'ti, the Sacred Pole.

De l'Isle's maps of 1703 and 1718 show the Omahas living near the Big Sioux River close to the present site of Sioux City, Iowa. They stayed in their earth lodges during the spring planting season and moved out onto the prairie to hunt buffalo in July, "the moon when the buffaloes bellow." Their ability to hunt as a tribe was an entirely new adaptation to the resource potential of the Plains, and was made possible through the use of horses. (See chapter 4 for a close description of the hunt.)

The Omahas were also becoming skillful at controling trade relations with Europeans, and realized that the inhabitants of a large village strategically located on the Missouri River trade route could wield considerable power. About 1720, the tribe established a village of earth lodges to the north and west of Bow Creek just south of the Missouri River. "Here the people remained," Fletcher and La Flesche write, "until a tragedy occurred which caused a separation in the tribe and an abandonment of this village by all the people" (85). Omaha tradition describes this tragedy as a violent dispute about the treatment of a woman who had been forced to marry an older man against her will. Following the violence, the village broke up and the warring factions moved to different locations. Despite the presence of the Sacred Pole among them, the tribe was not always able to speak as one voice. The old village site became known as Ton'wonpezhi (Bad Village). According to a story recorded by Fletcher and La Flesche, the warring factions were able to reunite into a single village a generation after the incident: "A new generation had grown up when a war party traveling east beyond the Missouri River encountered a village where the people spoke the Omaha language. Abandoning their warlike intents, the Omaha warriors entered the village peaceably, persuaded their new-found relatives to return with them, and so the Omaha people were once more united" (1911, 86).

Following this reunion, the tribe found itself vulnerable to attacks by the Sioux and began looking for a village site farther to the south. At first they settled on the west side of the Missouri near the present town of Dakota City,

Nebraska. The village was called Ti tan'ga jin'ga (lodge big little). According to Dorsey (1884, 213), it consisted of wood lodges (probably bark-covered wigwams) rather than the more elaborate and permanent earth lodges, indicating that the Omahas did not consider the residence permanent. By the early 1770s and no later than 1775, the entire tribe found a more suitable site about thirty miles to the south on the same side of the river. Omahas knew the place as *In'be zhunka monshonde te*, "the fork-tailed kites' hole," after a distinctive rock formation favored by kites as a nesting site. The site was ideally located for a mixed trading, farming, and hunting way of life. They called their village Ton'wontonga (Big Village). It was from this site, near the present town of Homer, Nebraska, that archaeologists removed the buried bones of more than a hundred individuals just before World War II and took them to the University of Nebraska–Lincoln. It was at Ton'wontonga that Omahas achieved their greatest prosperity, but also suffered some of their greatest adversity.

From this location in the low hills overlooking a broad flood plain of the Missouri River, the Omahas were ideally situated to manage relations with the traders who were beginning to move manufactured goods (particularly firearms) up and down the river. French trader Jean Baptiste Truteau described the location of Ton'wontonga in August 1794 as follows:

> The village of the Mahas is situated in a beautiful prairie about a league's distance from the Missouri and 289 leagues from the Illinois. From the Platte River to this village, the waters of the Missouri run less rapidly than in the lower part. The turns are long and frequent, so that a man on foot can travel a distance of land in one day that a well equipped pirogue could not make in 4 or 5 days by water. (Nasatir 1952, 264)

In response to trade opportunities, certain Omaha men with well-established intertribal connections became wealthy trading chiefs. Their power was not related to that of the pipe-holding council of chiefs. Perhaps the most famous trading chief was Blackbird (Wajinga-sabe), a man whose relations with other tribes began when he was captured by the Teton Sioux as a boy. Although his power approached that of great chiefs from the Mississippian tradition, it was based on personal achievement and shamanic power rather than hereditary and religious position. A disproportionate amount of information about this man has come down to us because of his direct and forceful involvement with traders who kept journals about their experiences on the Missouri. Not surprisingly, these outsiders did not experience the tribe's clan system or the ceremonies that took place during the buffalo-hunting phase of its yearly rounds.

In the summer of 1794, Jean Baptiste Truteau wrote extensively about the Omahas and their trading chief, Blackbird, but he makes no reference to the Sacred Pole, which must certainly have already been a venerable man by that time. He reports that he approached the big village of Ton'wontonga on August 24 with some caution, "afraid of being discovered by someone of that nation, who would have prevented me without fail from going further" (Nasatir 1952, 264). Truteau understood clearly that the Omahas, under Blackbird, were in a position to control all trade that passed by their village: "The policy of the savages of this river is to prevent communication between us and the nations of the Upper Missouri, depriving them of munitions of war and other help that they would receive from us if we made our way there easily. They keep these distant people in a continual fear of their fire arms" (Nasatir 1952, 264).

In light of Truteau's observations, it is not surprising that one of the Omahas buried at Ton'wontonga turned out to have been a gunsmith (see chapter 7). Truteau managed to pass by the Omaha village "at nightfall" on his way upriver, but was obliged to deal with Blackbird directly on his return in December. He writes at length about the great trading chief, whom he clearly considered to be a rival and adversary:

This great chief of the Omahas was the most shrewd, the most deceitful and the greatest rascal of all the nations who inhabit the Missouri. He is feared and respected and is in great renoun [sic] among all strange nations, none of whom dare to contradict him openly or to move against his wishes. They do not set out either for war or for the hunt unless he has given his consent to it. His name is recited in all assemblages and speeches are made in his absence in the most distant places to which they go. All the neighboring tribes hear his word and crown him with presents when he goes to visit them. If any of his men acquire beautiful merchandise or beautiful horses and he appears to desire them they instantly give them to him. He never goes about on foot, but is always mounted on the most beautiful horse in the village. He has slaves for his work, and better to say, they are all his slaves, for should he wish to sleep he has one or two hired attendants who gently rub his legs and feet while he sleeps. If these ordinary valets are absent, he presses into that service even the greatest and bravest of his tribe.

When it is time to awaken him it is necessary to do it with caution, being careful not to cry in his ears nor to stroke him with the hand, but they use a feather which they pass lightly over the face or tickle gently certain parts of his body. Finally he is a man who by his wit and cunning has raised himself to the highest place of authority in his nation and who has no parallel among all the savage nations of this continent.

He is able to do or cause to be done good or evil as it pleases him. It is not his warlike actions that have brought him so much power, for he has been inclined towards peace, but because of the fear that his men and his neighbors have of certain poisons which he uses, they say to kill off those who displease him. (Nasatir 1952, 282–83)

Truteau's description of Blackbird is perhaps colored by his distress at the Omaha chief's preventing him from making the exorbitant profits to which he was accustomed. He went on to comment that "the loss which this chief and his followers bring to the traders which takes from them the better or greater part of their effects at a low price, places them in a condition to make no gain. This Omaha post is about the most disadvantageous on the whole river at the present time as much through the great knowledge they have of trading through the English on the Mississippi, as through the evil disposition of this nation and their chiefs in our regard" (284).

Blackbird was said to have learned the use of arsenic following a trip to the trading post at St. Louis. Clearly, his position as chief derived from his personal charisma and his control of trade relations rather than from any status he had within the tribal government. According to a military officer who wrote about his experiences in Indian country, Blackbird was known as a prophet and shaman: "Blackbird was of undistinguished parentage; his earliest pursuits were those of a doctor. To this he soon added that of religious juggler; he became a 'medicine man.' . . . He next ventured to appear in the character of prophet; and . . . soon became a very distinguished one" (O'Shea and Ludwickson 1992, 24).

The Omahas were probably at their wealthiest and most influential during the era of Blackbird and other great trading chiefs. Grave goods from the Ton'wontonga burials are rich in material items obtained through trade. They include a variety of glass beads, copper coils used for bracelets, silver crosses imprinted with a maker's mark indicating they were made in Montreal, iron kettles, gun parts, clay pipes, and steel knife blades. Truteau wrote to other traders with some advice about the power Blackbird obtained from his control of Missouri River trade:

The man knows how to make the Frenchmen realize how much they are in need of him, perhaps in commerce with his nation, perhaps in the distribution of the credits which without his presence would be made long and noisily, perhaps also in getting payment. Having the policy of leaving the trader on such occasions in the embarrassment of disputes, threats, and robbery from his men, who are naturally brutal and ferocious and coming immediately to his aid, restores calm and order. The poor traders finding themselves fortunate for his support, are forced to load him with glory, with caresses and with good treatment, and no one dared to refuse what he desired. (Nasatir 1952, 283)

Omahas were able to support a large number of people in the single well-situated trading village of Ton'wontonga by growing corn in the nearby rich alluvial soils created by river flooding. They called the village they built at "the fork-tailed kites' hole" Big Village because it was probably the largest single settlement in their history. For a time, trade and farming gave them a steady source of wealth, but not to the exclusion of their other existence as mounted buffalo hunters. To complement the corn they grew in fields beside the Missouri, the Omahas headed west each summer to hunt buffalo. During the buffalo hunt, the tribe camped in a circle, the *hu'thuga*, according to clan membership (see chapter 4).

The tribe experienced its most prosperous years at Ton'wontonga between about 1780 and 1800. That prosperity was cut short by a smallpox epidemic that struck the tribe in the autumn of 1800 and lasted until 1803 (O'Shea and Ludwickson 1992, 30–32, 271; Reinhard 1994, 15). One casualty of the disease was the great chief Blackbird, who died during the winter of 1800–1801. The Omahas never fully recovered their position in the fur trade following the losses of that period. As the inhabitants of a single permanent village, they were more vulnerable to disease than people like the Sioux, who had a dispersed settlement pattern. Once their village had been weakened by disease, Omahas were prone to attack by the highly mobile Sioux.

The tribe continued to occupy Big Village intermittently until about 1819, when raids by the Teton Sioux forced them to relocate to a safer place. After several attempts to reclaim Big Village, the Omahas moved to a more secure site west of Bellevue, Nebraska, in 1845. From there they took up their present reservation land south of the former Big Village site under the terms of a treaty with the United States government, signed in 1854. The extent of this reservation has been considerably diminished since then, but today the Omahas continue to live in and around their modern town of Macy, Nebraska, only a few minutes' drive from the place where their ancestors made their home in the early 1770s. A copy of the 1854 treaty hangs on the wall of the present tribal office. Under the caption, *Articles of Agreement and Convention—1854 Treaty* is the treaty's text, followed by the signatures of seven chiefs: Logan Fontenelle, Joseph La Flesche, Standing Hawk, Little Chief, Village Maker, Noise, and Yellow Smoke.

Despite the enormous secular and supernatural power of chiefs like Blackbird, it seems clear that the tribe's ceremonial life remained within the control of chiefs and priests who derived their authority both from their position within the system of clans and from their ability to count their "hundred gifts" (known as *wathin'ethe*) for the benefit of the tribe. The tribe's sacred emblems retained their power independent of the power held by the trading chiefs. There is no evidence that the secular chiefs were involved in the priestly functions of the seven pipe-holding chiefs and the ceremonies conducted by the keepers of sacred objects. The ceremonial duties of the pipe-holding chiefs had to do with the preservation and renewal of the tribe as a whole. In this they were supported by the authority of the Sacred Pole. Fletcher and La Flesche write, "In the process of governmental development it became expedient to have something which should symbolize the unity of the tribe and of its governing power—something which should appeal to the people, an object they could all behold and around which they could gather to manifest their loyalty to the idea it represented (1911, 217).

It is not surprising that European traders wrote nothing about the Sacred Pole and the ceremonial life that centered around him. For one thing, the ceremonies took place on the prairie, far away from the usual riverine trade routes. For another, their interest lay in doing business with the trading chiefs, not in describing an indigenous system of government that would have been invisible to them because of its lack of formal hierarchy. We can only presume that the traditions continued, since they were clearly still in effect when La Flesche was young. Furthermore, it seems likely that emblems of tribal unity became particularly valuable during the dark days of epidemic disease. The Sacred Pole may have been needed then more strongly than ever before.

THE COMING FLOOD

Following the death of Blackbird a number of famous chiefs ruled. One of the most prominent chiefly names was Big Elk or On'pontonga. At least three individuals bore this name between 1815 and 1853. The last of them spoke to the tribe as a whole in 1853, warning them of "a coming flood" of white people. This is how his speech has come down to us:

> My chiefs, braves, and young men. I have just returned from a visit to a far-off country toward the rising sun, and have seen many strange things. I bring to you news which it saddens my heart to think of. There is a coming flood which will soon reach us, and I advise you to prepare for it. Soon the animals which Wakon'da has given us for sustenance will disappear beneath this flood to return no more, and it will be very hard for you. Look at me; you see that I am advanced in age; I am near the grave. I can no longer think for you and lead you as in my younger days. You must think for yourselves what will be best for your welfare. I tell you this that you may be prepared for the coming change. You may not know my meaning. Many of you are old, as I am, and by the time the change comes we may be lying peacefully in our graves;

but these young men will remain to suffer. Speak kindly to one another; do what you can to help each other, even in the troubles with the coming tide. Now, my people, this is all I have to say. Bear these words in mind, and when the time comes think of what I have said. (1911, 84)

Big Elk's speech, if we can trust Fletcher and La Flesche to have reported it accurately, turned out to be a prophetic warning which later generations remembered and recited word-for-word. Alice Fletcher reports a powerful moment that took place during her tenure as allotting agent for the federal government: "One day, in 1883, during the allotment of the land in severalty to the Omaha tribe, as a large group of Indians were gathered about the allotting agent watching the surveyor and talking of the location of allotments, there stood on a hill near by an old Indian. In a loud voice he recited this speech of Big Elk. At its close he paused, then shouted: 'Friends, the flood has come!' and disappeared" (84).

The flood came. But now, perhaps, it has begun to ebb. White people still dominate the continent, but new respect for Native American tradition is emerging. Although the buffalo are gone and will not return to the world as we know it, the Sacred Pole and the Sacred White Buffalo Hide are back among the Omaha people. They have come back through the stewardship of anthropology and the thought of the Omaha people. The ideas these emblems represent have been with the people since time immemorial and will be with them for generations to come. Fletcher and La Flesche point out that the idea of a sacred tree was with the people long before Umon'hon'ti came to represent Omaha tribal unity. The reality of that idea does not depend on the existence of a physical object, although it is immensely inspired when such an object does exist. They write that the tribe was already familiar with "the symbol of the tree as a type of unity" through their annual He'dewachi ceremony, the precursor of today's tribal pow-wow. During the years when Umon'hon'ti was in the Peabody Museum, the tribal pow-wow continued. The idea of tribal unity remained with the Omaha. Instead of the Pole, they placed the American flag at the center of the pow-wow dance arena. Photographs from the early part of this century show it flying prominently.

HE'DEWACHI

The idea of a pole to represent tribal unity existed long before Omahas found the Sacred Pole. The idea continued after he had gone to the Peabody Museum and is with them still. Long ago, and continuing into the late nineteenth century, Omahas honored another tribal emblem, the ancient Cedar Pole, also returned to them from the Peabody. When the tribe began its migration from the Ohio Valley to their present location on the Missouri River, they were well aware of the danger of splitting into smaller bands and losing

7. *Girl with tattooed Mark of Honor. From Fletcher and La Flesche,* The Omaha Tribe *(1911), figure 105. Photograph courtesy of the Smithsonian Institution National Anthropological Archives.*

the security of being a single and united people. One of their oldest ceremonies was probably already in existence when they began the migration. It is known as the He'dewachi and was traditionally held to celebrate the growing crop of corn and the passage of night into day. Omahas now know this harvest festival in English as the tribal pow-wow.

He'dewachi began early in the morning when a keeper of the ceremony "went forth, picked out a tall, straight cottonwood tree and then came back, returning as would a victorious warrior" (1911, 252). Following a ceremonial smoking of the tribal pipes, the keeper returned to the tree with a woman bearing the tattooed Mark of Honor (see chapter 5 for a complete description of this mark and its symbolism). Cutting the He'dewachi tree is remarkably similar to preparations for the present-day Sun Dance among other Plains tribes. It may reflect an ancient Siouan ceremonial practice from which the Sun Dance as we now know it evolved. The idea of a sacred white buffalo calf is also similar to the Lakota reverence for White Buffalo Calf Woman, who brought them their own Sacred Pipe. In Omaha ceremony, we may see an ancient tradition of ritual language from which other Siouan tribes developed their own distinctive stories and ceremonies. Hede'wachi is as much an ancestor of the Sun Dance as it is a precursor of ceremonies to renew the tribe and the Sacred Pole. Fletcher and La Flesche describe the cutting of the tree as follows:

> Then the woman bearing the "mark of honor," taking her axe, made four feints, one on each side of the tree toward one of the four directions, after which she gave four strokes, one on each of the four sides of the tree. Then the young men cut it down. As it was about to fall it was caught and held so that it would incline and fall toward the east.
>
> The leader now approached the fallen tree and said: "I have come for you that you may see the people, who are beautiful to behold!" The young men cut the branches from the tree, leaving a tuft of twigs and leaves at the top, stripped off the bark, then tied the tuft at the top together with a black covering. (253–54)

Following these preparations, two men with hereditary rights painted the pole in bands of black and red to signify night and day, thunder and death, and earth and sky. They dug a hole for the pole at the center of the *hu'thuga* and heaped the dirt from the hole to the east. Between this heap and the pole they cut a figure into the earth. It was a circle open to the east. This figure, known as *uzhin'eti*, was used as an earth altar. Every Omaha knew this form as a place in which family and tribal life takes place. It represents a tipi, the dwelling place of a family, and the *hu'thuga*, the dwelling place of the entire tribe. It is a dwelling place for the tribe's most ancient traditions. Its name refers to "the wistfulness of a child as when it stands before its parent waiting to share in some good thing." It is the dwelling place of ancient tribal traditions. Ceremonies conducted here were marked with special reverence for the generations of Omahas who had gone before. This same earth altar was also constructed by a priest of the Hon'ga (Leader) clan to conduct the tribe's most sacred ceremony, the painting of the Sacred Pole (see chapter 5). The remarkable catlinite platform pipe that accompanies the Sacred White Buffalo Hide also has the same form as *uzhin'eti*.

Fletcher and La Flesche complete their description of preparations for the He'dewachi as follows:

The keepers sat in a circle around the hole and again smoked the pipe, passing it four times. Down of swan, a water bird (the significance of water as connecting the Above and the Below has been given), and tobacco, the offering to Wakon'da, were sprinkled in the hole, which was thus made ready to receive the symbolically decorated pole. The leader said, "It is finished; raise him, that your grandfather may see him!" And the pole was set in the hole and made steady by tamping earth about it.

These preparatory ceremonies occupied three days. The dance and public festival took place on the fourth day. The pole simulated a man; the black covering on the top, his head. The decorations referred to the cosmic forces which gave and maintained life. As a tree it symbolized the tribe; the wands of the people were its branches, parts of the whole. Thus was the idea of unity symbolically set forth. (255)

The He'dewachi ceremony must have been familiar to members of the Omaha tribe at the time when they lived "in a village near a lake" (218). They knew that the He'dewachi pole represented the power of Thunder and the passage of night into day. These forces of nature are universal. They knew that the Pole represented tribal unity. People came together each year to sing and dance in celebration of their existence as a tribe. Omaha leaders also knew that the idea of tribal unity would be essential to their survival as they came into contact with many other tribes. They knew that the greatest threat to unity was rivalry between competing individuals and families, a problem they must still confront.

The Sacred Legend says that "the finding of the Pole is said to have occurred while a council was in progress between the Cheyenne, Arikara, Omaha, Ponca, and Iowa, to reach an agreement on terms of peace and rules of war and hunting, to adopt a peace ceremony" (218). Now, as in the past, Umon'hon'ti, the Real Omaha, is a single voice capable of speaking for the tribe as a whole if the Omahas can find a consensus within themselves. His return to the tribe has challenged contemporary Omahas to look at themselves as a vital link between past and future generations. He challenges them to think about themselves as a people moving together through time. He challenges them to stop and think about their situation, as they have done since the times recounted in the Sacred Legend. The seven pipes of the Nini'baton subclans have been scattered and will probably not be brought together again. Although the fate of the two tribal pipes is not public knowledge, the Sacred Pole and the Sacred White Buffalo Hide remain and have now come back to the people. Even more miraculously, the people themselves has survived disease and war and allotment and assimilation. They continue to be part of "an invisible and continuous life" that "permeates all things, seen and unseen."

Today, the tribe is governed by a tribal council of seven elected members and a tribal chairman. There is no longer any mechanism for appointing a council of seven chiefs empowered to act as religious officers. There are no public ceremonies in which to validate the priestly status these pipe holders once had. The Omahas remain divided on certain issues as they have throughout their past. They are divided, but they also continue to come together as they have for hundreds of years in the annual pow-wow. Now they have been joined in that gathering by the return of an ancient and respected elder, Umon'hon'ti and his companion, the Tethon'ha, the Sacred White Buffalo Hide. Also returned is the carved pipe belonging to the Sacred Pole and the ancient catlinite platform pipe of Tethon'ha, whose outline represents the stamp of a buffalo's hoof. Together, these ancient symbols are capable of speaking for the entire tribe with a single voice. Umon'hon'ti is a person of the people. He is Washa'begle, the Venerable Man. He is Waxthe'xe, "mottled as by shadows." He is Umon'hon'ti, the Real Omaha. Tethon'ha and her pipe remind people that even though the buffalo no longer nourish them physically, the idea they represent is still a source of power and inspiration.

Omaha history has not ceased as the tribe goes into the twenty-first century, any more than it ceased at any other point in the past. The physical forms of their sacred objects continue to represent points where Wakon'da has stopped, but they are as much beginnings as endings. As always, Wakon'da remains with them as a spirit of life and motion, an invisible and continuous life that permeates all things, seen and unseen. Now, the Sacred Pole and his companion, the Sacred White Buffalo Hide have moved from being unseen to having once again the potential for being central emblems of tribal identity. They have returned to view. As always, Omaha history continues to be made within a circle of stories.

CHAPTER THREE

A Tree That Stands Burning

My son has seen a wonderful tree.
The Thunder birds come and go upon this tree,
making a trail of fire
that leaves four paths on the burnt grass
that stretch toward the Four Winds.
When the Thunder birds alight on the tree
it bursts into flame
and the fire mounts to the top.
The tree stands burning,
but no one can see the fire except at night.
Fletcher and La Flesche (1911, 218)

A SACRED OBJECT AS TEXT

In this passage from Yellow Smoke's Legend of the Sacred Pole, a chief describes his son's encounter with the power of Wakon'da. From that encounter came the Sacred Pole of the Omaha tribe. Even today, Omahas agree that Umon'hon'ti is from Wakon'da. Omahas today have renewed contact with the story and with the Sacred Pole himself. Both can be read as texts from the past. Each reading of a text lifts the author's words from the inertia of their physical presence as lines of type on pieces of paper. Each reading brings the text into an altered context. Each reading of an ethnographic text transfers meaning from one culture to another. Each reading of a physical object reveals its relation to Wakon'da.

The son of an Omaha chief long ago read the object that was to become the Sacred Pole as "a wonderful tree." His father read the same object as "a tree that stands burning." The older man understood it as a sacred place where "the Thunder birds come and go . . . making a trail of fire that leaves four paths on the burnt grass that stretch toward the Four Winds." Fletcher and La Flesche read the same object as the relic of "a past once so full of human activity and hope." Now, more than a century has passed since that reading of the Sacred Pole as the relic of a dying culture. The Omahas have survived as a people. They still face the problem of devising "some means by which the bands of the tribe might be kept together and the tribe itself saved from extinction" through the forces of assimilation. In times gone by, Umon'hon'ti guided them toward the goal of cultural survival. Yellow Smoke told Fletcher and La Flesche that long ago "the wise old men thought how they might devise some plans by which all might live and move together and there be no danger of quarrels" (251). If people continue to come to Umon'hon'ti in the right mind, they may be gifted with his blessing for a long time to come.

The Twenty-seventh Annual Report of the Bureau of American Ethnology is a physical object as well as a written text. The Sacred Pole of the Omaha tribe is also a physical object. Both are messengers. Although the Pole does not contain written words, he is a rich container of meaning. Like a book, the Pole can be read as a text that carries meaning from one generation to another. Like a book, he speaks to people who understand his language. The Venerable Man communicates in a language of philosophy and ceremony, a language familiar to the experience of Native American people. Umon'hon'ti speaks prominently for his tribe as a whole. As a person who stands for all the people, he speaks with a single voice. As a knowledgeable elder of the tribe, he also speaks in the multiple voices of his various parts. He speaks in the intricate language of ceremonial exchange.

The Omahas have always thought of themselves as a tribe composed of complementary halves, the Sky people and the Earth people. Umon'hon'ti is a single person in whom these halves may join together. He is a venerable man, but he also reminds people of the compassionate female principle that Fletcher and La Flesche called "the great mother force." He speaks for men and for women. He speaks for Sky people and Earth people. He gives voice to Omaha sacred texts, in the way that scriptures give voice to the sacred traditions of other peoples.

Think of Umon'hon'ti as a person who has accumulated many stories during his long life. You can "read" some of these stories in his very appearance. My first impression was of his great antiquity. Now, I am impressed by his great vitality. Both are true to his nature. He bears the signature of much devotion. For many years, people "fed" him with buffalo meat. Each year they painted him with buffalo fat mixed with red pigment. They wrapped him with a piece of leather called *a'xondepa*, "the word used to designate the leather shield worn on the wrist of an Indian to protect it from the bowstring." Fletcher and La Flesche explain that "this name affords unmistakable evidence that the Pole was intended to symbolize a man, as no other creature could wear the bowstring shield. It indicates also that the man thus symbol-

8. *Doran L. Morris carrying Umon'hon'ti into the pow-wow arena, followed by Dennis Hastings and Edward Cline. Ian Brown is standing behind. Macy, Nebraska, August 20, 1989. Photograph © Ilka Hartmann, 1997.*

ized was one who was both a provider for and a protector of his people."
Omahas of long ago gave him a staff, *i'mongthe,* "such as old men lean on."
They lashed a piece of ash wood to his base and called it *zhi'be,* "leg." Upon
the top, or "head" of the Pole was tied a large scalp, *ni'ka nonzhiha.* Below the
head was a basketwork of twigs "now shriveled with age, which is lightly
filled with feathers and the down of the crane" (225). Around this receptacle
was a wrapping of tanned hide.

The Sacred Pole is remarkable because he is a physical object that has survived from a distant past. He is remarkable because he is sacred and alive with
meaning. He is remarkable because he is a person to members of the Omaha
tribe. He is remarkable because he represents Wakon'da, "a power by which
things are brought to pass." He is remarkable because he has led a long and
storied life. He has many names. He is Waxthe'xe, an object with the power
of motion, of life, that is "mottled as by shadows." This name, too, has stories
attached to it.

Originally, Waxthe'xe referred to the ancient Cedar Pole, associated with
war and the power of Thunder. "This venerable object," Fletcher and La
Flesche say, "was once the central figure in rites that have been lost." It fig-
ured in "creation myths associated with the advent of the human race." It
evoked the power of Thunder because "the Thunder birds were said to live
'in a forest of cedars'" (457). Fletcher and La Flesche continue: "There is a
tradition that in olden times, in the spring after the first thunder had
sounded, in the ceremony which then took place this Cedar Pole was painted,
with rites similar to those observed when the Sacred Pole was painted and
anointed at the great tribal festival held while on the buffalo hunt" (458).
Like the Sacred Pole, the Cedar Pole had a leg, was bound in the middle, and
"typified a manlike being." The Cedar Pole also went to the Peabody Museum in 1888 and has returned to tribal control a century later. The principal
difference between the two sacred objects is that *Umon'hon'ti* derives from a
particular visionary moment that spoke to a key episode in the tribe's history.
Like the key symbols of Christianity, he is both universal and particular.

Another name for the Sacred Pole is Washa'begle, "a dark chief whose
profile is seen as prominent against the horizon." The name evokes the
curved staff, *washa'be,* carried by the man chosen to lead the communal buffalo hunt (see chapter 4 for a complete description of this object in relation to
the hunt). It also suggests that the Pole is a spiritual chief of the tribe. Contemporary Omahas have chosen to call him Umon'hon'ti, "the Real Omaha."
He speaks to people today from a time in the tribe's past when "a great council was being held to devise some means by which the bands of the tribe
might be kept together and the tribe itself saved from extinction." He was

central to the tribe's ceremonies during their buffalo-hunting days. Now, he has returned to the tribe as a carrier of Omaha identity.

One of the stories Fletcher and La Flesche pass on describes an incident in his life that took place sometime early in the nineteenth century. It has to do with the honor and respect he was accorded even when the tribe was experiencing hard times:

> The keeper of the Pole had become a very old man, but he still clung to his duties. Misfortune had come to him, and he had no horse when the time came for the tribe to move out on the annual hunt. The old man and his aged wife had no one to help them to carry their tent and provisions, which, added to the Sacred Pole, made a heavy load for the old people. The old man struggled on for some days, his strength gradually failing. At last the time came when he had to choose between carrying food or carrying the Pole. The tribe had started on; he hesitated, then self-preservation decided in favor of the food, so leaving the Pole as it stood the old man slowly walked away.
>
> As he neared the tribal camp a young man saw him and asked what had happened that he was without the Pole. The old man told his story. The young man was poor and had only the horse he was riding, but he at once turned back to the deserted camp to rescue the Pole. The ride was a dangerous one, for there were enemies near. He risked his life to save the Pole by turning back. He found it where it had been left by the old man; then mounting his horse with it he made haste to rejoin the tribe. When he came near to where the people were camped he dismounted, took the Pole on his back, and leading his horse made his way to the old keeper, delivered to him the Pole, and at the same time presented his horse to the old man. This was the only time the Pole was ever carried on horseback.
>
> The act of the young man was at once known, and he was publicly thanked by the Hon'ga subgens that had charge of the Pole and its ceremonies. A few days later the Seven Chiefs were called to a council, and they sent for the young man, bidding him to come to them and to wear his robe in the ceremonial manner. He hesitated at what seemed to him must be a mistake in the summons, but he was told he must obey. When he entered the tent where the chiefs were sitting he was motioned to a vacant place beside one of the principal chiefs. The young man was thus made an honorary chief because of his generous act toward the Pole; he could sit with the chiefs, but he had no voice in the deliberations. (230)

The Sacred Pole's return to the Omahas is a challenge to anthropologists

9. *Studio portrait of Alice C. Fletcher. Photograph courtesy of the Smithsonian Institution National Anthropological Archives.*

as well as to contemporary Omahas. Anthropologists have kept descriptions of Omaha ceremonial life bound within the pages of their books. Now they must discover a language of translation that will bring the information they have been holding into the view of Omahas living today. They must provide a new reading of their old texts, just as Omahas must agree upon a new reading of the Pole himself. The Twenty-seventh Annual Report is now an old book. Like the Sacred Pole, the book itself has become the survivor of a past way of life. The culture of anthropology has changed as much as Omaha culture has in the years since 1911. As you read the stories in this book, think about the Sacred Pole as a living person, a Venerable Man of the Omaha tribe, and as a text from which you can receive a blessing if you "come to it in the right mind."

10. *Studio portrait of Francis La Flesche. Photograph courtesy of the Smithsonian Institution National Anthropological Archives.*

The Sacred Pole has stories to tell about life in our own times. Contemporary Omahas have touched him and prayed over him. Contemporary academics (like me and former Peabody curator Ian Brown) have marveled at the power of motion and of life that remains strong within him. The Venerable Man has aided the tribe in establishing positive relations with the university that had been holding the remains of their ancestors who lived at Ton'wontonga, the Big Village on the Missouri River. He continues to remind them of the power of Wakon'da. He continues to help them relate "the seen to the unseen, the dead to the living, a fragment of anything to its entirety." Even more than the Twenty-seventh Annual Report of the Bureau of American Ethnology, Umon'hon'ti offers himself as a text for the reading and interpretation of people alive today.

Francis La Flesche could not have known that the storied life of Umon'hon'ti would continue more than a century after he persuaded Yellow Smoke to send him to a "great brick house" in the East. As an employee of the Bureau of American Ethnology and as a practicing ethnographer, La Flesche struggled personally with the multiple and sometimes conflicting identities of being, at the same time, an Omaha and an anthropologist. He read both the Pole and his own biography in the vocabulary of these two traditions. In his book about his experience in a Presbyterian mission school, *The Middle Five*, La Flesche described how he came to understand the white man's world of books and writing. In *The Omaha Tribe*, he described the Indian side of his education.

The knowledge that Francis had of Omaha language and tradition was essential to the documentation of Omaha culture, which forms the core of the book he and Alice Fletcher wrote together. Most of the book is in Fletcher's voice, or at least in an academic voice upon which they both agreed. It reflects both a nineteenth-century belief in progress and Fletcher's particular fascination with the complementarity of male and female forces. The beautiful texts and translations of songs and ceremonies are the work of La Flesche. One section of the book is in his voice alone. It is a first-person narrative in which he remembers the lessons he learned when he took part in one of the last tribal buffalo hunts. He then describes his later negotiations, as an anthropologist, for the preservation of the Sacred Pole and Sacred White Buffalo Hide. His "Boy Memory" is a classic in the genre of Native American autobiography and complements his other autobiographical work, *The Middle Five*.

In the 1870s the buffalo disappeared from the prairies and Omaha life changed dramatically. The keepers of the Sacred Pole, the White Buffalo Hide, and other tribal emblems became discouraged. Because the tribe was no longer able to hunt buffalo, which was required for the great tribal ceremonies, the keepers were unable to find younger people willing to take responsibility for their sacred objects and their ceremonies. Finally, in 1888, Francis La Flesche approached Yellow Smoke with the proposal that the Venerable Man be given over to the Peabody Museum of Harvard University for safekeeping. In his "Boy Memory" La Flesche describes his own experience of the Pole during the tribe's last buffalo-hunting days and a final encounter with Yellow Smoke that resulted in the Pole's transfer. He calls his story "the boy memory of these ancient ceremonies of the Sacred Pole" and describes himself as "the only living witness who is able to picture in English those far-away scenes." It describes from personal experience one of the last occasions when the Pole's beautiful renewal ceremony was performed. Because of its unique value, it is worth reproducing here. Fletcher and La Flesche introduce it as follows:

> The following is the boy memory of these ancient ceremonies of the Sacred Pole, now forever gone, by one of the present writers, the only living witness who is able to picture in English those far-away scenes. (245)

A Boy Memory

One bright summer afternoon the Omahas were traveling along the valley of one of the streams of western Kansas on their annual buffalo hunt. The mass of moving people and horses extended for nearly half a mile in width and some 2 miles in length. There was an old man walking in a space in the midst of this moving host. The day was sultry and everybody around me was in the lightest clothing possible; but the solitary old man wore a heavy buffalo robe wrapped about his body. Around his shoulders was a leather strap the width of my hand, to the ends of which was attached a dark object that looked like a long black pole. From one end hung a thing resembling a scalp with long hair. One of my playmates was with me, and we talked in low tones about the old man and the curious burden on his back. He looked weary, and the perspiration dropped in profusion from his face, as with measured steps he kept apace with the cavalcade.

The horses that I was driving stopped to nibble the grass, when, partly from impatience and partly out of mischief, I jerked the lariat I was dragging with all the force I could muster in the direction of the horses, and the end of it came with a resounding whack against the sleek side of the gray. Startled at the sound, all of the five horses broke into a swift gallop through the open space, and the gray and the black, one after the other, ran against the old man, nearly knocking him over. My friend turned pale; suddenly he became anxious to leave me, but I finally persuaded him to remain with me until camp was pitched. He stayed to help me to water the horses and drive them to pasture and I invited him to dinner, which he seemed to expect.

While we were eating, the boy asked me if he should tell my father of the incident. I consented, for I thought that would relieve him from any fears of the consequences. As he was telling of what happened I watched the expression of my father's face with some trepidation, and felt greatly relieved when he smiled. We finished our dinner, but as we started to go out my father stopped us and said: "Now, boys, you must go to the Sacred Tent. Take both horses with you, the gray and the black, and this piece of scarlet cloth; when you reach the entrance you must say, 'Venerable man! we have, without any intention of disrespect, touched you and we have come to ask to be cleansed from the wrong we have done.'"

We did as we were instructed and appeared before the Sacred Tent in which was kept the "Venerable Man," as the Sacred Pole was called, and repeated our prayer. The old man who had been so rudely jostled by our horses came out in response to our entreaty. He took from me the scarlet cloth, said a few words of thanks, and re-entered the tent; soon he returned carrying in his hand a wooden bowl filled with warm water. He lifted his right hand to the sky and wept, then sprinkled us and the horses with the water, using a spray of artemesia. This act washed away the anger of the "Venerable Man," which we had brought down upon ourselves.

A few weeks later we were moving from the high hills down to the valley of the Platte river, returning from the hunt, our horses heavily laden with buffalo skins and dried meat. A beautiful spot was selected for our camp, and the crier gave in a loud voice the order of the chiefs that the camp be pitched in ceremonial form. This was done.

In the evening my playmate came and we ate fried bread and drank black coffee together. When we had finished the little boy snapped his black eyes at me and said: "Friend, let us go and play in the Holy (communal) Tent; the boys will be there and we will have fun." We went, and there was the Holy Tent, 60 or 70 feet in length. The two Sacred Tents of the Hon'ga gens had been united and a dozen or more other skin tents were added to them on either side, making a tent that could easily hold two or three hundred people. No grown people were there, so we youngsters had no end of fun playing hide and seek in the folds of the great tent, while the serious sages were taking the census of the people elsewhere, using small sticks to count with, preparatory to calling upon each family to contribute to the coming ceremony.

The next night we youngsters had again our fun in the Holy Tent. On the third night, when we went to play as usual, we found at the Tent two officers with whips, who told us that boys would not be permitted to play in the Tent that night. Still we lingered around and saw that even older persons were not allowed to come near, but were told to make a wide detour in passing, so as not to disturb the fresh grass in front of the Tent. Dogs were fired at with shotguns if they approached too near. The ceremony was to begin the next day, so the chiefs and priests, through the crier, requested the people to conduct themselves in such manner as the dignity of the occasion required.

Early in the morning I was wakened by my mother and told to sit up and listen. I did so and soon heard the voice of an old man calling the names of boys. Most of them I recognized as playmates. Suddenly I heard my own name distinctly called. I arose to make answer but was held back by my mother, who put in my arms a large piece of meat, with no wrapping whatever, regardless of my clean calico shirt, while she bade me go to where I was called. When I emerged from the tent with my burden the crier stopped calling my name, and called the boy in the next tent. As I neared the Holy Tent to which I had been summoned, an old man, wearing a band of buffalo skin around his head and a buffalo robe about his body, came forward to meet me. He put both his hands on my head and passed them down my sides; then he took from me the meat and laid it down on the grass in front of a dark pole standing aslant in the middle of the Holy Tent, a scalp dangling on the end of it. I recognized this pole as the one that was carried by the old man whom my horses ran against only a few weeks before. The calling of the names still went on; a man sat immediately back of the pole with two piles of small sticks before him; he would pick up a stick from one pile and give a name to the crier, who, leaning on a staff, called it out at the top of his voice; when this was done the stick was placed on the other pile.

When every family in the tribe excepting those of the Hon'ga gens had thus been called upon to make an offering, the priests began to sing the songs pertaining to this peculiar ceremony. I was now very much interested and watched every movement of the men who officiated. Four of the fattest pieces of meat were selected and placed just at the foot of the Sacred Pole. A song was sung and a man stood ready with a knife near the meat; when the last note died out the man made a feint at cutting and then resumed his position. Three times the song was repeated with its accompanying act, when on the fourth time the man in great haste carved out all of the fat from the four pieces of choice meat and put it in a wooden bowl. After the fat had been mixed with burnt clay and kneaded into a paste, another song was song, and the same priest stood ready with bowl and brush in hand beside the Pole. At the close of the song he made a feint at the Pole with the brush and resumed his former position. Four times this song was sung, each time followed by a feint. Then a new stanza was sung, at the end of which the priest touched the Pole lightly with his brush the entire length. This song and act were repeated four times. Then a different song was sung, the words of which I can remember even to this day: "I make him beautiful! I make him beautiful!" Then the priest with great haste dipped his brush into the bowl and daubed the Pole with the paste while the singing was going on. Four times the song was sung, the anointing was finished, and the Pole stood shining in fresh paint. Then many of the people cried: "Oh! how beautiful he is!" and then laughed, but the priests never for an instant changed the expression of their faces. I did not know whether to join in the merriment or to imitate the priests and maintain a serious countenance; but while I stood thus puzzled the ceremony went on.

A woman dressed in a peculiar fashion took the place of the priest who had painted the Pole. She wore on her head a band of buffalo skin and the down of the eagle, around her body a buffalo robe with the fur outside, and to her ankles were tied strips of buffalo skin with the hair on. In her left hand she held six arrows and stood ready with one poised in her right. A song was sung and at the close she made a feint with the arrow at the bundle of feathers in the middle of the Pole. Four times this was done; then other songs were sung and at the close of each song, with a quick movement the woman thrust an arrow through the bundle containing down tied to the middle of the Pole with such force that it passed through and as it dropped stuck in the ground, and the people shouted as with great joy. I joined in the shouting, although at the time I did not know why the people cheered. There were seven arrows in all; on this occasion every one of the arrows went successfully through the downy bundle. It is said that if an arrow failed to go through and bounced back, the gens which it represented would meet with misfortune; some member would be slain by the enemy.

After the singing of the songs and the anointing of the Pole, the meat was distributed among the families of the Hon'ga gens, the keepers of the Sacred Pole. The moment that this was done a man was seen coming over the hill running at full speed, waving his blanket in the air in an excited manner, and shouting the cry of alarm: "The enemy are upon us!" The horses were familiar with this cry and the moment they heard it they stampeded into the camp circle, making a noise like thunder. Men rushed to their tents for their bows and arrows and guns and were soon mounted on their best horses. Warriors sang the death song, and women sang songs to give the men courage. The excitement in camp was at its height, but the singing of the priests in the Holy Tent went on. Instead of going out to meet the enemy, the warriors gathered at one side of the camp circle opposite the Holy Tent and at the firing of a gun came charging toward it. It was a grand sight—four or five hundred warriors rushing on us at full speed. There was no enemy; the man who gave the alarm was only acting his part of a great drama to be performed before the Sacred Pole. The warriors fired their guns and shot their arrows at a number of figures made of bundles of tall grass and arranged before the Holy Tent. Shouts of defiance went from the tent and were returned by the charging warriors. This play of battles lasted nearly the whole day.

Years passed, and with them passed many of the brave men who told the tale of their battles before the Sacred Pole. So also passed the buffalo, the game upon which the life of this and other tribes depended. During these years I was placed in school, where I learned to speak the English language and to read and write.

Through a curious chain of circumstances, which I need not here relate, I found myself employed in the Indian Bureau at Washington. The Omaha had given up the chase and were putting all their energies into agriculture. They had abandoned their villages and were scattered over their reservation upon separate farms, knowing that their former mode of living was a thing of the past and that henceforth their livelihood must come from tilling the soil. To secure themselves in the individual ownership of the farms they had opened, the people petitioned the Government to survey their reservation and to allot the land to them in severalty. Their petition was granted by an act of Congress and the work of apportioning the lands was assigned to a lady who is now known among the scientists of this and other countries. I was detailed to assist her in this work, and together we went to the reservation to complete the task.

While driving over the reservation one day we came to a small frame house with a porch in front. Around this dwelling were patches of corn and other vegetables and near by was an orchard of apple trees with ripening fruit. In strange contrast with all this there stood in the back yard an Indian tent, carefully pitched, and the ground around it scrupulously clean. My companion asked, "What is that?" "It is the Holy Tent of the Omahas," I replied. "What is inside of it?" "The Sacred Pole," I answered. "I want to see it." "You can not enter the Tent unless you get permission from the Keeper." The Keeper was not at home, but his wife kindly conducted us to the entrance of the Tent, and we entered. There in the place of honor stood my friend, the "Venerable Man," leaning aslant as I saw him years before when I carried to him the large offering of choice meat. He had served a great purpose; although lacking the power of speech, or any of the faculties with which man is gifted, he had kept closely cemented the Seven Chiefs and the gentes of the tribe for hundreds of years. He was the object of reverence of young and old. When the United States Government had become indebted to the tribe for lands sold, he, too, was accounted as one of the creditors and was paid the same as a man of flesh and blood. He now stood before us, abandoned by all save his last Keeper, who was now bowed with age. The Keeper seemed even to be a part of him, bearing the name "Smoked Yellow," a name referring both to the age and to the accumulation of smoke upon the Pole. Silently we stood gazing upon him, we three, the white woman in the middle. Almost in a whisper, and with a sigh, the Keeper's wife said, "I am the only one now who takes care of him. When it rains I come to close the flaps of the Tent, at all hours of the night. Many were the offerings once brought to him, but now he is left all alone. The end has come!"

A few years later I went to the house of Smoked Yellow and was hospitably entertained by him and his kind wife. After dinner, as we sat smoking in the shade of the trees, we spoke of the past life of the tribe and from time to time in our conversation I pleasantly reminded him of important events within my own knowledge, and of others of which I had heard, where his knowledge guided the actions of the people. This seemed to please him very much and he spoke more freely of the peculiar customs of the Omaha. He was an important man in his younger days and quite an orator. I have heard him deliver an address on the spur of the moment that would have done credit to almost any speaker in either branch of our Congress. He was one of the signers of the treaty entered into between the Omaha and the United States.

As my visit was drawing to a close, without any remarks leading thereto, I suddenly swooped down upon the old chief with the audacious question: "Why don't you send the 'Venerable Man' to some eastern city where he could dwell in a great brick house instead of a ragged tent?" A smile crept over the face of the chieftain as he softly whistled a tune and tapped the ground with his pipe stick before he replied, while I sat breathlessly awaiting the answer, for I greatly desired the preservation of this ancient and unique relic. The pipe cooled and he proceeded to clean it. He blew through it now and then as he gave me this answer: "My son, I have thought about this myself but no one whom I could trust has hitherto approached me upon this subject. I shall think about it, and will give you a definite answer when I see you again."

The next time I was at his house he conducted me to the Sacred Tent and delivered to me the Pole and its belongings. This was the first time that it was purposely touched by anyone outside of its hereditary Keepers. It had always been regarded with superstitious awe and anyone touching even its Tent must at once be cleansed by the priest. Even little children shared in this feeling and left unclaimed a ball or other plaything that chanced to touch the Tent made sacred by its presence.

Thus it was that the Sacred Pole of the Omaha found its way into the Peabody Museum in 1888 but leaving its ritual songs behind. During these years I have searched for men in the Hon'ga gens who would be likely to know these songs but without success. The old priest, Tenu'ga, whose office it was to sing them, died before I came in touch with him.

By the use of the graphophone [a wax cylinder recording device] I was enabled in 1897 to secure the ritual songs of the Sacred White Buffalo from Wakon'monthin, the last keeper; and when the record was finished I said to him: "Grandfather, years ago I saw you officiating at the ceremonies of the Sacred Pole and from this I judge that you are familiar with its songs. May I ask if you would be willing to sing them for me?" The old priest shook his head and replied: "Eldest son, I am forced to deny your request. These songs belong to the opposite side of the house and are not mine to give. You are right as to my knowledge of them and you did see me officiating at the ceremony you referred to; but I was acting as a substitute. The man whose place I took was newly inducted into his office and was not familiar with its various forms; he feared the results of any mistakes he might make, on account of his children, for it meant the loss of one of them by death should an error occur. You must consult the keepers of the Pole."

Knowing that it would be useless even with bribes to attempt to persuade the priest to become a plagiarist, I refrained from pushing the matter further, trusting that circumstances in the future might take such a turn as to relieve him from his obligations to recognize any individual's ownership in the ritual songs.

In the latter part of June 1898, I happened to be on the Omaha reservation, and while there I drove over to Wakon'monthin's house. He was at home and after the exchange of greetings I addressed him as follows:

Grandfather, last summer, after you had taught me the songs connected with the ceremony of the Sacred Buffalo, I asked you to teach me the songs of the Sacred Pole. You replied that you knew the songs, but could not sing them for me, because they belonged to the other side of the house and were not yours to give. I respected your purpose to keep inviolate your obligations to maintain the respective rights and offices of the two houses that were so closely allied in the preservation of order among our people, so I did not press my quest for the knowledge of the songs at that time, believing that you would soon see that the object for which that Sacred Tree and its accompanying rites were instituted had vanished, never to return. Our people no longer flock to these sacred houses as in times past, bringing their children laden with offerings that they might receive a blessing from hallowed hands; new conditions have arisen, and from force of circumstances they have had to accede to them and to abandon the old. I have been here and there among the members of the opposite side of the house, to which you referred, to find some one who knew the songs of the Sacred Pole, so that I might preserve them before they were utterly lost; but to my inquiries the invariable answer was: 'I do not know them. Wakon'monthin is the only man who has a full knowledge of them.' Therefore I have made bold to come to you again.

After holding the pipe he had been filling during my speech, up to the sky, and muttering a few words of prayer, the old man lit the pipe and smoked in silence for a time, then passed the pipe to me and made his reply, speaking in low tones:

My eldest son, all the words that you have just spoken are true. Customs that governed and suited the life of our people have undergone a radical change and the new generation has entered a new life utterly unlike the old. The men with whom I have associated in the keeping and teaching of the two sacred houses have turned into spirits and have departed, leaving me to dwell in solitude the rest of my life. All that gave me comfort in this lonely travel was the possession and care of the Sacred Buffalo, one of the consecrated objects that once kept our people firmly united; but, as though to add to my sadness, rude hands have taken from me, by stealth [see chapter 7 for an account of the loss and return of this sacred object], this one solace, and I now sit empty handed, awaiting the call of those who have gone before me. For a while I wept for this loss, morning and evening, as though for the death of a relative dear to me, but as time passed by tears ceased to flow and I can now speak of it with some composure.

At this point I passed the pipe back to the priest and he smoked, keeping his eyes fixed upon the ground as if in deep meditation. When he had finished smoking, he resumed his address, cleaning the pipe as he spoke:

I have been thinking of the change that has come over our people and their departure from the time-honored customs, and have abandoned all hope of their ever returning to the two sacred houses. No one can now with reason take offense at my giving you the songs of the Sacred Pole, and I am prepared to give them to you. As I sit speaking with you, my eldest son, it seems as though the spirits of the old men have returned and are hovering about me. I feel their courage and strength in me, and the memory of the songs revives. Make ready, and I shall once more sing the songs of my fathers.

It took but a few moments to adjust the graphophone to record the songs for which I had waited so long. As I listened to the old priest his voice seemed as full and resonant as when I heard him years ago, in the days when the singing of these very songs in the Holy Tent meant so much to each gens and to every man, woman, and child in the tribe. Now, the old man sang with his eyes closed and watching him there was like watching the last embers of the religious rites of a vanishing people.

READING THIS STORY

What La Flesche begins as his "boy memory" he completes with accounts of obtaining the Sacred Pole from Smoked Yellow (Yellow Smoke) in 1888 and, a decade later, of recording the Pole's songs from Wakon'monthin (Mystery Walking), the last keeper of the Sacred White Buffalo Hide. La Flesche wrote his story in a simple first-person narrative style. It is full of vivid images and contains closely detailed descriptions of scenes to which he was a personal witness. Like both a novelist and a narrator within the oral tradition, he moves between material in his own voice and quoted excerpts of remembered or reconstructed dialogue. Unfortunately, La Flesche does not date the earlier scenes he describes, and the reader is left to guess when they may have taken place. Circumstantial evidence gives some clues. In an obituary in the *American Anthropologist*, Hartley B. Alexander says Francis was born on Christmas Day, 1857, although some scholars have disputed this date. Alexander notes that "in his youth the Omaha still followed the annual buffalo hunt, and when only fifteen he covered a hundred miles as a runner in some eighteen hours, discovering the first herd of the season. He also was a participant in ceremonial life, and in his early childhood filled the role of sacred Child when the Wa'wan (or Hako) ceremony was participated in by the Omaha and the Pawnee" (1933, 328–31).

Alexander's judgment, if not his credibility, is rendered somewhat suspect by the photograph of La Flesche that accompanies the obituary. A formal studio portrait of La Flesche wearing a buffalo robe over a white shirt and bow tie has been crudely retouched to make it appear that he is wearing only the buffalo robe, thus forcing him into the white stereotype of an Indian. To his credit, though, Alexander does report that La Flesche was president of the Anthropological Society of Washington in 1922–23 and held a law degree from National University. He also correctly describes his books on the Osage tribe as "certainly the most complete single record of the ceremonies of a North American Indian people" (Alexander 1933, 329–40).

The last renewal ceremony for the Sacred Pole probably took place in 1875 and the last buffalo hunt was the following year. Oral tradition has it that, unsuccessful in their hunt, tribal members were forced to return to the reservation by train. If the dates Alexander cites in his obituary are more or less correct, Francis would have served as a runner on the hunt of 1872, a few years after he attended the mission school, which closed in 1869 (Barreis 1963). La Flesche reports in *The Middle Five* that he was unable to go on the buffalo hunt while attending school. He describes how he once during that time attempted to run away to join the people and was brought back by a relative. Thus, his dramatic encounter with the Sacred Pole must have taken place sometime after 1869, when he was nearing his early teens. His role as sacred child in the Wa'wan may have taken place before his school days. This evidence contradicts his statement in the narrative that it was in the years following the passing of the buffalo that, "I was placed in school, where I learned to speak the English language and to read and write." In fact, La Flesche must have been seventeen or eighteen when the buffalo disappeared, and he could have begun working as an interpreter as soon as two years after that, since Dorsey arrived on the reservation in 1878.

Whatever the dates of the events he describes, his narrative is the only available eye-witness account of the Pole's renewal ceremony available. What it lacks in historical particulars it makes up in literary and ethnographic detail. The woman who completes the renewal ceremony "wore on her head a band of buffalo skin and the down of the eagle." Around her body she wore "a buffalo robe with the fur outside." To her ankles were tied "strips of buffalo skin with the hair on." Finally, "in her left hand she held six arrows and stood ready with one poised in her right." Throughout his narrative, Francis describes the Pole as a person; "When the United States Government had become indebted to the tribe for lands sold, he, too, was accounted as one of the creditors and was paid the same as a man of flesh and blood." When the boy's horses nearly knocked the Pole and his keeper over, Francis made amends by speaking directly to the Pole himself, rather than to his keeper. Unfortunately, he does not say whether this keeper was Yellow Smoke or a predecessor.

The boy's description of the Pole's renewal ceremony is a fitting complement to the ethnographer's later account of its song texts and ceremonial order (see chapter 5). As a child, Francis and his friends imitated the servers of the ceremony by "taking census" with a count of small sticks. He remembers the Holy Tent being "60 or 70 feet in length," and he was privileged to be

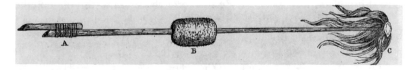

11. The "anatomically incorrect" drawing of the Sacred Pole. From Dorsey, Omaha Sociology (1884), figure 17.

one of the children entrusted with bringing meat "with no wrapping whatever" as an offering to the Pole, for which he received a blessing from a server of the ceremony. Here Francis saw the Pole in its position of honor for the first time. He listened carefully to hear each of four songs repeated four times, and was particularly moved by the ending words, "I make him beautiful! I make him beautiful!", to which the people reply, "Oh! how beautiful he is." He was present for the special moment when the keeper's wife completes the ceremony by shooting the seven sacred arrows through the Pole's bundle of swan's down. "I joined in the shouting," he writes, "although at the time I did not know why the people cheered." Francis never lost the sense of beauty and respect for ceremonial language that he first experienced at the Pole's renewal ceremony. Indeed, whatever compromises he may have made to the Lake Mohonk reformers, he subverted their Christian American chauvinism by dedicating his professional life to documenting the beauty of that language in his studies of Omaha and Osage ceremonial traditions.

Following the first part of his narrative, La Flesche describes how he obtained the preservation of the Sacred Pole and later recorded some of the songs belonging to the Pole from Wakon'monthin. His account of visiting the Pole with Alice Fletcher is sharply drawn. He describes their conversation novelistically, faithfully reporting the assertive side of Fletcher's character and revealing her supreme confidence in ethnography as an instrument of progress and civilization. This scene contrasts strikingly with the respectful and deferential encounter he describes in the boy memory.

"What is that?" Fletcher asks. "It is the Holy Tent of the Omahas," La Flesche replies, to which Fletcher responds with a command, "I want to see it." Francis responds by stating Omaha law: "You can not enter the Tent unless you get the permission of the Keeper." In an Indian context, that would have been a sufficiently strong statement of fact from which to draw a logical conclusion. To persist in the request would have denied the trust and respect necessary for shared discourse. Fletcher did not appear to understand what La Flesche had just told her. The Sacred Pole was an important ethnographic object and she was one of America's leading ethnographers. Francis must have known that Dorsey had earlier been unable to gain access to the Sacred

Pole, since the illustration he gives of it in 1884 (see fig. 11) is anatomically incorrect. He had probably shared his knowledge of this with Fletcher, who would have been particularly anxious to see what had been denied her predecessor. She was determined to enter. La Flesche simply reports next that Yellow Smoke's wife "kindly conducted us to the entrance of the Tent, and we entered."

Once in the Pole's presence again, La Flesche was clearly moved. "There in the place of honor stood my friend, the 'Venerable Man,' leaning aslant as I saw him years before when I carried to him the large offering of choice meat." It must have been awkward to be there without the keeper present. "Silently," La Flesche muses, "we stood gazing upon him, we three, the white woman in the middle." Yellow Smoke's wife tried to ease the moment. "I am the only one now who takes care of him. When it rains I come to close the flaps of the Tent, at all hours of the night. Many were the offerings once brought to him, but now he is left all alone. The end has come!"

What she said that day must have made a considerable impression on Francis. What she left unsaid must also have impressed him. Unlike Fletcher, he had grown up sensitive to the nuances of Omaha etiquette. In his introduction to *The Middle Five* he writes:

> Among my earliest recollections are the instructions wherein we were taught respect and courtesy toward our elders; to say "thank you" when receiving a gift, or when returning a borrowed article; to use the proper and conventional term of relationship when speaking to another; and never to address any one by his personal name; we were also forbidden to pass in front of persons sitting in the tent without first asking permission. (1963, xvi)

He knew that to pass in front of the Venerable Man without permission would have been improper. He also knew that the keeper's wife, who, in proper Omaha fashion, he does not call by name, had carried out the completion of the tribe's most awesome ceremony of renewal. For her to say that "the end has come," must have challenged him to think about how both the Pole and the tribe could continue their existence. He knew that the keeper's wife was a woman who once "wore on her head a band of buffalo skin and the down of the eagle." Around her body she had worn "a buffalo robe with the fur outside." To her ankles she had tied "strips of buffalo skin with the hair on." This was a woman who had once "in her left hand held six arrows and stood ready with one poised in her right." This was a woman whose success in thrusting the arrows through the swan's down bundle and into the earth had measured the tribe's well-being for each of many years.

Francis could not accept her pronouncement that "the end has come!" Although he clearly had no idea how his friend, the "Venerable Man" might find his way into the twentieth century and beyond, Francis seems then and there to have resolved to do whatever he could to further the life of the Sacred Pole. As he writes in describing a later conversation with Yellow Smoke, "I greatly desired the preservation of this ancient and unique relic."

The apparently simple incident La Flesche describes in a few paragraphs must in fact have been a defining moment in his life. It was wrong for Fletcher to persist in wanting to see the Pole without permission, and it was certainly wrong for her and other "Friends of the Indian" to support legislation banning Indian religious practices. But through this encounter, La Flesche tells us that he came to believe that it was wrong for the Sacred Pole to be abandoned entirely. Through it, he came to "greatly desire" its preservation. While he certainly accepted that a ceremonial tradition of renewing the Pole with gifts of buffalo meat had indeed come to an end, one part of him must have remained confident that the Pole was alive and was a person who stands for all the people.

Omahas today tell a story about La Flesche having taken the Pole when only the keeper's wife was at home. Doran Morris told me in no uncertain terms that this is tribal history. He and other Omahas I talked to are certain that La Flesche stole the Pole from the tribe. If this is true, La Flesche cannot be telling the truth when he states that, following their later conversations, Yellow Smoke delivered the Pole directly into his own hands. Perhaps tribal history reflects a memory of Fletcher having chosen to view the Pole without the keeper's permission. Perhaps people wish to blame La Flesche and absolve Yellow Smoke for having sold the Pole. I hope that Omahas reading what La Flesche wrote about the Pole will conclude, as I have, that he did the right thing, although perhaps in the wrong way and for the wrong reasons. Because of his actions, Omahas today have renewed contact with their Venerable Man. For this, they should be grateful to La Flesche. I would like to think, too, that the Pole himself saw fit to choose Francis as a respectful substitute for his traditional keeper in a time of crisis, as he seems to have chosen Doran Morris and Dennis Hastings in our own time.

A letter from Alice Fletcher to Peabody Museum Director F. W. Putnam may shed some light on the controversy surrounding the Pole's removal. It begins:

Winnebego Agency, Neb.
Sept. 26, 1888
My dear Prof. Putnam,
    Waiting for the spare moments when I could write you in detail has caused my silence and now I have only time for a brief note. I tell you an important ethnological matter. Francis when here last month se-

cured the Sacred Pole from the Hunga gens. This is a great prize. It cost us $45 and it is cheap. We have it at Mrs. Farley's (his sister) in Bancroft, and it is proposed, although this is a secret for it is by no means certain it can be brought about, to have next summer the full ceremonies so that F. and I can photograph them and take down all the songs and all the details. This will cost something but be a great thing for science. Francis has told Mr. Dorsey that we have the Pole and he is quite excited over it. There is but one more article and that is the white buffalo cow skin. We may get that. These two articles were kept in the two sacred tents in charge of the Hunga gens, one subdivision having one, another subgens the other. I spent three days at Francis' Father's having there old Yellow Smoke the old Hunga chief who kept the Pole, and I took down a hundred pages of notes. So far so good, save for a great grief and disaster.

(Fletcher to Putnam, Sept. 26, 1888, Peabody Museum Papers)

Yellow Smoke told the Sacred Legend of the tribe to Alice, Francis, and his father, Joseph (Iron Eye), in September of 1888. From the notes she referred to in her letter to Putnam, she abstracted a handwritten document on lined paper entitled "The Legend of the Sacred Pole." Below is a reading of both the handwritten version from 1888 and the one eventually published in 1911, followed by the continuation of her September 26 letter to Putnam.

THE SACRED LEGEND

After Yellow Smoke gave over the Sacred Pole, both Francis and Alice wished to obtain the Sacred Legend that normally would be passed on only to another keeper in the Hon'ga clan. Dorsey appears to have heard only a brief paraphrase of traditions relating to the Sacred Pole. Although he was acquainted with Yellow Smoke, he was not told the spiritual significance of the Pole's origin. Without identifying the source of his information, he writes that "the Omahas tell the following":

At first there were no chiefs in the gentes, and the people did not prosper. So a council was held, and they asked one another, "what shall we do to improve our condition?" Then the young men were sent out. They found many cotton-wood trees beside a lake, but one of these was better than the rest. They returned and reported the tree, speaking of it as if it was a person. All rushed to the attack. They struck it and felled it as if it had been a foe. They then put hair on its head, making a person of it. Then were the sacred tents made, the first chiefs selected, and the sacred pipes distributed. (1884, 234)

Fletcher and La Flesche were able to obtain more detailed information following Francis's purchase of the Pole for $45 on behalf of the Peabody Museum in 1888. They report that Yellow Smoke told them the tribe's Sacred Legend at the home of Joseph La Flesche that September, and that Fletcher "took down a hundred pages of notes." Nowhere in *The Omaha Tribe* do they give the full text of the Sacred Legend. Rather, they present isolated passages as they deem them relevant to particular topics. The 1888 manuscript in Fletcher's hand entitled "The Legends of the Sacred Pole," now in the National Anthropological Archives, is incomplete. The archive catalog lists it as "1888, 20 handwritten pp. by A. C. F." However, it is not dated in her hand and could be a compilation of notes written earlier. Her statement that the narratives "were written down on the spot just as they were given by him" is ambiguous. Her use of passive voice begs the question of who did the writing and how it was accomplished. Presumably, though, La Flesche heard it in Omaha and then gave Fletcher the passage in English to write down. There is no indication that they attempted to transcribe the text in the Omaha language. This is what Fletcher wrote about Yellow Smoke's narrative in her 1888 manuscript:

> The narratives of Shu-dae-na-the on these memorable days were written down on the spot just as they were given by him, and they are here transcribed with all their native flavor and fragmentary character in the belief that they will give a true insight into Indian thoughts and feeling and thus prove of value in the study of the race.
>
> While the old man talked he continually tapped the floor with a little stick he held in his hand, making the rhythm peculiar to the drumming of a man who is invoking the unseen powers according to certain Indian rites. His eyes were cast down, his speech was deliberate and his voice very low as if speaking to himself, so that one had almost to hold one's breath to catch the words. The scene was unpretentious, but even in the absence of all outward form there was a deep solemnity in these obsequies of a past once so full of human activity and aspirations. (1888 ms.)

Fletcher here characterized Yellow Smoke's narratives as having a "native flavor and fragmentary character" that "will give a true insight into Indian thoughts and feeling." She does not explain just what she means by the "fragmentary character" of Indian oral tradition. Perhaps because of her uncertainty about how Native American stories tie together, Fletcher experienced them as fragmented and consequently attempted to parcel out Yellow Smoke's narrative in bits and pieces as she and La Flesche worked them into their own narrative, *The Omaha Tribe*. But perhaps she had begun to understand what La Flesche had always known about the language of myth and ceremony. Each fragment is at the same time an entirety and a manifestation of Wakon'da. Each one connects to every other in a circle without beginning or end. Garrick Bailey, in commenting on La Flesche's documentation of Osage myth and ceremony, wrote that for La Flesche "the story did not exist as a single narrative but was presented in fragments scattered throughout the rituals." La Flesche called these songs, narratives, and ceremonies "the allegorical story of the tribe" (Bailey 1995, 63).

Whatever their reasons may have been, the authors chose not to present a single complete text of the narrative in their book. According to the 1888 manuscript, Yellow Smoke began his narrative with the following admonition: "The teachings of the pole are not for everyone; only to those who make gifts. These are taught." The 1888 manuscript does not report what gifts, if any, Fletcher and La Flesche brought to Yellow Smoke, but the letter to Putnam indicates that they paid him the relatively insignificant sum of forty-five dollars. Fletcher's comment to Putnam was "it is cheap." La Flesche would have clearly understood that such a momentous transfer of information would have required "the giving of gifts," for he later gave Wakon'monthin payment for telling him the ritual of the White Buffalo Hide. He must also have known that the sum of forty-five dollars did not match the value of this priceless cultural emblem. Because the 1888 manuscript is very similar to the one published in 1911, it seems likely that Fletcher wrote out both accounts, while La Flesche provided a simultaneous translation. She situates her 1911 account of what happened in Iron Eye's house at the top of the page facing a photograph of the Sacred Pole. Her words describe her recollection of an event that was one of the most important in her life. On the two preceding pages, set opposite to one another, are portraits of Iron Eye and Yellow Smoke.

Iron Eye looks stiff and formal, with short hair and a western suit. Yellow Smoke, by contrast, has long hair and an earring, and wears a medal as a pendant. Iron Eye must have been photographed in Nebraska, while Yellow Smoke was photographed by Roland Bonaparte on a trip to France. Both men were among the seven chiefs who signed the 1854 treaty. Both must have received medals for their participation. Fletcher and La Flesche chose to use Bonaparte's photograph of Yellow Smoke wearing his medal, but portrayed Iron Eye as an assimilated "make-believe white man."

Fletcher and La Flesche were well aware that Yellow Smoke's disclosure of information previously known only to keepers in the Hon'ga clan was sufficient cause for the sadness and anxiety they report he experienced. He was sad because the Pole was on its way to the Peabody Museum, the "great brick house" in the East. He was apprehensive for more immediate reasons. Omaha tradition demanded a strict adherence to proper ceremonial order.

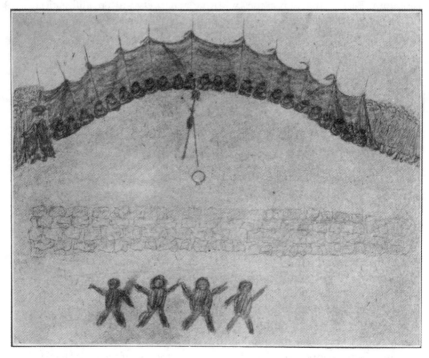

12. *Communal ceremonial structure (Holy Tent)—grass figures in foreground (native drawing). From Fletcher and La Flesche,* The Omaha Tribe *(1911), figure 58.*

Telling the Sacred Legend to outsiders broke all the rules he had lived with for many years. Fletcher and La Flesche report:

> If by any chance a mistake occurred during the ceremonies connected with the Sacred Pole, and one of the songs was sung out of sequence, then the following ceremony became obligatory: All the Waxthe'xeton subgens of the Hon'ga, they who had charge of the Sacred Pole and its rites, arose, lifted their arms, held their hands with the palms upward and wept. After a few moments one of the official servers came forward, passed in front of the line of standing singers, and wiped the tears from each man's face. Then the singers resumed their places, and the ceremony began again from the beginning as though for the first time. (232) [see fig. 12]

Yellow Smoke had lived with the knowledge of these obligations for most of his long life, but now he was alone. There were no members of his subclan at hand to wipe away the tears. The Pole was no longer the center of Omaha ceremonial life. Fletcher was a white woman, and Iron Eye, an adopted member of the Elk clan, had opposed the traditional ceremonies. Francis was young and was Omaha by blood only through his mother. All three remembered full well that Joseph La Flesche had suffered the consequences of interrupting the ceremonial order during his tenure as principal chief of the tribe.

Yellow Smoke was aware that Iron Eye had strongly advocated a policy of assimilation to American culture. He had led a faction known as "the young men's party." He and his followers had abandoned the earth-lodge villages and built frame houses, known by more traditional factions as "the village of the make-believe white man." More significantly, Yellow Smoke knew that Iron Eye had once refused to support the annual renewal ceremony for the Sacred Pole. Not long after that event, he developed an infection in his leg which resulted in its amputation. Dorsey reports that "when Joseph La Flesche lost his leg, the old men told the people that this was a punishment which he suffered because he had opposed the greasing of the Sacred Pole" (1884:235).

Fletcher gives more detail in notes for an unpublished manuscript entitled "Life History of Joseph La Flesche:"

Joseph La Flesche traded with his father out of the post at Bellevue and ran a ferry over the Missouri. He married and two years later his father died. He gave two horses to Big Elk, who later adopted him as his son and gave him the name of Inshta'maza and his title of chief. He was to raise Big Elk's son and make him chief when he came of age. He called all the chiefs and told them, "I have adopted Joseph La Flesche as my son, and I have placed him above my own son and in the spring I wish him to occupy my place as your head chief." The chiefs were willing and gave their consent. La Flesche gave the chiefs several feasts and gave them horses also, as was the custom among the Indians when a man desired a chieftainship.

Big Elk died before the spring. He was made head chief and Big Elk's successor by the whole tribe. Big Elk's son died in 1866. Joseph La Flesche gave the papers and medals Big Elk had given him to No Knife after holding the chieftainship for several years. La Flesche asked all the chiefs what their wishes were in regard to his chieftainship—that if they did not want him it was alright. They gave unanimous consent.

After, he received recognition in Washington as chief. Cattle given by trader who was La Flesche's rival and La Flesche told people to reject it and press for money owed. Ceremony of Sacred Pole performed—camp moved—heads of families called to contribute buffalo meat—La Flesche would not give away and the omission of the contribution was considered a sacrilege and was followed by punishment for the offense. That fall after the camp arrived home he stepped on a rusty nail, his leg was amputated and the tribe claimed this was the punishment for the omission of the contribution. When the people heard of this refusal to contribute to the ceremony, knowing him who was so free with his gifts, they all said, "They always get punished. Why did he do so?" The amputation of the limb took place about 1861. (Fletcher—La Flesche Papers, n.d.)

By the time Yellow Smoke and Iron Eye came together in Iron Eye's house on that September day in 1888, they had known one another for a long time. All present must have been acutely aware of the former chief's troubled relationship to the Sacred Pole, and of the danger that could result from causing a break in the ceremonial order. On the other hand, Iron Eye may have seen the occasion as an opportunity to do right by the Pole and make amends for his former slight. It is clear that while Yellow Smoke acknowledged that the ceremonies associated with the tribal buffalo hunt would never be repeated, he was certain that the Pole and its stories remained alive and powerful. Fletcher knew that the occasion was momentous and hazardous. She began her published account of the session with the simple words, "It was a memorable day," but quickly moved on to assert that "the past was irrevocably gone." She then acknowledged the concerns Yellow Smoke had expressed: "The old man had consented to speak but not without misgivings until his formal principal chief said that he would 'cheerfully accept for himself any penalty that might follow the revealing of these sacred traditions,' an act formerly held to be a profanation and punishable by the supernatural" (1911, 224). Her handwritten text of 1888 reveals more of the tension that made the day memorable:

> During the summer days of September 1888, when the harvest was ended and the tall stacks of wheat cast their shadows over the stubble fields and the wind rustled the yellowing corn, the writer was at the home of Joseph La Flesche, the last head chief of the tribe and who had passed through nearly all the rites and had gained all the honors possible to an Omaha. Thither came Shu-dae-na-the, a chief of the Hun'ga gens and Keeper of the Wa-thae-thae or Sacred Pole. This Sacred Pole had already been committed to the care of the two writers, and the old chief had come to tell us of the traditions which belonged to it. To speak of these things except when the ceremonies demanded it would have been in old times a sacrilege. But the past was irrevocably gone, so the old man (who had accepted Christianity and was already a citizen

of the United States) declared his willingness to part with these traditions even as he had laid away his office as Keeper of the Sacred Pole.

In her 1911 account of these events, Fletcher quoted Iron Eye as saying that he would "cheerfully accept for himself any penalty that might follow the revealing of these sacred traditions." In 1888, she emphasized his legitimacy within Omaha tradition by describing him as having "passed through nearly all the rites" and having "gained all the honors possible to an Omaha." Conversely, she described Yellow Smoke in 1888 as a man no longer bound by past tradition "who had accepted Christianity and was already a citizen of the United States." She later crossed out the passage and omitted it from the 1911 published text. She notes in 1888, though, that despite Yellow Smoke's apparent conversion, he was "a little sad withal, and somewhat anxious for, according to the belief of his tribe, the penalty for profanation of the Pole was death. But his (old) head chief was present and encouraged the old man to give forth these treasures, taking upon himself the risk of the penalty" (1888 ms.).

We will never know just what Iron Eye and Yellow Smoke may have been thinking that day and what sort of understanding they reached regarding Iron Eye's relationship to the Pole. What happened shortly after their meeting, though, is shocking and unequivocal. Iron Eye took ill immediately following the transfer of information and died two weeks later in the very room in which Yellow Smoke had told the Sacred Legend. Both of Fletcher's accounts record the drama of this turn of events. In 1888 she wrote:

> By a singular co-incidence the touch of fatal disease fell upon Joseph La Flesche almost at the very close of this interview, which lasted some days, and in a fortnight he lay dead. The old men and many others still under the influence of the traditions of the tribe, believed he had forfeited his life in giving away the Sacred Pole and that the sanctity of the faith of their fathers had thus been attested afresh.

By 1911 she described what happened as follows:

> The scene in that little room where sat the four actors in this human drama was solemn, as at the obsequies of a past once so full of human activity and hope. The fear inspired by the Pole was strengthened in its passing away, for by a singular coincidence the touch of fatal disease fell upon Joseph La Flesche almost at the close of this interview, which lasted three days, and in a fortnight he lay dead in the very room in which had been revealed the Sacred Legend connected with the Pole. (224)

In 1888 Fletcher recorded the opinion of "the old men and many others still under the influence of the traditions of the tribe," that Iron Eye's death was a demonstration of the "sanctity of the faith of their fathers." In 1911 she called his death simply "a singular coincidence" and refrained from presenting the Omaha interpretation of its meaning. The letter she sent to Putnam on September 26 is more succinct. After recounting to him that Francis had successfully purchased the Sacred Pole for forty-five dollars, she continued:

> So far so good, save for a great grief and disaster. Francis' father lies dead. He died Monday and F. is in route, too late to see his father alive. Joseph La Flesche was to spend the winter in Washington and F. and I were to get all we needed from him. How this one calamity will affect our work I can't tell. Poor F. will be heartbroken. His father was his idol and I fear the boy will hardly have courage to go on, but he is noble and manly and his father's great interest in this work will be a help. Mr. Dorsey said if he knew what F. was doing he would have got Maj. Powell to have Francis' leave extended so he could have worked longer this year, but as it has proved, that would have been useless since his father took sick two days after Francis left and died in two weeks. I was with the family staying up the last and I'll go back to attend the funeral. I was very much attached to Joseph La Flesche.
>
> He lies silent, while the winds rustle through his hundred acre field of ripe corn and play about his towering stacks of wheat all ready for the thresher. He had over 140 acres under cultivation, had builded him a house and barn, and all this since he left his old farm in the bluffs and came out on the prairie among the white settlers four years ago. He was the last head chief of the tribe, but died the leader of his people still. He cast his first vote as a citizen last fall and made an address to his tribesmen at Bancroft on the fourth of July this year. Both white-men and Indians respected him and many loved him as a father. Civilization and science have lost a friend in Joseph La Flesche.
> Goodby—Sincerely
> Alice C. Fletcher
> When convenient will you send check to Francis for the $45.
> (Fletcher to Putnam, Sept. 26, 1888, Peabody Museum Papers)

On December 3, 1888, Francis wrote Putnam regarding the death of his father. In the letter he assumed a curiously dispassionate objectivity, referring to his people as Indians "yet in the shackles of superstition."

> My dear Professor,
>   Your note with check for fifty dollars through Miss Smith is received. I write this only to acknowledge and send you my thanks for the same, as no doubt Miss Fletcher has written you how I secured the

sacred pole, *idol,* or whatever name it can be given, and why we did not send it to the Museum and kept it out there. The question of securing the full ritual and songs of that sacred article has become a serious and a puzzling one since the death of my father shortly after the *passage* of that relic out of the tribe.

The people are yet in the shackles of superstition and it will be hard to make them believe that my father's death was in no way the result of the taking away of the pole. Father once met with an accident which crippled him for the rest of his life. It happened soon after he refused to *regard* certain of the ceremonies *connected* with this very article and Indians said that it was from his disrespect for the sacred pole. But still there may be some way of getting a few of the songs at hand. Of these we have two.

Sincerely,

Francis La Flesche

AND THE PEOPLE THOUGHT

The Sacred Legend that Yellow Smoke told during those three days in September 1888 constitutes a history of the Omaha tribe. His narrative was punctuated, Fletcher and La Flesche say, with the words "and the people thought." Omaha oral tradition describes the events of their history as resulting from the power of thought as well as from emotion. I obtained my first glimpse of that power when I turned my thoughts to the meaning of the Sacred Pole. From thinking about the Pole at a distance and in isolation, I suddenly found myself involved in the story of his life as I joined my thoughts with those of Omahas living today. More generally, the Omaha Sacred Legend explains tribal history as the result of the people's thought. The events of the Sacred Legend are introduced with the refrain, "and the people thought." Thought, to the Omahas, is one of the places where humans encounter the power of Wakon'da. Thought is part of "a power by which things are brought to pass." Thought is one of the ways through which "all things are related to one another and to man." Thought helps explain "the seen to the unseen, the dead to the living, a fragment of anything to its entirety." The Sacred Legend tells about the people's suffering. It tells about their pride. It tells about the compassion of Wakon'da. It recounts how the people emerged to a primary level of consciousness by learning to see.

The Sacred Legend begins with an explanation of how the Omahas came to be human and how they thought about satisfying their physical needs. It goes on to say that they left an original homeland near a large body of water and came to be farmers and buffalo hunters of the Missouri River. It is not possible now to identify the exact location of that homeland, but it was prob-

ably east of the Ohio River and farther south than their present location. As
the tribe began to move, they confronted a problem they still think about today; that is, how to keep together as a single people who can, as Edward
Cline put it when he renewed contact with the Sacred Pole in 1988, "talk as
one person; think and do as one group of people," in the midst of change and
diversity.

In the seventeenth and eighteenth centuries the tribe had to stay together
as they moved from one place to another. It is possible to locate many of the
places they remember on a modern map (see chapter 2). In the nineteenth
and twentieth centuries, they have faced a similar problem, that of staying together as they move forward through time. During all those years, the Sacred
Pole has stood for the tribe's unity. For many years they honored the American flag as a reminder of the Sacred Pole. The Pole's return to them in 1989
was both a comfort and a challenge. The spirit of unity remains an objective
that can only be attained through attention to the power of Wakon'da. The
Sacred Legend that Yellow Smoke told Fletcher and La Flesche in 1888 begins with water. Yellow Smoke's telling of this episode may possibly have
been influenced by his having, as Fletcher says, "accepted Christianity." He
may have chosen to narrate the story in terms he knew a Christian listener
would understand.

> In the beginning the people were in water. They opened their eyes but
> they could see nothing. From that we get the child name in the Hon'ga
> gens, Nia'di inshtagabtha, "eyes open in the water." As the people
> came out of the water they beheld the day, so that we have the child
> name Ke'tha gaxe, "to make (or behold) the clear sky." As they came
> forth from the water they were naked and without shame. But after
> many days passed they desired covering. They took the fiber of weeds
> and grass and wove it about their loins for covering. (Fletcher 1888
> ms.)

Fletcher may be suspected of selectively organizing the material Yellow
Smoke told to present Omaha tradition as a tale of progressive evolutionary
betterment that would resonate well with the nineteenth-century American
belief in progress. In unpublished lecture notes she wrote that the Sacred
Legend "touches only upon the epochal points in the onward progress of the
people from a naked and precarious life, to the complete organization of the
tribe as it was at the advent of our own race" (Fletcher MS Box 19, item 65,
no. 3). The Legend as she has organized it goes on to describe where the
Omaha lived before finding the Sacred Pole:

> The people dwelt near a large body of water, in a wooded country
> where there was game. The men hunted deer with clubs; they did not

know the use of the bow. The people wandered about the shores of the great water and were poor and cold. And the people thought, What shall we do to help ourselves? They began chipping stones; they found a bluish stone that was easily flaked and chipped and they made knives and arrowheads out of it. They had now knives and arrows but they suffered from cold and the people thought, What shall we do? A man found an elm root that was very dry and dug a hole in it and put a stick in and rubbed it. Then smoke came. He smelled it. Then the people smelled it and came near; others helped him to rub. At last a spark came; they blew this into a flame and so fire came to warm the people and to cook their food. After this the people built grass houses; they cut the grass with the shoulder blade of a deer. Now the people had fire and ate their meat roasted; but they tired of roast meat, and the people thought, How shall we have our meat cooked differently? A man found a bunch of clay that stuck well together; then he brought sand to mix with it; then he molded it as a vessel. Then he gathered grass and made a heap; he put the clay vessel into the midst of the grass, set it on fire, and made the clay vessel hard. Then, after a time, he put water into the vessel and it held water. This was good. So he put water into the vessel and then meat into it and put the vessel over the fire and the people had boiled meat to eat. (1911, 70–71)

The Legend then goes on to describe how they learned to use corn and the buffalo. It also tells about how they met people from other tribes, and finally white men. The most remarkable story, and the one for which Iron Eye may have sacrificed his life, concerns the tribe's first encounter with "a tree that stands burning." Fletcher and La Flesche say that "there are two versions of the story of the finding of the Sacred Pole. Both have points in common" (217). Fletcher avoids disclosing whether both are from Yellow Smoke's narratives of September 1888, and if so, how he understood the connection between them. Portions of the 1911 second version appear in the 1888 manuscript, as well as passages that were not published. The version first published is not in the 1888 manuscript. The following is the 1888 manuscript version, beginning with an account of how the tribe devised a mechanism for negotiating intertribal peace through the use of peace pipes or calumets. Some passages in the 1888 manuscript were crossed out and an alternative text written in. For instance, the original refers to the Sacred Pole as "god" which was later crossed out and replaced by "Wakon'da." I have indicated the crossed out passages in parentheses.

The 1888 Manuscript

The chiefs made the two peace pipes to secure peace. The chiefs of other tribes agreed that there should be peace among the people and pipes were made to represent the first pipes and these were for the people to make peace among the people. All the pipes have eagle feathers and red streamers and owl feathers and duck heads.

And the chiefs said, "These pipes are from (god) Wakon'da. Whatever we say shall be as from (god) Wakon'da and shall govern the people. The words are from (god) Wakon'da who appointed them. The chiefs are slow to speak; Each word comes after much thought; no word is without meaning; every word is spoken in soberness so the words of a chief are few.

The people dwelt in their village of sod houses and they said it is not good to be without leaders. At this place we made chiefs (formed a government and had chiefs). Seven chiefs. The two pipes of the chiefs were made. One had a flat stem ornamented with porcupine quills. On the top [was] a woodpecker head with the bill turned back and underneath was tied a piece of buffalo hair. The other pipe had a plain flat stem (upon which was tied) with seven woodpeckers heads tied on it in line. These represented the seven original chiefs.

The words of these chiefs were as from (god) Wakon'da. When one of the chiefs utters a word the other chiefs believe the word was spoken after much thought and deliberation, accept it and follow it. They believe that the words are from Wakon'da. So they have all one head, one mouth.

When any question comes before the chiefs the seven pass the word, each asking the other what shall be done, until the question comes back to the first man. Again the question passes around the seven. Again and again. All day is spent (passed) in thinking (the deliberation) one man fearing to take the responsibility of directing. At last all agree and all take (accept) the responsibility and carry it together as one man.

After that (the question is decided) the old man who is the herald of the chief goes about the camp circle and (proclaims) cries aloud to the people the decision and none of the people dare dispute this word for they say, it is the voice of our chiefs and it must be (done) obeyed.

At this time the Poncas, Ioways, Cheyennes, Pawnees and Arikaras were with the Omahas and these tribes held a great council and agreed what they should do in hunting and in war. During this time a young man who had been wandering came back and said:

"Father, I have seen a wonderful tree," and he described it.

The old man kept silent until all was settled (the regulations were agreed upon) between the tribes. The young man visited the tree again and again told his tale. The old man waited in silence.

When all was settled between the chiefs of the tribes the old man sent for the chiefs and said:

My son has seen a wonderful tree. (Four paths from the four winds lead to it.) From the four winds the thunder birds come toward the tree leaving their trail of fire across the grass like four paths. They sit upon the tree and it bursts into flame and the fire mounted to the top. Still the tree was not consumed but stood burning, though no man could see the fire except at night.

Then the chiefs sent runners to see what this might be. And the runners came back (returned) and told the same story, how this tree stood burning in the night. Then all the people had a council and they agreed to run a race for the tree and attack it (like an enemy) as if it were an enemy. The chiefs said, "We shall run for it; put on your ornaments, prepare as for battle. So the young men (warriors) stripped themselves, painted themselves, put on their ornaments and set out for the tree.

The tree stood near a lake. The men ran. A Ponca reached it first and struck it as he would an enemy. Then they cut the tree down. Four men walking in line carried it on their shoulders to the camp (village). And the people sang four nights the songs which they had composed while they held their council (which had been composed for the reception of the tree while the people held their council). These songs were made in honor of the tree.

The tree was taken inside the circle and a tent was made for it. The chiefs marked upon the tree and shaped it and spoke of it (called it) as a human being. They made a sash of basketwork of twigs and feathers and tied it on the middle of the pole for (its) a body and then they said, "The head (or top) has no hair." So they set out to get a large scalp and they put it on for the hair. (They painted the pole. When all was completed they sent out a crier to. . . .) They sent out a crier to tell the people when all was completed they should see the pole. Then the pole was painted and the scalp and other things (articles) put on it and the chiefs took a crotched stick and set the pole up before the tent and called all the people. All the people came. Men, women and children.

When all the people were (assembled) come together the chief (arose) stood up and said.

"You now see before you your god. Whenever we meet with troubles we shall bring all our troubles here. Here you shall make your offerings and prayers. You must bring gifts with you when you come to pray. (All your prayers must be accompanied by gifts.) This (pole) belongs to all the people, but it shall be in the keeping of one family (and the leadership shall be with them) and if any one wishes to lead (take responsibility) among the people he shall make gifts to these keepers."

And the people began to pray to the pole. They cried (for courage). "Help me to have courage in battle that I may secure a trophy from my enemy." And their prayers were answered.

The pole became the friend of thunder, our helper in war and stood for the chiefs (and assisted with war and the chiefs and hunting).

And they said there must be something to go with the pole to give us success in hunting. Then they got the Tae-thon-ha [Sacred White Buffalo Hide]. The pole was helpful in war, the Tae-thon-ha helped in hunting and both were prayed to by the people.

They took the hide of the White Buffalo cow, left upon it the ears and horns, the hoofs and tail and on the hump placed a shell disc.

When this was done the people said, "Let us appoint a time when we shall again paint the pole and act before it the battles we have fought." So they fixed upon the month when the buffaloes bellow (July). The chiefs said to the people, "If there is any battle and you are victorious be sure and secure a large scalp to renew the hair of our god."

It happened that when the people were out on the hunt after they had camped four times a man said:

"I desire to put my eyes on the Tae-thon-ha." The skin was set upon a framework before its tent, and the man made gifts to it and all the people did the same and prayed for success in hunting. They were successful.

Then the people were told to get tongues and a heart for the pole.

Again they found a herd of buffalo. The report of them was first told to the Pole, then to the chiefs. The people were told (him) in what order they should go on the hunt. They sent the crier to tell the people. Two young men were told to go before the others, one to get the heart and the other to get the tongues. When the buffalo were killed these two made haste, one to get the heart, the other to get the tongues—twenty tongues, one heart. The two young men carried them to the pole.

Of these tongues and heart the chiefs, a part of the *hunga* (people) gens eat. If any is left over then all the people are asked to eat (and told if). If they eat of this sacred food they will have long life and health. Four times during the hunt the gathering of tongues and heart takes place. Then it is done no more.

The following are the two versions of the story Fletcher and La Flesche published in *The Omaha Tribe*:

A Tree That Stands Burning

1911: Version One

A great council was being held to devise some means by which the bands of the tribe might be kept together and the tribe itself saved from extinction. This council lasted many days. Meanwhile the son of one of the ruling men was off on a hunt. On his way home he came to a great forest and in the night he lost his way. He walked and walked until he was exhausted with pushing his way through the underbrush. He stopped to rest and to find the "motionless star" for his guide when he was suddenly attracted by a light. Believing that it came from a tent, the young hunter went toward it, but on coming to the place whence the welcome light came he was amazed to find that it was a tree that sent forth the light. He went up to it and found that the whole tree, its trunk, branches, and leaves, were alight, yet remained unconsumed. He touched the tree but no heat came from it. This mystified him and he stood watching the strange tree, for how long he did not know. At last day approached, the brightness of the tree began to fade, until with the rising of the sun the tree with its foliage resumed its natural appearance. The man remained there in order to watch the tree another night. As twilight came on it began to be luminous and continued until the sun again rose. When the young man returned home he told his father of the wonder. Together they went to see the tree; they saw it all alight as it was before but the father observed something that had escaped the notice of the young man; this was that four animal paths led to it. These paths were well beaten and as the two men examined the paths and the tree it was clear to them that the animals came to the tree and had rubbed against it and polished its bark by so doing. This was full of significance to the elder man and on his return he told the leading men of the mysterious tree. It was agreed by all that the tree was a gift from Wakon'da and that it would be the thing that would help to keep the people together. With great ceremony they cut the tree down and hewed it to portable size. (217–18)

1911: Version Two

During this time a young man who had been wandering came back to his village. When he reached his home he said, "Father, I have seen a wonderful tree!" And he described it. The old man listened but he kept silent, for all was not yet settled between the tribes.

After a little while the young man went again to visit the tree. On his return home he repeated his former tale to his father about the wonderful tree. The old man kept silent, for the chiefs were still conferring. At last, when everything was agreed upon between the tribes, the old man sent for the chiefs and said: "My son has seen a wonderful tree.

The Thunder birds come and go upon this tree, making a trail of fire that leaves four paths on the burnt grass that stretch toward the Four Winds. When the Thunder birds alight upon the tree it bursts into flame and the fire mounts to the top. The tree stands burning, but no one can see the fire except at night."

When the chiefs heard this tale they sent runners to see what this tree might be. The runners came back and told the same story—how in the night they saw the tree standing and burning as it stood. Then all the people held a council as to what this might mean, and the chiefs said: "We shall run for it; put on your ornaments and prepare as for battle." So the men stripped, painted themselves, put on their ornaments, and set out for the tree, which stood near a lake. They ran as in a race to attack the tree as if it were a warrior enemy. [Note the resemblance to the charge upon the He'dewachi tree also in the manner of felling and bringing the tree into camp.]

Then they cut the tree down and four men, walking in a line, carried it on their shoulders to the village. The chiefs sang for four nights the songs that had been composed for the tree while they held a council and deliberated concerning the tree. A tent was made for the tree and set up within the circle of lodges. The chiefs worked upon the tree; they trimmed it and called it a human being. They made a basketwork receptacle of twigs and feathers and tied it about the middle. Then they said; "It has no hair!" So they went out to get a large scalp lock and they put it on the top of the Pole for hair. Afterward the chiefs bade the herald tell the people that when all was completed they should see the Pole.

Then they painted the Pole and set it up before the tent, leaning it on a crotched stick, which they called *i'mongthe* (a staff). They summoned the people, and all the people came—men, women, and children. When they were gathered the chiefs stood up and said: "You now see before you a mystery. Whenever we meet with troubles we shall bring all our troubles to him [the Pole]. We shall make offerings and requests. All our prayers must be accompanied by gifts. This [the Pole] belongs to all the people, but it shall be in the keeping of one family (in the Hon'ga gens), and the leadership shall be with them. If anyone desires to lead (to become a chief) and to take responsibility in governing the people, he shall make presents to the Keepers [of the Pole] and they shall give him authority." When all was finished the people said: "Let us appoint a time when we shall again paint him [the Pole] and act before him the battles we have fought." The time was fixed; it was to take place in "the moon when the buffaloes bellow" (July). This was the beginning of the ceremony of Waxthe'xe xigithe, and it was agreed that this ceremony should be kept up. (217–19)

THEY MAKE HIM HOLY

The story of a chief's son finding "a tree that stands burning," the Pole's removal to the Peabody Museum, and the story of his return to tribal control in 1989 are defining moments in the life of the Omaha tribe. Each of these events reflects a challenge brought on by changing times. Initially, the tribe sought to keep itself together as it moved west. Now, it seeks unity as a nation within American and global culture. In each case, the Pole and his companion, the White Buffalo Hide, challenge Omahas to adopt a change in perspective. A young man lost his way while the chiefs were devising "some means by which the bands of the tribe might be kept together and the tribe itself saved from extinction." He looked to the heavens for direction. He looked toward "the motionless star" around which all the others turn. Beneath this star, the center of the night sky (which we know in English as the pole star), he discovered "a tree that stands burning." They cut the tree down, brought him into the *hu'thuga*, and called him a person. He gave the people direction. "When we meet with troubles we shall bring all our troubles to him," they said. Now, the Pole reminds people of a shared history. He is a person who stands for a people. That is why they call him Umon'hon'ti, the Real Omaha.

What a young man of long ago experienced as a mystery, his father understood as a revelation. The chief observed that four animal paths led to the tree. This was full of significance to him. When he told the other chiefs of his son's discovery, they all agreed "that the tree was a gift from Wakon'da and that it would be the thing that would help to keep the people together." In the latitude occupied by the Omahas, the pole star is about forty degrees above the horizon. No one can see the star except at night, but when the Pole is leaning upon his staff, he inclines toward that unseen and motionless center. In times gone by he reminded people of the star around which the night sky turns. He continues to remind people of Wakon'da. He reminds people of an unseen spiritual center. He reminds them of tribal unity. Lawrence Gilpin prayed to the Real Omaha upon his return in 1989:

Wakon'da, Most Holy Spirit above, you sit above us all.
Umon'hon'ti!
From way back, our forefathers, there was a tree.
There was a tree that grew from the earth.
Dadeho, Wakon'da Xube (Father, Most Holy Spirit above).
Whatever, how it was that he took it.
Somebody took it.

Through you, he received the tree from the earth.
From way back they used him for our lives.
It's been over a hundred years, past a hundred years,
In a strange place with strange people.
Dadeho, Wakon'da Xube.
Today the head of the people (the council),
Have brought him home,
Brought him home.
Dadeho, Wakon'da Xube.
Umon'hon'ti, they made him holy.
From way back in our camp he was the center,
Lived in the center of the people.
And whatever they did, how they lived,
They did it with him, through *Wakon'da*.
Wakon'da made life in that tree from the earth.
Dadeho, Wakon'da Xube.

Several hundred years ago, the young son of an Omaha chief saw a tree that stands burning. His father recognized the tree as a gift from Wakon'da. Toward the end of the eighteenth century, Omahas came to live in Ton'won-tonga, the big village not far from their present location. The Sacred Pole was with them then. Late in the nineteenth century, a young man named Francis La Flesche heard the last keeper's wife say, "The end has come!" He took advantage of the only means he saw as available to him at the time to save the Venerable Man for future generations. Housed as an ethnological specimen in Alice Fletcher's "great brick house," the Pole continued to exist as an object which can be read as a sacred text. A century after La Flesche accepted the Pole from Yellow Smoke, Omaha hands once again touched the Sacred Pole, whom they now call Umon'hon'ti, "the Real Omaha." It will be up to Omahas of the twenty-first century to rediscover a meaningful relationship to their Venerable Man. As Lawrence Gilpin told them when the Pole first returned to the reservation, "You have an undivided interest in him."

CHAPTER FOUR

The Beauty of an Indian Camp

The beauty of an Indian camp at night . . . can never be forgotten by
one who has seen it and it can hardly be pictured to one who has
not.
Fletcher and La Flesche (1911, 279)

Ever since human hunters appeared on the Great Plains more than eleven
thousand years ago, they have maintained a special relationship with that
country's vast herds of animals. For thousands of years the buffalo gave life to
people there, but only since native peoples took possession of horses in the
eighteenth century were former woodland dwellers like the Omahas able to
take up the hunt as part of their seasonal rounds. When Omaha people first
made their way to the edge of the prairies they found sheltered and fertile
river-bottom land on which to build earth-lodge villages and plant crops of
corn, beans, and squash.

The land was hardly an unoccupied frontier. The Caddoan-speaking Arikaras already occupied these lands, and the Omahas both borrowed from them
and displaced them. According to Fletcher and La Flesche, the Omahas learned
to make earth lodges from the Arikaras and participated in the great intertribal
peace ceremony symbolized by the awesome power of feathered stems known
as calumets. Dorsey reports that the Omaha name for this ceremony, Wa'wan,
means "to make a sacred kinship" (1884, 276). The contemporary phrase, "All
My Relations," reflects the spirit of that ancient ceremony.

To the west of the Omaha fields near the Missouri River, the vast grass-
lands stretched beyond the horizon. Each summer the tribe traveled to these
lands as a single group. Each summer they made contact with the buffalo
herds. Each camp they made was a human circle within the larger circles of
prairie land and sky. Unlike Siouan tribes such as the Lakota, for whom the
working social unit was a local band, the Omahas camped together as a tribe
during their annual buffalo hunt. They camped according to clan membership. Each clan had a clearly defined place in the camp circle. During the buf-

13. Ga-hi-ge's tipi. Photograph by William H. Jackson, 1868–69, courtesy of the Smithsonian Institution National Anthropological Archives.

falo hunt, the tribe's social organization was literally imprinted on the ground. Like the impression of one buffalo hoof, a single tipi's stamp on the grass stood for the entire tribe, as did the earth altar, *uzhin'eti*, in which the most sacred ceremonies took place. Each of these forms laid out the tribe's essential structure for all to see. The camp was a circle of lodges, the *hu'thuga*. In it, the Omahas gave their social order a physical presence. Within it, they enacted their most sacred ceremonies of representation and renewal.

THE HU'THUGA

Alice Fletcher wrote about the Omaha camp circle from personal experience:

The beauty of an Indian camp at night . . . can never be forgotten by one who has seen it and it can hardly be pictured to one who has not. The top of each conical tent, stained with smoke, was lost in shadow, but the lower part was aglow from the central fire and on it the moving life inside was pictured in silhouette, while the sound of rippling waters beside which the camp stood accentuated the silence of the overhanging stars. (1911, 279)

Her description of an Omaha camp reminds the reader that relations of family and clan organize every detail of Omaha life. The Omahas have always thought of their tribe as being like a single family. Like a family lodge which a man and woman bring about together, the camp circle was created in a spirit of cooperation. Like a single family, formed from the union of man and woman, the tribe was formed from the union of its "two grand divisions," the Sky people (Inshta'thunda) and the Earth people (Hon'gashenu). Within the tribe's singularity, there is always an idea of complementarity. That is why an orator addressed the people of the tribe by saying, "*Ho! Inshta'thunda, Hon'gashenu ti agathon'kahon!*" ("Ho Sky people, Ho Earth people, both sides of the house!"). This primary division of the tribe into halves of a circle reflects the Omaha idea that the process of creation is ongoing through the union of male and female principles in the cosmos at large. Fletcher and La Flesche explain further:

The Above was regarded as masculine, the Below feminine; so the sky was father, the earth, mother. The heavenly bodies were conceived of as having sex; the sun was masculine, the moon feminine, consequently day was male and night female. The union of these two forces was regarded as necessary to the perpetuation of all living forms, and to man's life by maintaining his food supply. This order or method for the continuation of life was believed to have been arranged by Wakon'da and had to be obeyed if the race was to continue to exist. (134)

Omaha philosophy represents both the tribe and the cosmos as a circle. An Omaha child could expect to grow up within a circle at every stage of his or her life. The earth lodge was a circle. The family lodge was a circle. And each summer, beginning in "the moon when the buffaloes bellow," a child experienced the circle of lodges, the camp circle known as the *hu'thuga*. The *hu'thuga* was an idea the Omaha people brought into being when they shared the gifts of the buffalo together. It was an idea they expressed when they acted together in ceremony. Making the *hu'thuga* a circle of the whole tribe helped them recall that creation is an ongoing process. They experienced the circle as a sign of the power of Wakon'da. That power is, in the words of Fletcher and La Flesche, "an invisible and continuous life" that "permeates all things, seen and unseen." In the camp circle they conducted ceremonies of renewal that expressed the "mysterious life and power" through which "all things are related to one another and to man."

The *hu'thuga* reveals the entire circle of creation, the continuous motion of an ongoing creative process. It expresses the thought that lies behind all outward appearance. It gives voice to the mythic idea that human beings were born of a union between the Sky people and the Earth people. This mythic union is not something that happened long ago and far away from everyday experience. Rather, it is enacted over and over again in the ceremonies through which the tribe renews its own existence, renews its form of government, and renews its relationship to the buffalo, to the maize, to the seasons, and to the forces of day and night.

The Omahas think about the circle of their own lives as an expression of the fundamental circles made by the union of earth and sky, night and day, male and female. The *hu'thuga* represents, to them, the form and motion of creation itself. During their buffalo-hunting days, it was a form all the Omahas could see because they lived and recreated it every time they set up their camps together during the communal buffalo hunt. Its physical form brought the "unseen forces" of the cosmos into the circle of everyday experience. Within its circle, keepers of the great tribal ceremonies further communicated with these same "unseen forces." Within its circle, the chiefs met in council. Within its circle, they renewed the Sacred Pole each year. They thought of the *hu'thuga* as being like the lodge of a single family. Just as each family member had his or her place within a family circle, each clan, they say, "had its place as had each member of the family within the lodge." Fletcher and La Flesche say of the *hu'thuga*:

> This form was circular, with an opening to the east, which represented the door of a dwelling. "Through it," the old men said, "the people went forth in quest of the game, and through it they returned with their supply of food, as one enters the door of one's home." (137)

Omaha elders described the entrance of the *hu'thuga* as "the door through which one entered the dwelling place of the tribe." During ordinary times, the entrance faced the direction of the tribe's movement, but symbolically, it "was always . . . to the east." When the tribe stopped to conduct its major ceremonies, the clans made their camps so that "the opening was actually toward the east." So strong was the idea of an "orientation" of the *hu'thuga*, that "the order of the clans was always as it would have been had the opening faced the east. This was effected by turning the tribal circle as on a hinge placed opposite the eastern opening, so that no matter in which direction the opening actually was, the Inshta'thunda and Hon'gashenu divisions were always as they would have been had the opening faced the east." Fletcher and La Flesche write:

> This interesting fact, of the carrying out of a symbolism in the manner of pitching the tents of the tribe on the wide unbroken prairie, indicates how deeply rooted in the minds of the people was the importance of the fundamental ideas represented in the *hu'thuga*—the two grand divisions and the orientation of the dwelling. In view of these and kindred ideas connected with the *hu'thuga*, it seems probable that in this form we are dealing with a symbol. (138)

The *hu'thuga* provided a place of refuge for the tribe. People felt safe within its circle because there they were "at home." Fletcher and La Flesche say that safety within the *hu'thuga* was a powerful symbol:

> That the idea of safety was involved in the form of the *hu'thuga* is probably true, but the dependence for safety was placed in the help to be derived through the recognition of cosmic forces and religious observances rather than in an advantageous arrangement of tents made in order to protect ponies and camp equipage. (138)

Fletcher and La Flesche explain why the Omaha word for "tribe" is *uki'te*, which as a verb means "to fight." The tribe, *uki'te*, could stand together against all outside enemies because it was a union of Earth people and Sky people, Inshta'thunda and Hon'gashenu. Fletcher and La Flesche distinguish *uki'te* from *hu'thuga*:

> This word is distinct in meaning from *hu'thuga*, the term used to designate the form or order in which the tribal organization ceremonially camped, in which each one of the villages, or clan, had its definite place. *Hu'thuga* is an old term and carries the idea of a dwelling. (137)

OMAHA CLANS

The *hu'thuga* was divided into halves or moieties that corresponded to the two "grand divisions" of the tribe. The Sky people camped in the northern half of the *hu'thuga*. The Earth people camped in the southern half. The entrance of the *hu'thuga* faced east when the tribe had stopped to conduct its ceremonies. Figure 14, adapted from Fletcher and La Flesche by Myers (1992), shows the positions of clans in the *hu'thuga*.

The Omahas have traditionally divided themselves into ten clans, five belonging to each side of the *hu'thuga*. Membership in an Omaha clan is determined by descent through the male line. A person belongs to the clan of his or her father, not the mother as in former Mississippian tribes like the Creeks, Natchez, and Cherokees. Fletcher and La Flesche and Dorsey used the now

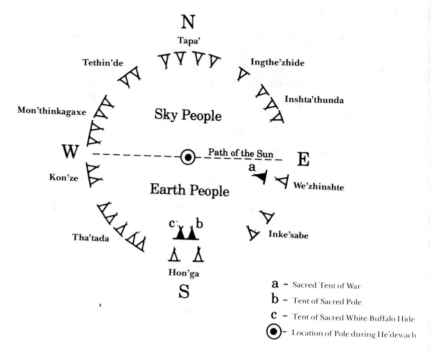

14. *Sacred camp (hu'thuga) circle of the Omaha during He'dewachi. Adapted from Myers,* The Birth and Rebirth of the Omaha *(1992), figure 3. Courtesy of the University of Nebraska State Museum.*

archaic anthropological term "gens" for clan, but the Omaha word is *ton'wongthon*, which also means "village," or more specifically, "a village of people who are kindred, of one kind, between whom marriage is prohibited." To distinguish between *ton'wongthon* meaning "settlement" and the same term as applied to clan, the Omaha language provides the word *uba'non*, which means "a group of a kind in a given place," and refers to clans camped together in the *hu'thuga*. Omahas use the word *ton'wongthon* meaning "place of residence" to describe white settlements like St. Louis and Washington, where people of many different kinds were also mixed together (1911, 135–36).

Earth-lodge settlements like Ton'wontonga contained people from different kinship "villages." A person's place of residence within the village did not follow any particular order based on clan membership. People lived with their relatives according to marriage alliances and friendships. The composition and identity of Omaha settlements changed as the people moved their fields and as family fortunes changed. Houses were owned by the women, and a man usually moved into the household of his wife and her family upon marriage. Thus, the people living in an earth lodge or a village of earth lodges could be members of more than one *ton'wongthon*. Ties of marriage brought them together. People of "different kinds" cooperated in planting and harvesting food. Because of clan exogamy, people of "different kinds" brought children into the world together. The community of earth lodges was a fertile and productive mixture of people. Fletcher and La Flesche describe the apparent lack of order in an earth-lodge village:

> In a village in which the entire tribe lived the lodges and tents were not arranged about a central open space nor were they set so the people could live in the order of their clans, an order observed when they were on the hunt and during their tribal ceremonies. Yet each family knew to what clan it belonged, observed its rites, and obeyed strictly the rule of exogamy. To the outward appearance a village presented a motley group of tribesmen. The dwellings and their adjacent corrals were huddled together; the passageways between the lodges were narrow and torturous. There was little of the picturesque. The grass and weeds that grew over the earth lodges while the people were off on their summer buffalo hunt were all cut away when the tribe returned. (99)

The Omaha system of clans came into view when all the people camped together in the *hu'thuga* for the annual buffalo hunt. What had been an informal mixture of people during the agricultural phase of the year became organized by clan for the hunt. Each clan had a particular place in the camp circle. "When the camping place was reached," according to Fletcher and La Flesche, "each woman knew exactly where to place her tent in the *hu'thuga* or tribal circle. The Sacred Tents were set up in their respective places and the sacred articles put at once under cover" (279). A woman set up her family's tipi next to those of her husband's clan relatives and in relation to the clan's ceremonial duties in the ritual life of the tribe. While village life during the agricultural year centered around women and things of the earth, during the hunt the patrilineal organization of the clans prevailed.

Fletcher and La Flesche explain that the question, "To what gens [clan] do you belong?" meant literally, "In which of the various (many) villages (of the tribe) are you there (have you a place)?" The answer to this question depended on whether the person asking it were an Omaha or Ponca, or a member of a different tribe unfamiliar with Omaha clan names.

If the questioner belonged to the Omaha or the Ponca tribe, he would know the names of the clans, so the reply would be: "Tapa', there I am;" that is, "I belong to the Tapa' clan." But if the question were asked by a stranger, a member of a different tribe, to whom the names of the Omaha clans were unknown, then the reply would indicate the symbol of the religious rite (the tabu) of the clan of the person questioned, and he might say: "I am a buffalo person" or an "elk person." (136)

Fletcher and La Flesche take care to point out that the reply does not mean "that the man thought of himself as a buffalo or elk, or as descended from one, but as belonging to a group which had charge of rites in which that animal was used as a symbol." Omahas continue to identify themselves in the manner that Fletcher and La Flesche described for their ancestors more than a century earlier. In addition to the ten formal clans, there are a number of subclans. It is subclans within the clans who are actually *nini'baton*, holders of pipes. Of the ten clans, only seven contain pipe holders. Similarly, subclans provide keepers for the Sacred Pole and Tethon'ha, the White Buffalo Hide, as well as important figures like the Wathon', the leader of the annual buffalo hunt. Those who care for the Sacred Pole and his ceremonies, for instance, belong to the Waxthe'xeton subclan of the Hon'ga or Leader clan. Another group, the Xu'ka, are a subdivision of the Washa'be itazhi (those who don't touch black bear) subclan of the Tha'tada, (those whose place in the *hu'thuga* was to the left of the Hon'ga). Members of the Xu'ka had the very important role of prompters and servers for the Waxthe'xeton priests during their singing of rituals pertaining to the White Buffalo Hide and the Sacred Pole. The name Xu'ka means "teacher or instructor in mystic rites." The Xu'ka were entrusted with wiping away the tears from each singer's face if one of the songs was sung out of sequence (160).

The social position a person derived through clan membership was more important than the geographical location of his residence in a particular village. Village residence could and did change, while clan membership and its attendant camping place within the *hu'thuga* was immutable. Each clan had charge of rites in which its animal "was used as a symbol." Every member of the tribe was a participant in the rites. Every person "had a voice in" the rites and "shared in (their) benefits." Clan identity was fundamental to the ritual order of the tribe during the buffalo hunt. Within the *hu'thuga*, people were "the same" as common members of a single tribe, but they were also meticulously differentiated into clans, subclans, chiefly councils, priesthoods, secret societies, and hunt officials. Each clan was responsible for the correct performance of rites that benefited the entire tribe. These rites were symbolized by the clan's particular animals. Members of a clan or subclan were "the same" in the way that animals of a single species are the same. Being a buffalo person or an elk person identified an individual as belonging to a group of people who were in some essential and spiritual way "the same." Clan names continue to pass from one generation to another within each clan.

CLAN CEREMONIES

Children were introduced to the tribe as clan members by a series of ceremonies. The first of these, called "Turning the Child," took place when a boy or girl was first able to take steps on its own. The ceremony sent the child "into the midst of the winds," which Fletcher and La Flesche identify as "that element essential to life and health." The child's feet were set upon stone as a reminder that the earth itself is old and wise. Then:

> "flames," typical of the life-giving power, were invoked to give their aid toward insuring the capacity for a long, fruitful, and successful life within the tribe. Through this ceremony the child passed out of that stage in its life wherein it was hardly distinguished from all other living forms into its place as distinctively a human being, a member of its birth clan, and through this to a recognized place in the tribe. As it went forth its baby name was thrown away, its feet were clad in new moccasins made after the manner of the tribe, and its *ni'kie* name was proclaimed to all nature and to the assembled people. (117)

The ceremony took place in springtime after the first thunders were heard, the grass was well up, and the meadowlarks had begun to sing. The ceremony not only sent a child "into the midst of the winds," but also bestowed on him or her a special kind of clan name, known as "*ni'kie*," which formalized clan identity. Fletcher and La Flesche translate *ni'kie* as, "those upon whom the people are thrown" or "who carry the people." A *ni'kie* name, they say, "always referred to the rites and tabu of the clan" (144). A child's *ni'kie* name thus connected him or her to the rights and obligations that belong to clan membership. Fletcher and La Flesche say that the word "signifies a declaration by the people or their chiefs of consent to a certain proposition. . . . It was the duty of a clan having charge of *ni'kie* rites to take care of the symbols and paraphernalia of the rite, and act as its priests. . . . Each of the sub-clans had its name, its rite, which was of the *ni'kie* class, its set of personal names, its tabu, and its place when the clan camped with the tribe in ceremonial order" (136–37).

Prominent men often decorated their tents with symbols relating to their *ni'kie* names. Dorsey published drawings of some of these in 1894 (see fig. 15). In addition to obtaining a *ni'kie* name belonging to his clan, an Omaha boy was consecrated to the power of Thunder in a ceremony called We'bashna, "to cut the hair" (122). Each clan owned the right to use a distinctive pattern of shaving the head, leaving only tufts of hair that immediately identified the

15. Tent of Te'san—sun and rainbow vision. From Dorsey, A Study of Siouan Cults *(1894), figure 170.*

boy as one of its members. Some of these patterns symbolized the clan's animal. For instance, boys of the Elk clan had tufts of hair representing the head, lock, and tail of an elk (145). Each clan or subclan provided hereditary priests who had charge of "carrying the people," through its *ni'kie* rites. The Washe'ton subclan of the We'zhinshte (Elk) clan had charge of cutting a boy's first lock of hair and consecrating it to Thunder. Francis La Flesche describes how he and other boys who entered the Presbyterian mission school were given short haircuts that obliterated all outward sign of their clan identities. This was just one of the many measures taken to enforce assimilation.

The entrance to the *hu'thuga* was flanked by the two clans or subclans of the Inshta'thunda and Hon'gashenu that had charge of particular rites having to do with the Thunder powers. People belonging to these groups camped immediately to the north and south of the *hu'thuga*'s entrance. The subclan that had charge of Thunder ceremonies belonging to the Sky people was the Washe'ton division of the Flashing Eyes (Inshta'thunda) clan. The other was a separate clan, the Elk (We'zhinshte) clan of the Hon'gashenu moiety, which had authority over the rites of war. Each of these two groups had special knowledge of the Thunder powers.

As members of the tribe passed in and out of the *hu'thuga*, they received the influence and protection of the awesome Thunder powers from both the earth and sky sides of the tribe. Moving from east to west, an Omaha entering the *hu'thuga* would have known that to the right was the Washe'ton division of the Flashing Eyes clan of the Inshta'thunda (also Flashing Eyes) half of the tribe. To the left, a person entering the *hu'thuga* would have felt the protective power of the first clan of the Earth people, the We'zhinshte clan of the Hon'gashenu. These were the two groups who conducted the initiation ceremonies called "Turning the Child" and "Introducing a Boy to the Thunders." Thus, each time a member of the tribe passed in and out of the *hu'thuga*, the influences of these Thunder powers of earth and sky recalled the experience of being sent by them "into the midst of the winds," as Omahas described these childhood initiations. The keeper of the Tent of War was always a member of the *We'zhinshte*. The name conveyed the idea that its members were "those through whom the tribe made known its displeasure or anger, because of some injurious act by another tribe" (1911, 142).

Omaha society was and continues to be organized through the symbolic associations of its clans and subclans. The system was probably always a good deal more fluid than the systematized version Fletcher and La Flesche present. In fact, the clans were constantly changing as family fortunes changed from one generation to another. As Fletcher and La Flesche describe the system, each clan and subclan carried with it particular rights, obligations, and taboos, some of which were known only through stories at the time of their work with the tribe. For instance, the following story fragment explains the red ear of corn taboo of the Nini'baton subclan of the Black Shoulder clan.

The Inke'sabe (Black Shoulder of the Buffalo) were the first of the Omaha to exist. There were one man and one woman. They lived together and children were born to them. The woman went out one day and found little mounds on the ground. In a few days she went again, and saw that out of the mounds plants were growing not known to her. From time to time she went to look at these plants. They grew tall, and by and by ears grew on them. These she gathered and took to her husband and children. They roasted the ears by the fire and ate them. These were the people to whom the corn was sacred; so to this day they do not eat the red ear of corn.(1911, 147)

The following is an outline of further information about the names, symbols, taboos, and ceremonies associated with each of the clans.

THE HON'GASHENU (EARTH PEOPLE)

We'zhinshte (Elk clan)

The name means literally "by whom to become angry." Through this clan "the tribe made known its displeasure or anger because of some injurious act by another tribe" (142). In order to accomplish these ends, the We'zhinshte had charge of the Sacred Tent of War and were keepers of the tribe's rites having to do with war and Thunder. According to Fletcher and La Flesche:

When any question arose as to the policy to be pursued in dealing with another tribe the members of which had committed acts of hostility, such as killing Omaha or stealing their horses or carrying away by force women of the tribe, it was the duty of the keeper of the Tent of War to call the Seven Chiefs and the leading men of the clan to a council. At this council the We'zhinshte presided. The Sacred Pipe of the Tent of War was filled by the keeper of the Tent and when, after due deliberation on the action to be taken, a decision was reached, the Seven Chiefs smoked this Pipe. This was a religious act and through it the decision became sanctified. Then the herald of the We'zhinshte proclaimed to the tribe the decision of the chiefs. If it was determined upon, the organization of volunteer war parties generally followed this authorization. (142)

Members of the Elk clan were responsible for welcoming the awakening of life-giving forces following the first peals of thunder in the spring. The keeper of the Tent of War offered smoke to Wakon'da after the first thunder of the year sounded. He then used human hair to tie four bunches of tobacco in bladder bags. These he fastened to a wand that he placed in the ground facing east from the crest of a hill. Elk clan members were obliged to honor the elk "on account of the service believed to have been rendered the people by that animal" (144). According to a story Fletcher and La Flesche relate:

When the pipes and the other articles belonging to the rites pertaining to war were made, the people sought for some skin to be used as a covering in which to keep and protect these things which were regarded as *waxube*, or sacred; but none could be found save that of the male elk. The fact that at that particular time only the skin of the male elk was obtainable was regarded as an indication that the male elk came to their aid by direction of Wakon'da. Therefore, in memory of this act of the male elk, this animal became tabu to the clan. (143)

Members of the Elk clan did not eat meat from a male elk or wear elk skin moccasins except upon death, when moccasins made of male elk hide were placed on the clan member's feet so that he would be recognized as We'zhinshte by relatives in the other world.

Inke'sabe (Black Shoulder [of the buffalo] clan)
According to Fletcher and La Flesche, members of this clan, which camped to the left of the Elk clan, were responsible for providing the Wathon', the leader of the buffalo surround. They report that "if the last Inke'sabe was an infant in its mother's arms, it would be carried to lead the people in the *wanon'ce* (the surround of the herd)." The hunt leader was known as "he who

is eyes for the people." The office was hereditary within the Wathi'gizhe or "hoop that becomes a buffalo" subclan (147).

Another subclan of the Inke'sabe was *nini'baton*. According to Fletcher and La Flesche, a family within this subclan had charge of the two Sacred Tribal Pipes. While its taboo was the touching of red ears of corn, the subclan was also responsible for providing sacred ears of red corn used by a subclan of the Leader clan in planting ceremonies (147). A group within the *nini'baton* subclan had the taboo of touching charcoal and was responsible for painting the pole used in the He'dewachi ceremony.

Hon'ga (Leader clan)

Contemporary Omahas sometimes describe the Hon'ga clan as being like Brahmans in the Hindu caste system in that they traditionally provided keepers for the tribe's most sacred objects, the Sacred Pole and the White Buffalo Hide. Two subclans, the Waxthe'xeton and the Washa'beton, were responsible for the Sacred Pole and for the Washa'be used in the buffalo hunt. Members of the Waxthe'xeton had charge of the Sacred Pole, whose name was Waxthe'xe, "mottled as by shadows." One taboo of the Waxthe'xeton was "*tezhu'*," the cut of meat from a side of buffalo "that was brought as an offering to the Sacred Pole at the great tribal ceremony when the Pole was anointed." The other Waxthe'xeton taboo was the crane or swan. Crane's down fills the wickerwork wrist shield of the Sacred Pole. The seven divining arrows used in the ceremony are fletched with crane feathers.

Members of the Washa'beton subclan had charge of making and decorating the Washa'be used by the Wathon', the leader of the tribal buffalo hunt. The Washabe'ton also had charge of Tethon'ha, the White Buffalo Hide, and its pipe and tent (155). Yellow Smoke was a member of the Hon'ga, as is his descendant, Doran Morris. Wakon'mon'thin, the last keeper of the Sacred White Buffalo Hide, was also Hon'ga.

Tha'tada (To the left of the Hon'ga clan)

According to Fletcher and La Flesche and Dorsey, the Tha'tada were a collection of subclans, each of which was like a clan with its own taboo and duties. Collectively, they camped between the Hon'ga and Kon'ze. One of the subclans was the Black Bear, which included the Xu'ka, prompters and servers for the Waxthe'xeton priests during their singing of rituals pertaining to the White Buffalo Hide and the Sacred Pole. Both Dennis Hastings and Edward Cline are members of the present-day Bear clan. Another, the Buffalo Head subclan (Te'pa or "those who do not touch the buffalo head"), was *nini'baton* and held one of the seven tribal pipes (160).

Kon'ze (Kansas clan—the name refers to the Kansa tribe)

The clan's taboo is verdigris, the greenish blue pigment found on weathered copper and brass. In more recent times, Kon'ze clan members are forbidden to wear lipstick or face paint. One subclan is called Tade'ata, "in the direction of the wind." When mosquitoes were thick a Kon'ze man was jokingly beaten with robes to call up a breeze. A second subclan was *nini'baton*. In former times, the Hethu'shka (warrior) society was led around the tribal circle by the Kon'ze "in recognition of the power of the wind to befriend warriors" (169). Lawrence and Alfred Gilpin were members of the Kon'ze clan, as is their sister, Elsie Morris.

THE INSHTA'THUNDA (SKY PEOPLE)

Mon'thinkagaxe (Earth Maker or Gray Wolf clan)

This clan has a special relationship to rock or stone as a symbol of wisdom acquired by age, and to the grey wolf, which Fletcher and La Flesche report is symbolic of "man's restlessness, his questionings of fate, his destructiveness." The Earth Maker clan once kept four sacred stones that were painted white, black, red, and green or blue. These were placed in a hole in the ground and covered with the down of the swan, a bird associated with water. Taken together, the symbols of the Mon'thinkagaxe give it the authority to interpret the stories of creation. One family within the clan was *nini'baton*. One of the names that this family could use was *nini'ushi*, "filler of the pipes." In times past, the person who bore this name was privileged to fill the pipes of the seven council chiefs. There are no subclans within the Earth Makers.

Tethin'de (Buffalo Tail clan)

The rites that this clan may have overseen are lost except for the ceremony that pertained to the crow. "In certain myths that speak of the Creation it is said that human beings were at first without bodies; they dwelt in the upper world, in the air, and the crow was instrumental in helping the people to secure bodies so that they could live on the earth and become as men and women" (175). Because of this association with the birth of people in bodily form, Tethin'de people were forbidden to touch the unborn young of an animal. "In later days the tabu applied especially to the buffalo young, and also to the lowest rib adhering to the backbone, as the head of the fetus was said to rest against this part of the animal; consequently the meat from this rib could not be eaten" (175). There are no subclans among the Tethin'de but one group of families were *nini'baton*.

Tapa' (Pleiades or Deer Head clan)

Like the Earth Maker or Grey Wolf clan, the Deer Head people had charge of rites dealing with the story of creation. Because of their association with the

Pleiades, a constellation of seven bright stars, their ceremonies related to the power of stars and the night sky. Tapa' rites involved the use of wildcat and fawn skins, because their spotted appearance suggested the night sky. A Tapa' baby was painted with spots like the fawn and sometimes also with red lines symbolic of lightning. There were no subclans among the Tapa', but particular families had charge of ceremonies relating to Thunder while others were *nini'baton*, bearers of the clan's pipe.

Ingthe'zhide (Red Newborn Buffalo Calf Dung clan, commonly known as Red Dung clan)

The name of this clan refers to the reddish dung of a newly born buffalo calf. Little is known about the rites it may have controlled, except that "traditions speak of these having been connected with the procreation of the race to insure its continuance through the medium of the sky powers" (183). The clan's taboo was touching the fetus of an animal, particularly the buffalo. There were no subclans and no pipe bearers among the Ingthe'zhide.

Inshta'thunda (Flashing Eyes clan)

The name refers to the lightning and its power. The Inshta'thunda camped opposite the Elk clan at the eastern side of the *hu'thuga* and shared with them rites connected with thunder and lightning. Perhaps because they were the first clan of the northern or sky half of the tribe, their name was used for the Sky people as a whole. Fletcher and La Flesche describe one *nini'baton* subclan and another called Washe'ton (to possess children). This subclan had charge of rites that consecrate a child's life to the life-giving power symbolized by thunder and lightning.

THE SACRED TENTS

Among the throng of people moving across the prairie, three were keepers of Sacred Tents containing objects used in ceremonies for the benefit of the entire tribe. Fletcher and La Flesche describe how these tents were set up among the others within the circle of lodges:

> When the camping place was reached, each woman knew exactly where to place her tent in the *hu'thuga*, or tribal circle. The Sacred Tents were set up in their respective places and the sacred articles put at once under cover. After the camp was made the daily life went on as usual; the ponies were tethered or hobbled and put where they could feed; wood and water were secured, and soon the smoke betrayed that preparations for the evening meal were going forward. (278–79)

The sacred Tent of War belonged to the south of the *hu'thuga*'s entrance.

The tents of the Sacred Pole and the White Buffalo Hide were set up next to one another just south of the circle's center. The Sacred Pole was always carried on the keeper's own back. In later years the White Buffalo Hide was packed on a pony, but in early days it, too, was carried on the back of its keeper. Both the White Buffalo Hide and the Sacred Pole were the focus of tribal rituals carried out during the annual buffalo hunt (see fig. 5).

TE'UNE: THE BUFFALO HUNT

The Omahas called their annual hunt Te'une. It took place "when the crops were well advanced and the corn, beans, and melons had been cultivated for the second time." This was in July, "the moon when the buffaloes bellow." Like other Plains Indians of historic times, the Omahas developed a way of life based on the mobility that horses gave them. Horses helped transport a family's belongings. Fletcher and La Flesche describe the tribe on the move as follows:

> The tent poles were fastened to each side of the pony by one end; the other trailed on the ground. The parfleche cases containing clothing, regalia, the food supplies, and the cooking utensils, were packed on the animal. Travoix were used, supporting a comfortable nest for the children, some of whom, however, often found places among the household goods on the pony's back. Men and women walked or rode according to the family supply of horses. Between the trailing tent poles, which were fastened to a steady old horse, here and there rode a boy mounted on his own unbroken pony, for the first time given a chance to win his place as an independent rider in this great cavalcade. Many were the droll experiences recounted by older men to their children of adventures when breaking in their pony colts as the tribe moved over the prairies on the hunt. (275)

Buffalo hunting required discipline and coordination. Like war, its success depended on a combination of individual skill and group cooperation. Omahas deeply respect the right of an individual to use his or her skills to the best possible advantage. They have always maintained a system of government that balances the authority of individuals, families, clans, and the two great tribal divisions, Inshta'thunda (Sky people) and Hon'gashenu (Earth people). They have maintained a council of seven chiefs. Even great leaders like Blackbird and Big Elk were empowered only to speak for the tribe rather than dictate to it. But there are times when the tribe is obliged to act in unison and to speak with a single voice. *Te'une*, the buffalo hunt, was one of these times. The Omahas recognized that their relationship to the buffalo was like that of two peoples who give away to one another. Like the buffalo, who run together as a single body, the Omahas prepared themselves to act within the authority of a single will and purpose during the hunt. They hunted buffalo by locating, approaching, and finally surrounding a herd of suitable size. Success depended upon each hunter knowing his place in relation to that of every other and to the overall plan of the hunt. They conducted every part of the hunt with respect, with a coordinated strategy, and with ceremony. To accomplish these objectives, they willingly (but only temporarily) gave over individual authority to that of a hunt director, a man called by the title of Wathon'. The last Omaha to hold the title was Inshta'thabi, "He who is Eyes for the People" (1911, plate 25). The symbol of his authority was a curved, feathered staff known as the Washa'be.

THE WASHA'BE

The name Washa'be comes from "*wa*," (sacred and alive with the power of motion) and "*sha'be*" (seen as a dark object raised above the horizon). Both *wa* and *sha'be* give voice to ideas that are deeply rooted in Omaha philosophy. *Wa* is the root from which the word *Wakon'da* is derived. It refers to what Fletcher and La Flesche described as "an invisible and continuous life" and a spiritual power that "permeates all things, seen and unseen." *Wa* is also a root of the name Fletcher and La Flesche give for the Sacred Pole, Waxthe'xe, a sacred power that is "mottled as by shadows." *Sha'be* is another Omaha root with spiritual and social meaning. In recent times Omahas have referred to the Sacred Pole by a related term, Washa'begle, "The Shadowed One." While *Washa'be* could be translated literally as "dark," Fletcher and La Flesche point out that it really means "raised above the horizon." As a reference to high position, *sha'be* names the highest order of chiefs, the Ni'kagahi sha'be or "Dark Chiefs." These were ranked among themselves and were raised above both ordinary people and above the other chiefs, the Ni'kagahi xu'de or "Brown Chiefs." All the Brown Chiefs were viewed as being on the same level, in the way that brown is "a uniform color, as of the brown earth, where all are practically alike, of one hue or rank" (202).

The highest ritual act a person could perform in order to become a member of the Dark Chiefs (Ni'kagahi sha'be) was known as Washa'be ga'xe, "to make the Washa'be." Making the Washa'be was under the control of a special hereditary group, the Washa'beton subclan of the Hon'ga or Leader clan. Collecting materials for the Washa'be was the first task of the man who was to take the office of Wathon', the hunt director. He made ritual preparations as the people prepared themselves physically to move out onto the prairies. The Washa'be was made of an ash sapling. In addition to the ash staff itself, the Wathon' assembled "two eagles, (one black and one golden), a crow, a swan skin, a dressed buffalo skin, two pieces of sinew, a shell disk, a copper kettle (formerly a pottery cooking vessel), and a pipestem" (275). He brought these to members of the Washabe'ton subclan who had charge of actually making the Washa'be. Fletcher and La Flesche describe how they put the materials together:

> The buffalo skin furnished by the aspirant was cut and a case made from it for covering the pole. All the coarse feathers were removed from the swan skin, leaving only the down; the skin was cut in strips and wound about the staff, making it a white object. On one side of the staff was fastened a row of eagle feathers, and a cluster of golden eagle feathers hung at the end of the crook. Crow feathers were arranged at the base about 10 inches from the end of the pole, which was sharpened. (276)

When the tribe was on the move, a virgin had the honor of carrying the Washa'be. When they formed the camp circle it was kept in the Sacred Tent of the White Buffalo Hide. Elders told Fletcher and La Flesche that it "belonged to" the Hide. Both the White Buffalo Hide and the Washa'be played important parts in the hunt itself.

PITY ME WHO BELONG TO YOU

> You are to go upon the chase, bring in your horses.
> Braves of the Inshta'thunda, Hon'gashenu,
> Pity me who belong to you!
> (1911, 280)

The person chosen to be Wathon' had extraordinary responsibilities and was held accountable for the tribe's fortunes and misfortunes. During the buffalo hunt he became like the Sacred Pole himself, belonging to the tribe "as a man's hand belongs to his body" (281). During his term of office, Fletcher and La Flesche say, "the entire tribe was placed under his direction and control." For the duration of the hunt, he was a part of the tribe who was granted authority to speak for the whole. The responsibility was awesome, and he prayed to the hunters, "pity me who belong to you." Even the council of seven chiefs followed his instructions and limited their role to providing advice. The Wathon' was responsible for selecting camping places, for sending out runners to locate the buffalo herds, and even for "the health and welfare of the people down to the quarreling of children and dogs." During the hunt, all Omahas were expected to live in harmony. Fletcher and La Flesche report:

> "Pity me who belong to you" constituted an appeal by the Wathon' to the honor and the compassion of the people to avoid all dissensions

and imprudence which might bring about trouble or misfortune, since any misdeed or mishap would fall heavily on the director, who was responsible for every action, fortunate or unfortunate, and who must suffer for the acts of the tribe, as through his office he belonged to them, was in a sense a part of them, "as," an Omaha explained "a man's hand belongs to his body." (281)

If conflicts did arise or if the winds blew toward the herds and frightened them away, the Wathon' was held responsible and might be required to resign his office. In order to deal with such problems in a less serious fashion, the chiefs appointed another man to take the name of Wathon'. It was his duty to act as a sort of humorous scapegoat and assume the blame for all quarrels and mishaps. Through this device, the tribe was able to talk about conflicts without having to disrupt the all-important hunt.

Fletcher and La Flesche provide a detailed description of the buffalo hunt and its rituals. Their description is based on two sources of information. One is provided by elders of the tribe whose knowledge of strategy, songs, and ceremony was fresh in the 1880s. The other is the personal experience of Francis La Flesche, who served as *wadon'be*, a runner in search of the herds, when he was a young man. The following is a description of the hunt based on their information. I have used the present tense and set the scene at the beginning of the nineteenth century to give the reader a sense of what it might have been like to be part of this great tribal event when the buffalo were still abundant.

THE MOON WHEN THE BUFFALOES BELLOW

It is the moon when the buffaloes bellow, the beginning of July. The day's first light touches scattered clouds east of the Missouri River. The sun is about to begin another circle above Ton'wontonga, the Omaha Big Village of earth lodges beside the Missouri River. The seven Dark Chiefs (Ni'kagahi sha'be) of the pipe-holding clans are meeting with a man who has been chosen to be the Wathon', the one who will direct them in the coming buffalo hunt. They have come together as spiritual leaders of the tribe. The men wear buffalo robes with the hair outside. The head end of each robe rests on the wearer's left arm. The tail is on his right. The men's heads are bowed and their arms are crossed so that the robes cover their heads like hoods. In the quiet of this sacred moment before dawn they look like a buffalo herd at rest and at peace with itself. In this ceremony, as in the one that begins the renewal of the Sacred Pole, Omahas show that they are one with the buffalo who give them life, and with the power of Wakon'da, the spirit of all life and motion.

Servers from the Inke'sabe and Tha'tada clans bring out the two Sacred

Tribal Pipes that are always kept together, even in ceremony. As the sun emerges from earth's darkness and takes to the sky, they fill the pipes and chant the ritual for beginning a hunt that will bring life to the entire tribe. The pipes remind the chiefs that the tribe is a union of Sky people, Inshta'thunda, and Earth people, Hon'gashenu. They remind the man who is to become the Wathon' that his authority during the hunt derives from the coming together of Sky people and Earth people in the *hu'thuga*, the camp circle. They remind everyone that no single chief can be head of the tribe. In following the Wathon', they do not submit to his will. Rather, they join their wills as individuals to the power they all know as Wakon'da. The chiefs smoke in silence.

When the smoking is completed, the servers clean the pipes. One of the chiefs then begins to speak. He explains how he is related to all the others present. Each person responds in a way that is appropriate to the relationship the chief has stated. By this way of speaking, they remind each other that the entire tribe is made up of relations between people, families, clans, and keepers of the sacred objects and ceremonies. They can see all these relations in the way the chief speaks and in the order in which the clans camp in the *hu'thuga*. The chief who speaks first explains how important the hunt is to the tribe as a whole. He calls on those present to express their opinions, but warns that any person who has "given way to violence" in the past year must keep silent. Because the people now have undertaken to act with a single voice for the duration of the hunt, the consequences of a single person's anger would be transferred to the people as a whole.

The chiefs talk about when to begin the hunt and what route to take. They continue the discussion throughout the day. As the need arises, they send out the tribal herald to consult women of the tribe about where wood and water might be available along the proposed route. Once a decision has been reached, the council members bow their heads. In this position of prayer, they are served a sacred feast in seven wooden bowls. The servers pass these around the council four times, each chief taking a mouthful from a black horn spoon. They remain seated with heads bowed until the sun finally returns to earth from his place in the sky. A circle has been completed.

Four days before the people are to leave for the hunt, the Wathon' begins a fast. He fasts and remains in seclusion until all but a few elders and caretakers have left the village. When all who are going on the hunt have departed, the Wathon' removes his moccasins and his weapons. Slowly, with bare feet, he follows the people to where they have made the first camp. He remains distant from them. He is attentive to a power that is unseen in the normal course of events. The people withdraw as he arrives so that he can enter his own tent alone and in silence. They recognize his actions as a form of prayer to

Wakon'da. He has withdrawn deeply into a spiritual place within himself. He prays for courage and for wisdom in directing the hunt for the benefit of all the people.

The Wathon' will continue to pray throughout the time he holds office. He will eat little and live apart from his family. The people call his sacrifice *non'zhinzhon*, the same term they use to describe the vision quest of a child who goes up "on the hill" for the first time and cries to Wakon'da for help. The people understand *non'zhinzhon* because every one of them experienced it directly when he or she became "old enough to know sorrow." The word means "to stand sleeping." Elders explain that the Wathon' has withdrawn from ordinary life and "stands oblivious to the natural world." In this spiritual state of mind, he is able to take his instructions directly from Wakon'da, the "great unseen power."

The people wait and watch for a signal from the Wathon'. It comes the following morning. He drops the cover of his tent. When the women can see the poles of his tipi standing out above the sky, they begin to unfasten their own tent covers. In a short time the camp becomes a memory and the people are "once more on the march, stretched out as a motley colored mass over the green waste" (1911, 279).

A great moment comes when the people see signs of buffalo for the first time. They hold another council. Again the Wathon' meets with the seven chiefs and the Washa'be subclan of the Hon'ga. This time their task is to appoint a number of men who will act as "soldiers" or marshals during the hunt. They choose these men "from among the bravest and most trusty warriors of the tribe, those who had won the right to wear 'the Crow'."

"The Crow" decoration is said to symbolize a battlefield after the conflict is over. The fluttering feathers on the pendants represented the dropping of feathers from the birds fighting over the dead bodies. Sometimes the wearer of "the Crow" added to the realism by painting white spots on his back to represent the droppings of the birds as they hovered over the bodies of the slain. The two arrow shafts had a double significance: they represented the stark bodies and also the fatal arrows standing in a lifeless enemy. The eagle was associated with war and with the destructive powers of the Thunder and the attendant storm. The wolf and the crow were not only connected with carnage but they had a mythical relation to the office of "soldiers," the designation given to certain men on the annual tribal hunt, who acted as marshals and kept the people and the hunters in order during the surround of the herd. (1911, 441–42)

The herald summons these men to the Sacred Tent of the White Buffalo

16. *"The Hunters Dividing into Two Parties to Circle the Herd of Buffalo." Engraved by C. W. Chadwick after a drawing by De Cost Smith. Courtesy of the Smithsonian Institution National Anthropological Archives.*

Hide. Here the chiefs tell them that their duty is to dedicate themselves entirely to the good of the tribe. They must apprehend any person, even a relative, whose actions might threaten the hunt. They tell these men, "You are to recognize no relations in performing your duty—neither fathers, brothers, nor sons." These rules come into effect, they tell them, "when the camp is within hearing distance of the herd selected for the coming surround." They tell them to prevent noises such as loud calls and the barking of dogs.

Now the Wathon' makes another selection. He chooses twenty swift runners from among the young men of the tribe. They are called *wadon'be*, "those who look." Their task is to search for a herd suitable for the tribe to surround. The herald calls each one by name. "This country," he says to each one. "Take action and explore it for me." If there is a danger of encountering enemies in the area, the runners go out in groups. Otherwise, each takes his own direction. The tribe waits in silence. They wait with the Wathon', with the seven chiefs of the council, and with the keepers of the two tribal emblems, the Sacred Pole and the White Buffalo Hide.

There is a general silence throughout the *hu'thuga*. The Inshta'thunda wait in the north. The Hon'gashenu wait in the south. The keepers of the Sacred Pole and the White Buffalo Hide stand by their sacred tents. Suddenly, they are not alone. A runner appears in the distance. He pauses for a moment on the first point of land from which he can be seen. He signals to the people first in silence. If he is by himself, he runs from side to side. If there are two runners, they run back and forth, crossing one another. The name for this

17. "The Return of the Runners" by De Cost Smith. Courtesy of the Smithsonian Institution National Anthropological Archives.

signal is *waba'ha*. As soon as watchers have received the signal, they pass it on to the Wathon' and to the keepers of the sacred tents. Immediately, the keepers pick up the Pole and the pack containing the White Buffalo Hide. They carry them to the edge of the camp in the direction of the returning runners. The seven chiefs follow after. The Wathon' returns to his tent and remains alone until he hears the voice of the herald calling the people together. (See figs. 16 and 17).

While the runners are closing the remaining distance to camp, the keeper of the White Buffalo Hide takes out the Hide and arranges it over a frame so that it looks like a buffalo lying down. The keeper of the Sacred Pole sets up Umon'hon'ti on his staff, a forked stick known as *i'mongthe*. The seven chiefs, the keepers, and the herald wait for the runners in silence behind these sacred objects. The first runner approaches them and delivers his message in a low tone. He tells them where he has found the herd and how many there are. He is careful not to exaggerate. The second runner follows the first with the same message. The chiefs then send the herald to tell the people. He returns to camp and announces, "It is reported that smoke (dust) is rising from the earth as far as the eye can reach!" The hunt is about to begin.

Now the Wathon' comes out of his tent. It is time for him to take command of the hunt. He joins the seven chiefs at the tent of the White Buffalo

Hide. He has now become leader of their council. It is he, now, who instructs the herald. It is he who selects two men to lead in the surround. One of these will carry the Washa'be. The other will carry the pipestem the Wathon' has secured. The Wathon' also selects two boys to secure the twenty buffalo tongues and one heart that will be required for a feast following the hunt. The herald then circles the *hu'thuga* in the sun's direction, the direction of the dance. He calls to the people on behalf of the Wathon' with the words quoted above:

> You are about to go upon the chase,
> Bring in your horses.
> Braves of the Inshta'thunda, Hon'gashenu,
> Pity me who belong to you!
> Soldiers of the Inshta'thunda, Hon'gashenu,
> Pity me who belong to you!
> Women of the Inshta'thunda, Hon'gashenu,
> Pity me who belong to you!
> (1911, 280)

If the herd is still some distance away, the tribe moves quietly and with reverence to a new location close to where the herd has been sighted. The keepers bearing the Sacred Pole and the White Buffalo Hide take the lead. Marshals ride on either side to keep people in order. They have the authority to enforce silence and to kill any barking dogs that might disturb the herd. Hunters prepare for the coming work in silence. Two boys on horseback attend each hunter. They lead the fast-running horses the hunters will use in the hunt. The herald circles camp to make sure that all is ready. His return to the tent of the White Buffalo Hide is taken as a signal to begin.

The two young men that the Wathon' has selected now begin to lead the hunters toward the herd. One carries the Washa'be. The other carries the pipestem. These sacred objects remind them of the reverence they must show for the buffalo and for the power of Wakon'da. They move slowly and with deliberation, maintaining a calm like that of the herd at rest. Their imitation of the buffalo continues the quiet mood that the chiefs began when they first put on their buffalo robes at the beginning of the hunt. The Wathon' and the seven chiefs follow the two young men. The rest of the hunters fall in behind. They speak softly to their horses, calling them father, uncle, or brother. They ask them to run well and not to fear the buffalo. They tell them to run close to the buffalo but to avoid the danger of their horns. The runners and riders wear only moccasins and breechcloths. They carry only their weapons. Their bodies are without ornament. In contrast to them, the marshals wear the highly prized bustle known as "the Crow," an emblem of the respect they have earned in defense of the tribe.

The solemn procession of spiritual leaders and hunters advances toward the herd in four stages. At the close of each stage, the Wathon' and the seven chiefs sit down and smoke. The four pauses remind people that the buffalo hunt is spiritual as well as practical. The chiefs and the Wathon' smoke as a prayer to Wakon'da. They smoke to quiet the haste and excitement of the hunters. They smoke to prevent any hunter from acting selfishly, rather than for the common good. They smoke so that each family may obtain its share of the food supply. As the hunters wait for their leaders to conduct these ceremonies, they have time to think about the four directions and the four winds. They remember that when they were children just old enough to move about unaided, the elders "sent them into the midst of the winds" in the ceremony of "turning the child." Like children, they are impatient for the hunt to begin. They are impatient, but they are also adults. They are men who have received the names of their clans. They have learned the importance of waiting. They are hunters.

As they wait, the hunters remember the story of an impatient man who once galloped up to where the Wathon' and the chiefs sat smoking during the third halt. He was unwilling to move toward the herd at the hunt director's slow pace. He was afraid that the herd was moving away from them and might escape if the hunters followed the Wathon's direction. The Wathon' answered the man quietly, "If your way is the better, follow it!" The hunters remember that the man dashed off and many hunters followed him. Without any plan or direction, they rushed upon the herd. They rushed upon the herd but succeeded only in driving it away. In the confusion, several of the hunters were injured and the man who led them was crippled for life by his horse falling on him. The memory of these events serves as a reminder that the hunt is part of the power of life and motion that is Wakon'da. To go against its direction would be like going against the winds.

The chiefs and hunt director complete the four pauses. They come to the place where the hunters will begin to circle around the herd. The Wathon' gives a command. The hunters divide into two parties. One party follows the young man with the Washa'be. The other follows the young man with the pipestem. The command of the Wathon' signals an abrupt change in mood. Now the time has come to move swiftly. The young men carrying the Washa'be and the pipestem run silently but at full speed to circle the herd. Older hunters on horseback follow them. The marshals ride beside them with whips to hold back any rider who might be tempted to break into the herd or advance beyond the Washa'be and the pipestem. The two young men meet to complete the circle. Before the buffalo have time to realize what has happened, they are surrounded by horses and men. The young man who carries the Washa'be thrusts it into the ground. The one who carries the pipestem ties it to the Washa'be. This is the signal for the hunt to begin. The marshals give a command and the hunters charge on the herd shouting. They drive the buffalo in circles toward the camp. The hunters choose their targets from among the moil of moving animals. Their arrows are powerful and it is not unusual for one to pass entirely through the body of a buffalo.

As soon as the first animal falls, the two boys selected to secure the tongues and heart for the sacred feast rush in, "for they must take the tongue from a buffalo before it had been touched with a knife." As a sign of their respect for the buffalo, servers of the ceremony had taught that "if a knife was thrust through the tongue to make a hole, it would bring bad luck." Instead of piercing the tongue, "an opening was made in the throat of the buffalo and the tongue pulled through and taken out; then the end of the tongue was bent over and the fold cut." The boys carry their bows unstrung and thrust the tongues onto them. When each boy has pierced ten tongues and strung them on his bow, and when together they have obtained a buffalo heart, they return to the tent of the White Buffalo Hide.

Through the hunt, the people have once again joined their lives to "an invisible and continuous force [that] permeates all things, seen and unseen." They have joined:

> The seen to the unseen,
> The dead to the living,
> A fragment of anything,
> To its entirety.

TETHON'HA: THE SACRED WHITE BUFFALO HIDE

While men are busy bringing meat into camp and women are cutting it into strips to dry, the seven chiefs, the Wathon', and members of the Washa'be subclan of the Hon'ga begin preparations for the feast of tongues and heart to be held in the tent of the White Buffalo Hide. Although members of this subclan prepare the food for the feast, they do not take part in it because the buffalo tongue is their taboo. Those who take part in this feast take their food "in the crouching attitude observed at the initial council when the Wathon' was authorized and the route to be taken on the hunt determined." The feast thus completes a circle which binds together the lives of people and buffalo. It also marks the beginning of a beautiful and stately ritual celebrating the birth and life of the buffalo.

The ritual of the White Buffalo Hide is a cycle of nineteen songs that celebrate the buffalo as a gift from Wakon'da. It was sung by the Hide's keeper and other members of the Washa'beton subclan. During the ritual, the Hide

18. Tent of the White Buffalo Hide. Figure is probably Wakon'mon'thin, or Walking Sacred One. From Fletcher and La Flesche, The Omaha Tribe *(1911), plate 27.*

was mounted on its frame in a place of honor in the back of the tent, facing the east. The tent itself was cared for by the Washa'beton and was painted with images of growing corn (see fig. 18). Fletcher and La Flesche suggest that the imagery reflects a time when corn was more important than the buffalo to the Omahas. Inside this gracefully painted tent, "the chiefs and the Wathon', muffled in their robes, sat with bowed heads and smoked the peculiarly shaped pipe belonging to the Hide" (283).

THANI'BAHA: THE HOLY PIPE

This pipe is unusual and must be very old. It is known as a discoidal platform pipe, the top surface of which is flat and circular. Similar pipes have been found dating from the fifteenth century (Thomas Myers, personal communication). If the pipe were to be turned over and placed on a bed of soft earth, it would mark the ground with a print like that of a buffalo hoof. Like the hoof which leaves a track that stands for the entire animal, the pipe leaves a track that stands for all the buffalos. It is a fragment that is also an entirety. The pipe is multiply symbolic. Its bowl has been drilled into the center of a perfect circle which is scribed with lobes that suggest the two halves of the *hu'thuga*. The lobes are set at a slight angle to one another so that the space between them forms a narrow wedge, opening out away from the stem. When the pipe is held up toward the White Buffalo Hide standing at the east side of the tent, it shows the form of *uzhin eti*, the sacred earth altar in which the Sacred Pole's renewal ceremony takes place. This holy pipe is one of the tribe's greatest treasures because it is very old and because it continues to be alive with meaning. According to Wakon'monthin (Mystery Walking or James Robinson), the Hide's last keeper, the lobed drawing on the top of the pipe specifically represents a buffalo's track.

As the chiefs and the keeper sit with their heads bowed, they pass this amazing pipe around their circle. The keeper begins the first of the nineteen songs that constitute the ritual. La Flesche was able to obtain the entire cycle from Wakon'monthin, and he recorded short versions of the songs on wax cylinders. These recordings have now been transferred to tape by the American Folklife Center of the Library of Congress. A sample of these and other Omaha songs are available on a handsomely illustrated album (Lee and La Vigna 1985). The ritual consists of four groups of songs, each one of which is sung four times. Performing the entire ritual "occupied the greater part of the night." One reason for this is that, like the songs performed for the Pole's renewal ceremony, "an error made it necessary to begin at the first song again, for the ritual must go straight through without any break in the order of the songs" (1911, 287). Perhaps because of this requirement, the first song suggests all the others. Like the pipe itself, it is both a fragment and an entirety. Fletcher and La Flesche were amazed at the levels of meaning found in both the pipe and in this single opening song. They write:

134

Although so simple and concrete, this song throws more light on the native thought and belief in the use of the pipe than any single song the writers have found. The pipe is here represented as infused with "movement," that special attribute of life, and "appears" to become the bearer of man's supplication to Wakon'da. The music fittingly clothes the thought expressed in the words and makes a majestic opening to the ritual. (288)

Because the song is so central to an understanding of Omaha ritual language, it is worth citing the Omaha text and the explanation that Fletcher and La Flesche give of it. Their understanding reflects the great sensitivity to Omaha expressive culture that La Flesche brought to their collaboration. The song has four lines as follows:

Thani'baha
[An old, ceremonial form of *nini'ba*, pipe.]
Xu'be hehe
[An object set apart from ordinary usage and made holy; some consecrated thing that is used as medium of communication with the supernatural.]
Thani'baha, e'thonbe
[Holy Pipe appears, comes into view, of its own volition, from a covered place, so as to be seen by all.]
Thani'baha. Don'ba
[Holy Pipe to see; the word as here used is a part of the phrase *don'ba iga* (*don'ba*, to see; *i*, plural sign, a number addressed; *ga*, command). The phrase is equivalent to "Behold ye!"]
(287–88)

Fletcher and La Flesche offer a free translation. While their English may sound a little archaic to the modern ear, I would not presume to suggest another reading. La Flesche, after all, was fluent in both languages and sensitive to the subtle shadings of ritual meaning.

Thani'baha	The Holy Pipe!
Xu'be hehe	Holy, I say.
Thani'baha, e'thonbe	Now it appears before you.
Thani'baha. Don'ba	The Holy Pipe, behold ye!

This song was repeated four times, as were all the others. What is important, even miraculous, about the song's language is that through it the pipe reveals itself, of its own volition, as a manifestation of Wakon'da. The song is a prelude to the chiefs and the Wathon' actually taking up the pipe. The song suggests that by taking up the pipe they acknowledge the gift of creation that will unfold through the remaining songs of the ceremony. They must have been very much aware that the pipe appears of its own volition in the same way that "a tree that stands burning" showed itself as a mystery to a young man long before. They were certainly aware that the entire cycle of nineteen songs gives voice to the tribe's accumulated knowledge of the complex interdependence of humans and the buffalo from whom they obtain life.

The second song carries on the story from its opening invocation of creation as a miraculous appearance to the point at which humans discover a means of participating in it. Fletcher and La Flesche translate the second song's text as:

> Holy Pipe, most holy, appears; it appears before you.
>   Now I bid ye
> Within your lips take this holy Pipe, holy Pipe.
> The Pipe, it appears, appears before you, I say.
>   Now I bid ye
> Within your lips take this holy Pipe, holy Pipe.
> The Pipe it appears, appears before you, I say.

With this song, "the chiefs, representatives of the people, are bidden to accept the holy Pipe, take it within their lips, that the fragrant smoke may carry upward their supplication." (289) With this song, the pipe literally springs to life in their hands. While the first song suggests that the Pipe stands apart as something "clothed with mysterious power," the second song proclaims that the Pipe has now come near enough to touch the people in whose hands it rests:

> It now comes near and in touch with the supplicants and lends itself to service. These two songs complement each other and show both dramatic and musical form. (289)

The ceremony goes on through three other parts, speaking to what Fletcher and La Flesche call Supplication, Assurance of Wakon'da, and the Hunt. The seventeen songs in these three parts tell the story of how the buffalo "come from every direction and cover the face of the earth" (286). The first song of the four that represent supplication completes a circle that unites the pipe, the buffalo and the Omaha people:

> In this song the creation of the buffalo is depicted. "Movement" is synonymous with life. The living embryo moves of itself. According to native reasoning it moves because it is endowed with consciousness. As breath is a sign of life, the nose, whence the breath issues, is the first to "move." Next the face moves, then the eyes, and so on until all the parts of the body "move" because of conscious life. Then the little one,

the calf, is born. Finally as the feet move they leave on the earth a sign of life—"tracks." Observe in this connection the peculiar pipe belonging to the Hide, in the shape of a track of a buffalo hoof. The music is recitative and in a minor key. The emphasis on the keynote, of the last word, *Thigthe*, "tracks," indicates the finality of creation. (290)

Fletcher and La Flesche go on with another nineteen pages of close description, carefully unfolding the symbolism by which the songs of this ceremony set out a grand story of how the buffalo and the Omahas are related to one another. The songs give people a chance to reflect upon the cosmic significance of the hunt they have just experienced. Hearing the ceremony performed perfectly must have been immensely satisfying to the chiefs and particularly to the Wathon', who is now released from his cry of "pity me who belong to you!"

This ceremony of the White Buffalo Hide is a remarkable example of how Native American theater, philosophy, and literature combine to form a powerful expressive language. Each song line is subtly stated but immensely suggestive. Each song furthers an episode in the story. Each episode of the story is familiar to the participants, because they have just completed the hunt. They know the story because they have experienced it. The images of song and ceremony reproduce and intensify what these people already know. Like the holy pipe of the White Buffalo Hide, they are capable of imprinting experience with enduring meaning.

Today, the buffalo hunt is gone and there are no members of the Washa'beton capable of singing the story into existence. The Sacred White Buffalo Hide and its holy pipe, though, have returned to join the Real Omaha. A time of separation has ended. Once again, the pipe has stamped its imprint onto Omaha experience. A time of return and renewal has begun. The people are being challenged to discover themselves once again in the sacred objects that led their ancestors long ago. The objects themselves are calling out with the cry of long ago, "pity me who belong to you." The people are listening to that call.

CHAPTER FIVE

A Fragment of Anything to Its Entirety

Tears were made by Wakon'da as a relief to our human nature.
Wakon'da made joy and he also made tears.

> Through this mysterious life and power
> All things are related to one another
> And to man.
> The seen to the unseen,
> The dead to the living,
> A fragment of anything
> To its entirety.

Ceremony is a language, with its own particular syntax and vocabulary.
Omaha ceremonies had to be performed perfectly and without pause in order to be considered properly done. Ceremonial order and song texts are the
equivalent of books for the preservation and practice of Omaha knowledge.
Like the sacred objects themselves, they can be read as texts. Francis La
Flesche documented ceremonies that belonged to the Omaha people during
their buffalo-hunting days. He reported the end of those days with "the wistfulness of a child as when it stands before its parent," an attitude Omahas of
all ages felt when they were witness to the annual ceremony that renewed the
Sacred Pole, the life of the buffalo, and the well-being of the tribe as a whole.
This renewal ceremony was known as Waxthe'xe xigithe, "the Sacred Pole to
tinge with red." Omahas looked to the Pole's renewal as they did the sacred
earth altar in which it took place, with the anticipation of a child, "waiting to
share in some good thing."

La Flesche experienced wistfulness as he documented the ending of
Omaha traditions, for he was not certain that giving up all memory of cere-
monial knowledge would be a good thing for the tribe. Like many other
Omahas who saw the end of the buffalo-hunting life with their own eyes, La
Flesche may have feared that a failure of Waxthe'xe xigithe meant a failure of

the tribe's ability to renew itself. However, he never gave up a trust in the power of Wakon'da, despite his long sojourn in the white man's world. Perhaps because he believed that the Omaha ceremonies he knew as a child were the only possible ways of maintaining tribal identity, he made it his life's work to record and preserve a memory of them for future generations. Because of his work, Omahas today may read the language of their sacred objects and ceremonies as texts that take them back to the tribe's essential philosophical principles.

Waxthe'xe xigithe was a ceremony of great power and complexity. The keeper who directed it was responsible for knowing all the songs and prayers that supported it. Like the ritual of the White Buffalo Hide, this ceremony had to be performed perfectly from beginning to end. The ceremony took place over the span of several days and involved the participation of people from each tipi of the *hu'thuga*, as well as the pipe-bearing chiefs, the Pole's keeper, the keeper's wife, and singers from the Waxthe'xeton subclan of the Hon'ga. The ceremony culminated when the wife of the keeper shot seven sacred arrows through the Pole's wickerwork wrist shield filled with swan's down and into the ground of the sacred earth altar, known as *uzhin'eti*. The ceremony reminded Omahas that their lives continue through the power of Wakon'da, the power of life and motion. It reminded them that each person is both a complete whole and part of the larger whole that makes up the tribe. It reminded them that each living being, like each clan of the *hu'thuga*, is part of a circle that makes up the universe. As Fletcher and La Flesche put it when writing about Wakon'da, the ceremony connected "a fragment of anything to its entirety."

Following the end of buffalo hunting in 1876, Omahas experienced a challenge to the fundamental ideas on which they based their identity. Fletcher and La Flesche report that the renewal ceremonies "needed the buffalo for their observance, and its disappearance, which in its suddenness seemed . . . supernatural, had done much to demoralize [them] morally as well as socially" (244). In desperation, "the tribe sought to make their appeal to Wakon'da through the old ceremonies connected with the anointing of the Sacred Pole by purchasing beef as a substitute for buffalo meat" (635). In fact, the tribe was under considerable pressure from the Indian agent, who wrote disparagingly to the Interior Department that "the Omahas have a tradition that when they do not go on the buffalo hunt they should at least once a year take the lives of some cattle and make a feast" (244). Fletcher and La Flesche comment on his remark:

> This interpretation of the Indian's desire to spend his money for the purchase of the means by which he hoped to perform rites that might bring back the buffalo and save him from an unknown and dreaded fu-

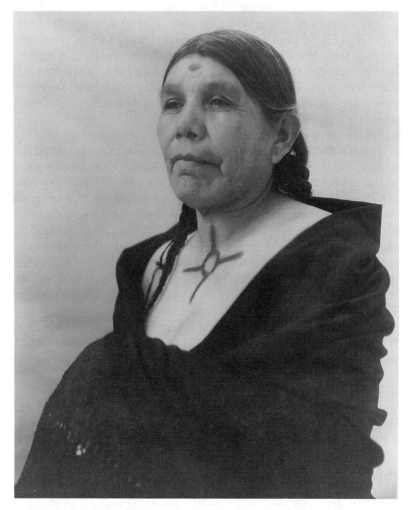

19. Mary Mitchell McCauley showing the "Mark of Honor," August 24, 1925. Courtesy of the Nebraska State Historical Society.

ture is a significant gauge of the extent to which the Indian's real life had been comprehended by those appointed to lead him along new lines of living and thinking. The cattle were bought at a cost of about a thousand dollars. The ceremony took place; but, alas! conditions did not change. A second and third time the tribe spent its money, but to no avail. New influences and interests grew stronger every year. The old customs could not be made to bend to the new ways forced on the people. Opposition to further outlay for cattle to hold the old ceremony arose from the Government and also from some of the tribe; so years passed when the Pole stood untouched in its tent, dreaded as a thing that was powerful for harm but seemingly powerless to bring back the old-time prosperity to the people. (244).

Fletcher and La Flesche report that "in 1875 the last ceremony was performed and the wrapping put on as it remains today." In the years following the buffalo's disappearance, government officials came increasingly to view ceremonies like Waxthe'xe xigithe as a reversion to "savage and barbarous practices" (Prucha 1973, 295). In 1882 Secretary of the Interior Henry M. Teller wrote to the commissioner of Indian affairs complaining that "a few non-progressive, degraded Indians are allowed to exhibit before the young and susceptible children all the debauchery, diabolism, and savagery of the worst state of the Indian race." He went on to say:

I desire to call your attention to what I regard as a great hindrance to the civilization of the Indians, viz, the continuance of the old heathenish dances, such as the sun-dance, scalp-dance &c. These dances, or feasts, as they are sometimes called, ought, in my judgment, to be discontinued, and if the Indians now supported by the Government are not willing to discontinue them, the agents should be instructed to compel such discontinuance. These feasts or dances are not social gatherings for the amusement of these people, but, on the contrary, are intended and calculated to stimulate the warlike passions of the young warriors of the tribe. (Prucha 1973, 296)

Like many Omahas who lived through these hard times, La Flesche may have been persuaded that when Waxthe'xe xigithe and the other tribal ceremonies disappeared from living memory, the tribe would also assimilate into the American melting pot. It is understandable that he held such an opinion. He lived under the authority of the assimilationist Dawes Act. Indeed, his adopted mother and academic collaborator, Alice Fletcher, was one of its principal authors and a leading figure among the "Friends of the Indian" (Mark 1988, 116–21). Despite his support for the assimilationist project, La Flesche was also persuaded that it was essential to document Omaha ceremonial knowledge, both for future generations of Omahas and to dispel the prevailing prejudice that "the Indian" is "a simple child of nature with mental faculties dwarfed and shriveled" (Prucha 1973, 194). La Flesche ended his "boy memory" with the sad thought that watching Wakon'monthin perform songs of the Sacred Pole and White Buffalo Hide for a wax-cylinder recording machine "was like watching the last embers of religious rites of a vanishing people." With the Sacred Pole gone, the tribe's continued identity as "something distinct to be seen by all the people" seemed impossible. Perhaps as a balance to his gloomy account of the Omahas as "a vanishing people," La Flesche poured his energy into documenting knowledge that was rapidly passing out of the oral tradition.

Omahas today no longer think of themselves as a vanishing people. They know that they have survived as a tribe and will continue to maintain themselves as individuals, as families, as clans and as a community. Omahas today have a renewed opportunity to discover how Umon'hon'ti, the Real Omaha, may represent them as a people. La Flesche was comfortable with the past, but uncertain about the future. Omahas today are certain about their future, but they are still looking for ways to complete the circle of connection to a past they apprehend as much with fear as with understanding. The Sacred Pole has come among them again, but the ancient ceremonies of renewal are lost from living memory. All that remains of their intricate form is what Fletcher and La Flesche wrote down from the elders of their time, the songs they recorded, the ceremonial order, the sacred objects themselves, and what recollections may have come down through oral tradition.

Perhaps Omahas of today can learn from the mistakes that La Flesche made as well as from the wonderful information he recorded. When his horses nearly knocked over the keeper of the Sacred Pole, La Flesche took cloth offerings to Umon'hon'ti, the Venerable Man himself. The old keeper wept and sprinkled water on the boy from a wooden bowl with a spray of sweet sage. He wept for a break in the order caused by the boy's impetuous ways. He wept and the break was healed. Now the Pole has returned after a break from his people that lasted a century. The Omahas who helped him return wept when they saw him for the first time. It is the responsibility of other members of the tribe to wipe away the tears. As an old man told Fletcher and La Flesche, "Tears were made by Wakon'da as a relief to our human nature. Wakon'da made joy and he also made tears." Tears of compassion and tears of joy are at the heart of renewal. In renewing their relationship to the past through the return of Umon'hon'ti, the Omahas can once again say, "I make him beautiful, I make him beautiful."

Although the buffalo disappeared long ago, the Omahas have remained together as the years go by. After all, their buffalo-hunting days were just one episode in a rich and varied tribal history. More important than their coming together with the buffalo was their coming together with one another as a tribe. This they have continued to do without a break. Each summer they have celebrated He'dewachi, also known as pow-wow. Historic photographs document the remarkable continuity of these events from year to year, generation to generation. Each year, families have continued to give away to one

20. Woods family on way to the pow-wow at Macy, Nebraska, September 1922. Maggie Johnson is seated on the left. Courtesy of the Nebraska State Historical Society.

another in ceremony. Recently, old and young alike have played out the stately dancelike movements of the Omaha hand game. Since the old ceremonies were abandoned, Omahas have become active leaders of the Native American Church, which continues to be an important part of reservation life today. Lawrence Gilpin was a past national president of the church. Each year, children have been born to replace the elders who passed away. Even without the old ceremonies, the tribe continues to renew itself.

I MAKE HIM BEAUTIFUL

The Sacred Pole has the power of motion, the power of life. The tribe once renewed its contact with this power during the "moon when the buffaloes bellow." They called the renewal ceremony "Waxthe'xe xigithe." Francis La Flesche knew these rites from personal experience. As a boy of fifteen, he served as a runner to locate the buffalo herd during one of the last tribal hunts. The renewal ceremony took place after the fourth communal hunt of the season; it followed the four ceremonies connected with the buffalo tongues and hearts and the ritual of the White Buffalo Hide. Its name, "the Sacred Pole to tinge with red" reminded all the people of their undivided interest in the Pole as an emblem of tribal unity. La Flesche described the ceremony beautifully in his boy memory, quoted in chapter 3.

With Alice Fletcher, Francis La Flesche documented the ceremonial events that made up Waxthe'xe xigithe more fully in their BAE report. La Flesche was particularly successful in obtaining texts of the songs and prayers he had witnessed as a boy. The following is a summary of their description. As in describing the buffalo hunt, I have written about the ceremony in a way that may help the reader discover some of its symbolic and spiritual meanings. I have changed the tense of their description from past to present in order to create a feeling for the ceremony's actuality. This ceremony is as real as the Sacred Pole it honors. It is as real as the Omaha people, who have kept themselves together during the years since Yellow Smoke and his wife performed this powerful ceremony.

WAXTHE'XE XIGITHE

When the time for renewal has come, the Waxthe'xeton subclan of the Hon'ga calls the seven chiefs of the tribe's governing council to the Sacred Tent. Inside the closed tent, they sit clad in buffalo robes. They let their hair flow down their backs outside the robes to mingle and blend into a single protective covering. Each of the seven chiefs lets his head fall onto his left arm. Each chief crouches on the ground in imitation of a buffalo. The actions they take together evoke the spirit of the buffalo herd at peace. "Without a knife or spoon, in imitation of the buffalo's feeding," the seven chiefs eat the food provided for them by the keeper of the Pole and his clan. Any food that falls to the ground is pushed toward the fire. "No one," the legend says, "must take anything claimed by the Pole."

The seven chiefs then decide on the day of renewal. They consecrate this decision by smoking the pipe belonging to the Pole. This pipe, which has also been returned to the tribe from the Peabody Museum, is of red catlinite and is incised on the sides with a design resembling a stylized eye. The lines that form the pipe's design are filled with a black substance, giving an effect of a black inlay against the red pipestone. The manner in which the chiefs smoke this pipe is unusual. When it passes from one man to another in the circle, the stone end is never lifted from the ground but is dragged by the stem. To prevent the stem from pulling out from the bowl, a sinew cord is secured to a flange at the end of the stone, and the other end of the cord is attached to the pipestem (see fig. 21a).

When the chiefs have finished smoking and decided the day on which the

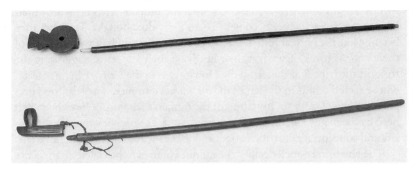

21a. Pipe of the White Buffalo Hide (top) and Pipe of the Sacred Pole (bottom), both with stems. From the Omaha Tribal Collection, curated by the University of Nebraska State Museum. Photographs courtesy of the Omaha Tribe.

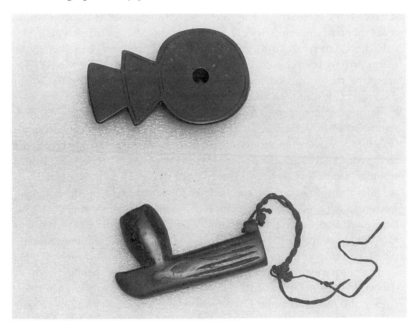

21b. Pipe of the White Buffalo Hide (top) and Pipe of the Sacred Pole (bottom).

ceremony will be held, the herald announces the decision to the tribe. They then send runners to locate a herd of buffalo. In preparation for the ceremony, the herald wears a headband of matted buffalo wool, to which is attached a single downy eagle feather.

The chiefs have prepared for the renewal ceremony by establishing their identity, and hence that of the tribe, with the buffalo herds on which their lives depend. Each chief becomes like an individual buffalo. Together they become like the herd at rest. They merge their unbound hair with the hair of their buffalo robes. They rest their heads on their left arms, suggesting the support the tribe will gain from the Hon'ga clan of the Hon'gashenu moiety, whose sacred tent is to the left of the *hu'thuga*'s entrance. They eat food prepared by the *Hon'ga* "in imitation of the buffalo's feeding." Once the sacred herd has been located, the chiefs and priests enact a series of rituals that intensify and concentrate the tribe's attention on the idea of itself as a single family.

The chiefs in council decide "the number of men to be called on to secure poles for the communal tent." Each of the seven chiefs then takes a reed from a bundle kept throughout the year in the Sacred Tent. There is a reed in the bundle for each man of the tribe. Each reed stands for a man and each man stands for his family, in the same way that Umon'hon'ti, the Real Omaha, stands for the entire tribe. The chiefs call out the names of the men whose reeds they have chosen. They call out the accomplishments of each man. The tribal herald then takes the reeds out into the *hu'thuga* and gives them to the men who have been chosen. Each man takes his reed back to the Sacred Tent, accepting the distinction conferred on him by the seven chiefs. Each man then places his reed back in the bundle held by the keeper.

The movement of reeds from the *hu'thuga*'s center to its edges and back reminds the people that each individual, each family, and each clan is responsible for the well-being of the entire tribe. Each one is a part that is connected to the entirety through the power of Wakon'da. The chiefs take reeds from a singular bundle that represents the tribe as a whole. They distribute them to singular individuals among the circle of clans that make up the *hu'thuga*. Each man who is chosen carries his reed from where he is camped with his family and clan to the common center that all of them share. The travel of each reed back and forth between the circle edge and its center reminds people of their responsibility to one another and to a common center.

This movement between center and circumference parallels that of dancers in the Sun Dance of other Plains tribes. Both the Omaha renewal ceremony and the Lakota Sun Dance present ancient Siouan ideas about how the individual may achieve union with the collectivity and with Wakon'da (or Wakan Tanka). Sun Dancers blow eagle-bone whistles as they dance from their positions in the arbor's circle toward the Sun Dance Pole, just as Omaha men, represented by reeds in a common bundle, move from their clans' places around the edge of the *hu'thuga* toward the Sacred Pole at its center.

After returning their reeds to the bundle, the chosen men go back to the circle of lodges. From each they select a single pole to be used in the construction of a long sacred tent in which the ceremony of renewal, Waxthe'xe xigithe, will take place. They strike the chosen poles as they would an enemy warrior, replicating the action of men who cut down the He'dewachi pole. Their action also replicates the rush of men toward the "wonderful tree" long ago as told in the Sacred Legend, and it anticipates a similar rush that will end the renewal ceremony. They then recount their valiant deeds. Other men and women of the Waxthe-xeton subclan carry the selected poles toward the Sacred Tent. Near it, they construct a semicircular lodge open toward the center of the tribal circle. La Flesche describes this "Holy Tent" as being "60 or 70 feet in length" (see fig. 12). When the chosen men strike a pole of each lodge in the *hu'thuga*, their actions remind people of how men in the Sacred Legend struck the Thunder bird tree that gave off light beneath the "motionless star" long ago. When they take these poles to where the Holy Tent is being constructed, they remind people that each family stands for the tribe as a whole.

The ceremonial lodge created from the poles thus consecrated represents all the families of the tribe. It is called *waxu'be*, "holy" or "sacred," because within its circle the tribe will be renewed. It is a sacred center within the sacred circle of the *hu'thuga*. The entire process of selecting and redistributing the reeds and poles teaches people that each part of the tribe is responsible for the well-being of the whole. A single reed stands for a man of the tribe, a single lodge pole stands for a family of the tribe, and the Sacred Pole stands for the tribe as a whole. The ceremonial repetition of the idea that parts make up a whole concentrates and intensifies its power, bringing what is known, but normally unstated, into public view for all to see. Fletcher and La Flesche translate the Pole's ancient name, Waxthe'xe, as "the power of motion, of life; mottled as by shadows (bringing into prominence to be seen by all the people as something distinctive)" (219). Thus, the ceremony actualizes the power of that ancient name.

The tribe now comes to a halt for the duration of the ceremony. Guards are stationed at the opening of the *hu'thuga* to ensure that people and horses will not move casually across its entrance, which has become sacred. The seven chiefs, the keeper of the Pole, and the leaders of each clan, wearing buffalo robes "in the ceremonial manner," walk quietly into the sacred tent and take their places. Members of the Xu'ka act as servers in this and every other ceremony conducted by the Hon'ga. They are a division of the Washa'be itazhi or Bear clan of the Tha'tada, a clan that camps to the left of the Hon'ga. Although the formal ceremonial system is no longer in place, it is interesting to note that both Dennis Hastings and Edward Cline belong to this clan. Their roles in supporting the Pole's return are a modern equivalent of their traditional clan roles.

After each song is sung, a marker stick is laid aside. If the ritual order should be accidentally disturbed, the keeper of the Sacred Pole is obliged to rise and weep until the servers of the ceremony come to wipe away his tears. Throughout the ceremony of renewal, the Hon'ga support the tribe's identity in the same way that the keeper physically supports the Pole as he carries it from camp to camp. That support is not possible without a reciprocal support from the tribe itself, a function that is performed by the Xu'ka. They are there to wipe away the keeper's tears.

The wife of the Pole's keeper carries the Pole to the edge of the Sacred Tent. There, the keeper leans it on its "staff" toward the center of the *hu'thuga*. It also inclines toward the unseen motionless star that centers the night sky. The seven chiefs pull reeds from the bundle, one by one, and speak the name of the man each represents. As each name is spoken, the herald advances to the Pole and shouts the man's name so that it can be heard throughout the *hu'thuga*. If the man named is a chief, the herald shouts the name of his son. Every man called is expected to send one of his children to the Pole with a special offering of buffalo meat.

It is this part of the ceremony in which Francis La Flesche took part as a boy, taking from his mother "a large piece of meat with no wrapping whatever" and carrying it to the Holy Tent where "an old man, wearing a band of buffalo skin around his head and a buffalo robe about his body" received it and "put both hands on my head and passed them down my sides." He recalled that "the calling of names still went on; a man sat immediately back of the Pole with two piles of small sticks before him; he would pick up a stick from one pile and give a name to the crier, who, leaning on a staff, called it out at the top of his voice; when this was done the stick was placed on the other pile" (1911, 246).

The ritual song begins with words that Fletcher and La Flesche translate literally as "here are they (the people); an object that has power; touching what is theirs" (233–42). They offer a free English translation but retain the Omaha exclamation *tho ho!*, which they say is used here "in the sense of a call to Wakon'da, to arrest attention, to announce that something is in progress relating to serious matters."

> The people cry aloud—*tho ho!* before thee.
> Here they prepare for sacred rites—*tho ho!*
> Their Sacred, Sacred Pole,
> With reverent hands, I say, they touch the Sacred Pole.

The words of this song remind people again of a reciprocity between the tribe's parts and its whole. They suggest that through the exchanges of reeds, poles, and buffalo meat, the people are "touching a power that is theirs." The song serves to focus attention on the ceremony of renewal that is to begin. It

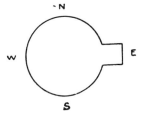

22. *Uzhin'eti. From Fletcher and La Flesche,* The Omaha Tribe *(1911), figure 59.*

reminds people that the Pole stands for both a person of the tribe and for the tribe as a whole.

As a member of the Waxthe'xeton subclan of the Hon'ga advances toward the Pole and unties the skin which conceals the wickerwork object bound to its middle, the Hon'ga keepers sing the next stanza of the ceremony's opening song:

> We now unloose and bring to view, *tho ho!* before thee,
> We bring to view the sacred rites, *tho ho!*
> This sacred, sacred thing,
> These sacred rites,
> This sacred thing comes to view before thee.

The figure of a circle, open to the east, is now cut into the prairie sod immediately in front of the Pole. It is called "*uzhin'eti*" (see fig. 22). Fletcher and La Flesche say that *uzhin* refers to "the wistfulness of a child as when it stands before its parent waiting to share in some good thing." *Ti*, they say, means "house." Thus, the name of this altar before which the tribe's renewal is enacted marks it as a place where each person receives the blessing of being a child born of the cosmic union that brings about the tribe as a whole. Fletcher and La Flesche reinforce the message of their translation by quoting an old man who said, "As I stand before *uzhin'eti* I seem to be listening for the words of the venerable ones who gave us these rites." The form of *uzhin'eti* is also echoed by the catlinite platform pipe sacred to Tethon'ha, the White Buffalo Hide.

This "keyhole shaped altar" is probably of great antiquity among Plains Indians. It is a powerful symbol because it reproduces both the form of a single lodge and that of the camp circle. It concentrates the collective energy of an entire people into a single place. Its name in Omaha reminds each person of his or her connection to the tribe's collective traditions. It suggests an interdependence between generations. The renewal to be completed within its enclosure ensures that each person stands before the tribe with "the wistful-ness of a child as when it stands before its parent waiting to share in some good thing."

After this symbolic figure is cut into the earth, the Hon'ga keepers begin the second song of the ceremony:

> I here declare our work to be completed,
>> Done our task!
> I here declare that all our work is now completed,
>> Done our task!
> I here declare that all our work is now completed,
>> Fully completed!

On the following day, the wickerwork object, called the "wrist shield," af-ter the wrist guard of a bowman, is fully opened. It contains the down of a crane or swan. Songs repeat the attributes of the Pole: "unity of the Tribe, unity of the Seven Chiefs which made them 'as one heart, as one voice,' the authority of Thunder." A song celebrates the wrist shield as a "round object," like the sun, and refers to its power as being like that of a man's bow, "used for the defense of life and to secure the game that gave food, shelter, and clothing." Fletcher and La Flesche say that a literal translation of the song is difficult because it does not do justice to the song's associations through rep-etition. "To the Indian mind," they say, "the repeated words brought up the varied aspects of the Pole":

> It represented the unity of the tribe; the unity of the Council of Seven Chiefs, which made them "as one heart, as one voice"; the authority of the Thunder. It was a being—a man; it was a bow, the weapon of a man which was used for the defense of life and to secure the game that gave food, shelter, and clothing. As this song (which referred to the shield—the article that protected the wrist of a man when he pulled the bow string) was sung, the wickerwork containing the down was fully opened, preparatory to the ceremonies in which it had a part.

The authors conclude that "the full meaning of the lines of the song does not appear from the literal words, but must be found in the symbolism of the ceremonial acts connected with this 'round object'," the wickerwork wrist shield. The Omaha words are:

> Axondepa ha ha! win the thon
> Axondepa ha ha! win the thon
> Axondepa ha ha! win the thon
> Axondepa ha ha! win the thon
> Axondepa ha ha! win the thon

Axondepa refers to the bowman's wrist shield. *Ha ha!* is an exclamation, *win the* means "one, here this," and *thon* refers to the round shape of the wrist shield. Opening this wickerwork and exposing the swan's down within is like pulling a bow string in preparation for shooting an arrow. As the singers complete the lines of this song, the Pole is seen to be both a man who is ready to launch his arrows on behalf of the tribe and the bow he holds in his hand. Once again, the Pole is read as a part that stands for the whole, "a fragment of anything" connected to its entirety.

Following the wickerwork's opening, the fourth song is sung. The keeper arranges on the ground in front of the Pole, side by side, four of the best pieces of buffalo meat (called *tezhu*) that have been brought to honor the Pole. These represent four buffaloes, four hunts, and "the four ceremonial offerings of hearts and tongues which have preceded this ceremony." Sometimes the meat offerings are offered in four parallel rows. From these offerings, the keeper later cuts the fat that is to be mixed with paint to anoint the Pole. Once again, the keepers of the ceremony repeat the first song eight times:

> The people cry aloud—*tho ho!* before thee.
> Here they prepare for sacred rites—*tho ho!*
> Their Sacred, Sacred Pole,
> With reverent hands, I say, they touch the Sacred Pole.
> The people cry aloud—*tho ho!* before thee.
> Here they prepare for sacred rites—*tho ho!*
> Their Sacred, Sacred Pole,
> With reverent hands, I say, they touch the Sacred Pole.
> We now unloose and bring to view, *tho ho!* before thee,
> We bring to view the sacred rites, *tho ho!*
> This sacred, sacred thing,
> These sacred rites,
> This sacred thing comes to view before thee.

Once the meat has been arranged in rows along the front of the Holy Tent, the singers repeat the second song:

> I here declare our work to be completed,
>> Done our task!
> I here declare that all our work is now completed,
>> Done our task!
> I here declare that all our work is now completed,
>> Fully completed!

Repetition is important to the success of the ceremony. Each song has its place in the ritual order. Each repetition intensifies its message, in the same way that the movement of reeds and men back and forth between center and circumference intensifies the idea that each part of the tribe stands for its entirety. Each new song furthers the keeper's progress toward the ceremony's completion. The sixth song exhorts him to show the knife with which he will cut the fat and to hold it up to view. Its words "Do thou show thy knife standing there!" are repeated nine times.

While the songs for the Pipe of the Sacred White Buffalo Hide tell an epic narrative that literally sings the buffalo into life, the songs for the Sacred Pole authorize the keeper's studied and ritualized preparation of the meat and fat with which the Pole and the tribe itself will be renewed. Song texts and actions move forward together in a kind of stylized dance. In the seventh song, the Hon'ga singers repeat their clan's authority over the ceremony and give their blessing for the keeper to continue. After the first stanza has been sung four times, the keeper lowers his knife in anticipation of the action that the second stanza authorizes with the words, "I make or authorize him to cut." As these words are being repeated four times, he begins to cut the fat from the four *tezhu'* now lying in front of the Pole. He then drops the fat into a wooden bowl held by his wife.

Fletcher and La Flesche say that "fat was the emblem of abundance; red, the color of life. The mixture therefore symbolized abundant life." As the eighth song is sung, the keeper takes the brush with which he will paint the Pole and makes a ceremonial approach toward it, while his wife approaches holding the bowl with its offering of buffalo fat. The song's lines are:

> Abahe he the abahe he the
> Te ehe the
> Abahe he the abahe he the

The words mean literally, "to hold toward this; buffalo, I say, this." The second line "was explained to mean that the buffalo was here declared to be a life-giving gift from Wakon'da, and that the buffalo yielded itself to man for his abundant food and also to provide him with shelter and clothing." Thus, the ceremony gave thanks to the buffalo and to Wakon'da as well as honoring the Pole.

The second stanza of the eighth song refers to touching and then repeats the line, "buffalo, I say, this." As it is being sung, the keeper touches the Pole with a brush on which he has placed sacred red pigment. He paints four lines down the Pole's length in a deliberate and reverent manner. He repeats these motions as his clan members begin to sing the ninth song, the first two stanzas of which La Flesche translates literally as, "I cause the paint to adhere; I make it to be red." The melody of the third and final stanza of the ninth song will later accompany the ceremony's completion by the keeper's wife. It is this song that La Flesche quoted in his "boy memory." Its words in Omaha are "*Konpi akithe, Konakithe he he.*" La Flesche translates them as "I make it beautiful." He notes that *Konpi* "here refers to man, the most comely of all creatures endowed with life, to whom Wakon'da has given the promise of abundance." In the boy memory, he translated the words more coloquially as, "I make him beautiful! I make him beautiful!" The people respond to this line with joy and laughter, and cry out, "Oh how beautiful he is!"

The people reach out to the Pole through this part of the ceremony. They reach out to him with their offerings. They reach out to him with their gifts of buffalo meat and fat. They reach out to him through the intermediary of their children, wistfully standing before them "waiting to share in some good thing." They reach out to the Pole with fat that comes from the teeming energy of the buffalo herd. They reach out to the Venerable Man for the purpose of tribal renewal. Their cry of praise to the Pole's beauty also praises the beauty of their coming together as a people in ceremony. It praises the beauty they see in their life together as a tribe.

When the Hon'ga singers and the keeper have completed their painting of the Pole, the ceremony's focus turns toward the earth altar, *uzhin'eti*. It also turns from the keeper to his wife, a member of the opposite, Inshta'thunda, moiety. In addition to meaning Sky people, Inshta'thunda also means flashing eyes, a reference again to the power of Thunder. At the center of the altar, "where a fireplace would be in the lodge," the Hon'ga servers of the ceremony place a buffalo chip, light it, and burn bundles of sweet grass and sage. (In a similar fashion, Lawrence Gilpin burned sweet-smelling cedar to welcome Umon'hon'ti back to the tribal arena, which is also a circle open to the east.)

The priest's wife holds seven arrows to represent the seven chiefs. Fletcher and La Flesche say that she "stood for the mother of the race and her share in the rites was a prayer for its continuation and prosperity." La Flesche remembered her holding six of the arrows in one hand and a seventh in the other. She wears a ceremonial costume, like that of her husband, and a buffalo robe around her waist, skin side out and painted red. "Across her cheeks and her glossy black hair red bands were painted and to the heel of each moccasin was attached a strip of buffalo hair like a tail." She holds the seven arrows above the sweetgrass smoke as the singers complete the tenth song, which repeats the first stanza of the eighth song, "to hold toward this; buffalo, I say, this." The singers now sing the eleventh song, which is the same as the sixth. They repeat its words nine times. "A number multiplied by itself," Fletcher and La Flesche say, "as 3 times 3 or 4 times 4, as not infrequently occurs in ceremonials, indicates completed action." Every detail of this complex and beautiful ceremony reveals multiple layers of meaning. Repeating lines and songs has the force of both intensifying and punctuating key moments in the ceremony.

The ceremony draws near to completion as the singers begin the twelfth and last song. Its music is the same as in the ninth song, which accompanied the painting by the Pole's keeper, but its words are different. They are *Baxon akithe, baxon akithe, he he*, which means "to thrust; I cause it." The singers repeat these words seven times, once for each of the arrows the keeper's wife holds in her hands. As they complete the first line, the woman "makes a feint with the arrow at the bundle of feathers in the middle of the Pole." Four times she repeats this motion with the arrow she holds in her right hand. Then, suddenly, she thrusts the arrow through the down enclosed by the wickerwork wrist shield and into the ground, using the Pole as if it were a bow. "In this act the Pole became the bow, and the basketwork the wrist shield on the arm of the man who grasped the bow." She then repeats this act with the other six arrows, following the singing of each additional line of the song. When all seven arrows are safely lodged within the soft earth of *uzhin'eti*, the tribe is assured that they and the buffalo will prosper during the coming year. Following the woman's act of holy divination, the Pole is folded together with its staff "and tied in its skin covering until the next year, when the ceremony would be repeated."

The act of shooting the seven arrows embodies a number of complex symbolic transformations. The Pole, who is the Venerable Man, for a moment becomes both a man's bow and his shooting arm, parts that stand for his whole. The woman, normally the recipient of buffalo meat, now takes on the role of hunter. Her act of thrusting the arrow toward the ground also suggests an obvious sexual reversal that Fletcher and La Flesche choose not to mention directly. They do explain that performing the ceremony successfully had momentous consequences for the tribe's well-being: "The woman shot the arrow along the bow, simulating the shooting of the buffalo, to secure the gift of abundance. When the arrow was not checked by the wickerwork or down, but passed clear through the bundle with sufficient force to stand in the ground on the other side, a shout of joy arose from the people, for this was an augury of victory over enemies and of success in hunting" (242).

Fletcher and La Flesche note that the renewal ceremony is divided into two parts. In the first part, performed by a man, the Pole represents "an authority granted and guarded by the supernatural powers." In the second part, performed by a woman, he stands for "the men of the tribe, the defenders and providers of the home." They point out that "the same songs are used for both parts, but in the first part the ceremonial acts are performed by a man; in the second part the ceremonial acts are performed by a woman." The division of the ceremony into two parts, they say, "reflected the fundamental ideas on which the tribal organization is based, the union of masculine and feminine." Their analysis shows the renewal ceremony as a means of expressing a complementary reversal of male and female activities. While the ceremony is prepared by men of the tribe, the actual shooting, on which success in hunting depends, is done by the keeper's wife, a woman of the complementary Inshta'thunda moiety. Because the ceremony is performed in public, it is an oral and performative analog to scripture in one of the "great traditions," suggesting something that people of all ages and social positions can understand and feel connected to.

After the two parts of the ceremony have been completed and the buffalo meat taken away, "four images made of grass and hair were set up before the Pole." These represent enemies of the tribe. This concluding ritual, in which the public participates, is known as "shooting the Pole." It is considered to be "an act intended to do public honor to the defenders of the home and the tribe. It begins when the tribal herald shouts for all to hear: "Pity me, my young men, and let me [speaking to the keepers of the Pole] complete my ceremonies!" In response to his call, all men who have won honors in defense of the tribe put on the regalia they have earned the right to wear, and make ready for the final act of this long and complex ceremony. Meanwhile, all the young men of the tribe ride away from the *hu'thuga* on their horses. "Suddenly some one of them turned, and crying, 'They have come! they have come!' the whole company charges on the camp." This was done, Fletcher and La Flesche say, "in so realistic a manner as to deceive the people into the belief of an actual onslaught of an enemy, to the temporary confusion of the whole tribe." The chiefs and leaders remain in the Holy Tent, in front of which the Pole inclines, while the warriors charge grass images of the enemies they have encountered during the past year. As Waxthe'xe xigithe comes to an end, the tribe begins to prepare for the more secular He'dewachi ceremony, which will commence the following day.

The Pole, the Venerable Man, is associated with the power of Thunder, the Thunder bird that in Omaha imagery empowers the male creative energy. In ceremony, the Pole is supported by its staff at a forty-degree angle, the elevation of the pole star above the horizon in the latitude occupied by the Omaha. The Pole may also suggest the phallic power of male procreation. Certainly the wrist shield serves as a symbolic reminder that the Pole is simultaneously a whole man and his various parts, just as the tribe is a single entity made up of many complementary parts. The song's evocation of the round sun extends this image to include the power of the sun itself as an attribute of the Pole. This, in turn, reinforces the idea that day and night, male and female, sky and earth, complement one another. The Pole was discovered as a blessing of the night, "the great mother force," but he shows himself with a power like that of the sun.

The story of the Pole's origin begins with a council among chiefs of the tribe "to devise some means by which the bands of the tribe might be kept together and the tribe itself saved from extinction." The ceremony of renewal ends with a temporary scattering of the tribe, a reminder of the ever-present danger of dissolution. This scattering is reversed when the warriors charge grass images of past enemies, and remind people of how men of the tribe long ago charged the "wonderful tree" that became their Sacred Pole. Now that Umon'hon'ti has returned to his people, he reminds the tribe of the ancient challenge to devise some means by which the tribe may be saved from extinction. "It held the tribe together," Fletcher and La Flesche say; "without it the people might scatter."

Omahas have been meeting the challenge of staying together in the years that Umon'hon'ti spent in the care and keeping of anthropologists. Their challenge now is to devise some means by which the Venerable Man from their past may continue to receive honor in their lands. The seven arrows that the keeper's wife shot through the Pole's wrist shield long ago have now come back into Omaha control. So has the Pole's pipe, with its lanyard for dragging it between the chiefs sitting in ceremony together. Omaha hands have again held Umon'hon'ti. The old ceremonies are gone, but their spirit remains.

XTHEXE: THE MARK OF HONOR

The Sacred Pole was known to Omahas of past generations as Waxthe'xe (something sacred, mottled as by shadows, bringing into prominence to be seen by all the people). Xthexe is also the name they gave to the blue spot or "Mark of Honor" tattooed on a girl whose father qualifies for membership in the Hon'hewachi (Night Blessed or Night Dancing) Society. The Mark of Honor consists of cosmic symbols tattooed (in blue in modern times) on the forehead and throat of the Hon'hewachi initiate's daughter. According to Victor V. Robinson Sr., each clan had its own version of the Mark of Honor. Inke'sabe and Tapa women had a round tattoo at the center of the forehead. Hon'ga women had a star on the breast. Tha'tada women had the star on the left lower arm with a circle in the middle and a band around the arm. (Robinson 1982, 124). The blue spot on the girl's forehead represents the sun. The star sign at her throat "is emblematic of the night, the great mother force," according to Fletcher and La Flesche. "Its four points," they say, represent "the life-giving winds into the midst of which the child was sent through the ceremony of Turning the Child" (505). These two cosmic signs represent the complementary principles of night and day that are fundamental to Omaha thought and experience.

Membership in the Hon'hewachi represents a man's "recognition of Night, of the feminine force or principle" (507). Every member of the Hon'hewachi society must compose a song in the Hon'hewachi rhythm. The song must express the initiate's personal experience, and frequently it refers to "a dream or vision that came in answer to his supplication" (503). Initiation into the Hon'hewachi society represents a man's contact with "dramatic rhythmic movements for the expression of personal emotion or experience." It places him in position "for the presentation of mythical teachings" (393). It recognizes that he has been blessed by the night. The Hon'hewachi songs, ceremonies, and symbols "refer to the creative cosmic forces typified by night and day, the earth and the sky." They empower him to present mythic teachings to the tribe. They represent "the fundamental ideas on which the tribal organization rested" (495).

THE HON'HEWACHI FEASTS

The ritual of tattooing the Mark of Honor is part of a four-day set of ceremonies initiating a girl's father into the Hon'hewachi society. In their speeches, society members address their fellows as Hon'ithaethe, "those blessed by the night" (Fortune 1932, 148). The ceremonies begin with Watha'wa, the Feast of the Count, in which the initiate recounts from memory the hundred or more gifts or sacrifices he has made over a period of years. During the feasting he must also give away the entire contents of his lodge. At the climax of the ceremonies he presents his daughter to the life-giving power of the sun.

The gifts and sacrifices of the initiate's count are brought to mind by a bundle of willow sticks he has been accumulating over the years. Each stick represents one of his *wathin'ethe* gifts. Chiefs from each of the two sides of the *hu'thuga*, the Hon'gashenu and Inshta'thunda, sit at the back of the lodge. They are Ni'kagahi U'zhu, "principal chiefs" who have counted the largest number of *wathin'ethe*. They face east toward the entrance of the lodge. They face the rising of Mithon, "the sun, the round sun" (504). They represent the female and male principles that combine to make up the tribe as a whole. Each is known as a "chief to the left" because of the direction in which he passes the bundle.

First, the Hon'gashenu chief takes the bundle and passes it to his left. He passes it in the direction of the sun's travel. He passes it to his complement, the Inshta'thunda chief. The bundle moves from hand to hand around the circle of Hon'ithaethe, those blessed by the night. They are seated according to the rank of their *wathin'ethe* gifts. When the bundle has completed its circle and returned to the Hon'gashenu chief, the herald carries it back to the initiate sitting at the eastern entrance of the lodge. He must then begin to "count" his hundred gifts entirely from memory and without error or hesitation. Fletcher and La Flesche report that "it was a severe tax on a man's memory, for these gifts often extended over a period of ten or twenty years" (498).

The Feast of the Count is followed by the Feast of the Hon'hewachi. On the evening before the tattooing, chiefs of the tribe and the Hon'ithaethe assemble to receive the record of the initiate's count. They sing a song in recognition of the candidate's steps toward initiation. The rhythm of this song is a model for all other songs in what Fletcher identified as the Hon'hewachi rhythm. The song indicates that the Hon'ithaethe accept the initiate's count of one hundred *wathin'ethe* gifts. Many of these gifts are the products of women's labor and because of this they represent the female cosmic principle. The song's words sum up the purpose that brings the society's members together. They mean literally:

> Thidon be shaya ma
> Thidon be shaya ma
> [See you
> as the result or outcome of a decision
> coming, they]
> Egon shon don uthudon be taya ma
> [To look into, to consider, to judge]
> Thidonbe shaya ma
> Thidonbe shaya ma
> Thidonbe shaya ma
> [coming for that purpose, they]
> (502)

As the chiefs and Hon'ithaethe sing the final stanzas of this "judgment song," the initiate's daughter enters and dances before them. She is the young woman who will receive the Mark of Honor. She is the young woman who will one day send her children into the midst of the winds. She and the other "woman chiefs" will dance at meetings of the Hon'hewachi. She will carry Xthexe, "mottled as by shadows," among her people when she is an old woman. Her dance before the Hon'hewachi members, Fletcher and La Flesche tell us, "dramatized the awakening of the feminine element—an awakening everywhere necessary for a fulfillment in tangible form of the life-giving power" (502).

The girl wears a tunic embroidered with porcupine quills. Her hair is parted in the middle, pulled back across her forehead, and braided behind the ears into thick buns that rest upon her shoulders. Three young women who have already received the Mark of Honor dance with her, singing Hon'-

hewachi songs. Fletcher and La Flesche point out that the song to which the girl dances in preparation for receiving the Mark of Honor "gives the rhythmic model after which all songs that pertain to the Hon'hewachi were fashioned. "It therefore represented," they say, "the fundamental rhythm that expressed the musical feeling concerning those ideas or beliefs for which the Hon'hewachi stood" (502). It is both a fragment of that feeling and its entirety.

THE CRY OF THE LIVING CREATURES

The chiefs and Hon'ithaethe spend the night preceding the tattooing in the lodge of the girl's father. They continue to be his guests until the tattooing is completed. On the morning following the Feast of the Hon'hewachi, the sun emerges from a point on the eastern horizon behind where the girl's father stood to recite his count. It begins to move toward the zenith point. It moves in the direction the bundle of willow sticks took in its circle around the hands of the Hon'ithaethe. It moves toward the moment when the tattooing will be consecrated.

The initiate's daughter begins her preparations to receive Mithon, the sun, the round sun. Early in the morning, servers of the ceremony set up scaffolds on either side of the entrance to the initiate's lodge. On these they suspend the articles given as fees to validate the ritual. These articles must include a hundred knives and a hundred awls. The knives and awls are required as emblems of male and female activities, and in honor of the hundred count the initiate has accomplished in the Feast of the Count.

The tattooing begins later in the morning when the sun is already high enough to bring heat and to shorten shadow. Two woman already bearing the Mark of Honor prepare food for the assembled guests. The lodge has been emptied of all the initiate's possessions during the preceding days of feasting. Only the final gifts remain on the scaffolds that frame its entrance to the east. Only the young woman remains to be given away to the life-giving power of the round sun. Servers of the ceremony then thrust the hundred knives and hundred awls into the ground on either side of the morning fire. The time for the presentation of mythical teachings is approaching.

Behind the hearth at the place of honor, servers of the ceremony lay out "a bed of the costliest robes." They place a pillow toward the east, the direction of the sun's first appearance. The initiate and his guests take their morning meal in the lodge that has been prepared for the work of tattooing. The young woman takes her meal with her family in a lodge adjoining the one in which the ceremony is to take place. Then the Hon'ithaethe and women who have received the Mark of Honor sing a song to the young woman. Its words are:

They are coming for you
They are coming to tell you
Because it is time
(Lee and La Vigna 1985)

The morning meals have been completed. Servers of the ceremony escort the young woman into the lodge of her father. They lay her with great care and dignity upon the fine robes on the bed of honor. She faces west, as does the sun in his path across the sky, "for, being emblematic of life, she had to move as if moving with the sun" (503). She wears "a skin tunic embroidered with porcupine quills" (502). When she has taken her place of honor with the chiefs and members of the Hon'hewachi society, two heralds stand at the entrance of the lodge. Mithon, the round sun, moves in his slow and certain circle closer to the zenith point. The heralds call the names of those who are to sing during the tattooing. They give voice to the war honors achieved by the men who are to sing. Some of these men are already in the lodge when the herald addresses them. Others enter following his salutation.

A ring of silence encircles the lodge and extends outward into the places where people are living. They respect the blessing of the night that is come here among them. They respect the silence into which the round sun will speak. They are careful to keep children, dogs, and horses at a distance. The Hon'ithaethe speak among themselves in gentle voices. The lodge has become a holy place. It is to become a center of the cosmos. It has become a place of waiting for the presentation of mythic teachings. One of the Hon'ithaethe, those blessed by the night, has been chosen to perform the tattooing. He may be considered for the task by right of inheritance. He must also be blessed and protected with power from a vision of the serpent whose "teeming life 'moves' over the earth" (506). He must be able to suck the blood and charcoal pigment from the young woman's freshly tattooed skin without harm. He must be in contact with the serpent's flashing eyes and moving cry which, in Omaha symbolism, is the noise of teeming life that "moves" over the earth.

Servers of the ceremony prepare charcoal pigment in a wooden bowl. The tattooing chief outlines the sun circle and the star with a flattened stick dipped in a charcoal solution. He takes up a tightly bound bundle of flint points. To the flints are fastened rattlesnake rattles. In later times these implements were replaced with needles and small bells. The young woman lies on her bed of honor in absolute silence. She must make no noise throughout the ceremony. "If she should do so," Fletcher and La Flesche say, "it was considered as evidence that she had been unchaste. If the healing process was rapid, it was considered a good omen" (506).

Silence surrounds the lodge. The Earth people and Sky people who make up the tribe keep their distance in respect for the sacrifice that is taking place for their well-being. The chiefs and Hon'ithaethe begin to chant the sun song:

Mithon shui the tha
Mithon shui the tha
Mithon shui the tha
Mithon shui the tha
Mithon gathu ti thon de shui thetha
Mithon shui the tha
Mithon shui the tha

These words mean literally:

The sun the round sun
Comes—speaks—says
The sun the round sun
Comes—speaks—says
The sun the round sun
Comes—speaks—says
The sun the round sun
Comes—speaks—says
The sun the round sun
Yonder point
When it comes—speaks—says
The sun the round sun
Comes—speaks—says

"This ancient song," according to Fletcher and La Flesche, "refers to the sun rising to the zenith, to the highest point; when it reaches that point it speaks" (504).

The tattooing chief begins to prick the sun sign into the skin of the young woman's forehead. Against the rhythm of the Hon'hewachi song evoking the power of the sun at its zenith point, she can hear the dry rhythmic percussion of the rattlesnake piercing her skin and drawing her blood with its flickering fangs of flint. She endures and waits in perfect silence. Above the lodge of her father the sun, Mithon, moves silently westward, toward his zenith point and beyond. He moves toward the moment of their meeting. When the sun reaches that point, "it speaks, as its symbol descends upon the maid with the promise of life-giving power" (504).

The dry sound of rattling stops. The young woman's forehead is hot with a circle of her own blood. It is hot with the promise of the Hon'hewachi song. It is hot with anticipation of the round sun's movement to the zenith point. The momentary silence that surrounds her anticipates the sun, as it comes, speaks, says. Her silence reaches out to receive the life-giving power of his voice as he reaches the highest point. The song promises her the sun, Mithon, the round sun. The round sun comes, speaks, says, to her at his zenith point.

The tattooing chief bathes her forehead with a cooling charcoal solution. The rattling begins again. The rhythm of the Hon'hewachi again surrounds her. The chief's bundled flint fangs inject the pigment beneath her skin. They complete the sun sign as the Hon'hewachi song comes to an end. Both the song and the sign promise life-giving power when the moment arrives for the sun to descend upon her.

The tattooing chief moves toward the young woman. His lips move toward where she is hot with the round sun sign and her own hot blood. He is protected from harm by the blessing of his serpent vision. He sucks the mixed blood and charcoal from the freshly tattooed surface of her skin. With his action, the sun sign is ready to receive the teeming cry of the living creatures. Her sign is ready to receive the round sun as he moves like living wind in the trees.

There is a pause in the ceremony. The young woman can feel the sun sign pressing into her skin at the center of her forehead. The people will know her by this sign when she is an old woman. They will honor her for it always. She can hear the sound of her own breathing, moving in a rhythm like living wind in the trees. She knows that in time she will send her children "into the midst of the winds" in the ceremony of Turning the Child. In silence, the Hon'hewachi rhythm continues to surround her. Her father, the chiefs, the women who serve her in ceremony, and the Hon'ithaethe are suffused with the rhythm of the great mother force. They are filled with her emotion. They are filled with an "awakening of the feminine element." They are ready to experience the mythic teachings of Hon'he, the "creative acts" by which, "through the mysterious power of Wakon'da, night brought forth day" (494).

The shadow cast by the initiation lodge creeps up into itself as the sun, the round sun, arches toward the point of midday. The tattooing chief picks up his flint bundle. Its rattles shake her silence like the flickering tongues of heat lightning and distant thunder that penetrate the mystery of a sultry summer night sky. The rattling sound reminds the young woman of serpent power, the teeming life that moves over the earth. It reminds her that the name of the Sky people, Inshta'thunda, means "flashing eyes." It reminds her that the Sky people "in union with the Earth people, gave birth to the human race" (185). It reminds her that the sky powers bring forth life by descending upon the earth in the form of lightning, thunder, and rain.

The time has come for the Hon'ithaethe, those blessed by the night, to think about the night sky and its promise of day to come. The singers give voice to the rhythm of the night dance:

Honthin the tha
Honthin the tha
Honthin the tha
Umba ia tho
Umba ia tho
Umba ia tho

The song's words mean:

Night moving
Going
Night moving
Going
Night moving
Going
Day is coming
Day is coming
Day is coming

Fletcher and La Flesche translate the meaning of these words as "night moves, it passes, and the day is coming" (505). As the singers chant these words in the Hon'hewachi rhythm, the tattooing chief resumes his rhythmic penetration of the young woman's skin with his bundle of flints. The rattles shake in response to his motions. The rattling sound blends with the words of the song. They penetrate her consciousness as well as her skin. The figure that takes form in hot bright blood upon her throat is a four-pointed star.

"The star," according to Fletcher and La Flesche, "is emblematic of the night, the great mother force. . . . Its four points represent," they say, "the life-giving winds into the midst of which the child was sent through the ceremony of Turning the Child" (505). The star also evokes the pole star beneath which a chief's son discovered the luminous tree that was to become Waxthe'xe, the Sacred Pole. The Hon'ithaethe know that "the name of the Pole, Waxthe'xe, signifies that the power to give the right to possess this 'mark of honor' was vested in the Pole" (219). According to the sacred legend Yellow Smoke told in 1888, "the Thunder birds come and go upon this tree, making a trail of fire that leaves four paths on the burnt grass that stretch toward the Four Winds" (218). Membership in the Hon'hewachi comes to a man who has been "pitied (compassionately helped) by night. . . . The feminine cosmic force was typified not only by night but by the heavenly bodies seen by night, as the masculine cosmic force was symbolized by day and the sun" (494).

The shadow of the initiation lodge has nearly vanished. Mithon, the round sun, has nearly reached the zenith point. He is nearly in line with the day and night signs of the young woman's body. The Hon'ithaethe sing a song of completion as the moment of alignment draws near. Its words are:

> Gathin xue tha
> Gathin xue tha
> Eda tonda ha xue tha
> Gathin xue tha
> Gathin xue tha
> Hio

The words mean literally:

> Yonder unseen is one moving
> Noise
> Yonder unseen is one moving
> Noise
> For that reason
> Over the earth
> Noise
> *Hio*—The cry of the living creatures

The rhythmic rattling that gives voice to the flint's repeated piercing pauses. The tattooing chief bathes the young woman's star sign with soothing charcoal. Then he picks up the bundle of flints for the last time. He pricks the pigment into her skin with a final dry rattling of the serpent-tailed flint fangs. He removes the remaining blood and charcoal by sucking with his mouth. The designs are now part of her body. They have taken the places they will occupy on the body of a young mother. They have become centers of the universe that will honor the Omaha tribe throughout the long life of an old woman. Out of fragments, they have become an entirety.

The sun moves directly into line with the young woman's body. His rays come down to her through the smoke hole's shadowless shaft of light. They fall upon her. She receives his light as "the cry of the living creatures." It is the serpent-like noise of teeming life moving over the earth. It is the noise of the Sky people come to join the people of Earth. The energy of their union passes through the woman's young body and into the earth. It passes through the sun sign. It passes through the star sign. It passes through her young womb and into the ancient and constantly fertile womb of the Earth. It passes through her and into the earth like the seven arrows that the keeper's wife shoots through the Sacred Pole's cradle of swan's down. It passes through her and it becomes her. Through her, it becomes a moving center worthy of carrying the same name that is given to the Sacred Pole.

UNION OF NIGHT AND DAY

"By the union of Day, the above, and Night, the below," Fletcher and La Flesche tell us, "came the human race and by them the race is maintained. The tattooing [is] an appeal for the perpetuation of all life and of human life in particular" (507). Women bearing the Mark of Honor were still alive among the Omaha people when the Pole returned to them. The spirit of Xthexe, mottled as by shadows, continues to unite Sky people and Earth people into a single tribe. The creative rhythm of the Hon'hewachi is still very much alive among the Omaha people. Its emotion is still among them for the presentation of mythical teachings.

A young woman receives the sun's power when she is at a point on the earth's surface directly between the earth's center and the highest point in the sun's heavenly arc. Her complement, the young man in the story of the Sacred Pole's origin, receives his power by recognizing the star around which all others turn, a center of the night sky. He finds his center burning beneath a steady star around which the star-world reels as he watches it, amazed, through the night. He is able to see "a tree that stands burning" through the compassion of the night. A young woman is able to hear "the cry of the living creatures" as they pass through her body when it is aligned with the zenith, the center of the sun's path across the sky. These revelations of the sacred to a young man and a young woman complement one another. Through them, the tribe as a whole becomes centered. One center may be found in many places. The Pole is a center who travels as the people travel. The Mark of Honor worn by a young woman is also such a center. The young woman finds her center in the sound of all living things moving through her like a great wind. In ceremony, she finds herself centered between earth and sky. Like the tribe, she finds her center in the union of Earth people and Sky people.

Vision comes through a shift in perspective. The young man's lonely vigil through the night shows him how stars circle around a single point of light among their multitude. The tree beneath that central star burns itself into his mind. The night force and his isolation reveals this sky-world to him. "The whole tree, its trunk, branches, and leaves, were alight, yet remained unconsumed." But by day, "the brightness of the tree began to fade, until with the rising of the sun the tree with its foliage resumed its natural appearance."

The young woman gains her shift in perspective by day, when the sun is at the highest point in its arc. During the tattooing she "strove to make no sound or outcry." The sharp rattle of the serpent-tailed flint, "representative of the teeming life that 'moves' over the earth," writes its signature on her silence. "Because this life is 'moving,' it makes a noise. Even the sun as it 'moves,' it is said, 'makes a noise,' as does the living wind in the trees." The four points of the tattooed star stand for "the life-giving winds into the midst of which the child was sent through the ceremony of Turning the Child." They bring to mind the "trail of fire that leaves four paths on the burnt grass that stretch toward the Four Winds." The symbols of night and day are aligned with the sun's path across the sky, with the young woman's face, with the part in her hair, with her waiting womb, and with the earth itself. As the tattooing is completed, the Hon'hewachi singers chant the following words:

> Yonder unseen is one moving
> Noise
> Yonder unseen is one moving
> Noise
> For that reason
> Over the earth
> Noise
> *Hio*—The cry of the living creatures

The ceremony for tattooing the Mark of Honor perfectly aligns the young woman's body with male and female cosmic forces. It channels the very energy of creation into the life of the tribe. The ceremony centers the young woman who is to become a protector of those in need. It centers her directly beneath the zenith point, the sky's center and the center of day. It centers her, and through her renews the spirit of life. "By the union of Day, the above, and Night, the below," according to Fletcher and La Flesche, "came the human race and by them the race is maintained." "The Tattooing," they say, is "an appeal for the perpetuation of all life and of human life in particular."

When Dennis Hastings invited Jillian Ridington and me to attend our first Omaha tribal pow-wow in 1985, we had every reason to believe that the Mark of Honor had been abandoned, like the Sacred Pole, many years before. Fletcher and La Flesche wrote about it as a thing of the past. Margaret Mead wrote in 1932 that "the last hereditary tattooer died some twenty years ago; his place was taken, for a time, by a pretender who abandoned the old method of tattooing and used India ink. . . . The society [of Blue Spot women] has now practically disintegrated, and there is no place in the aboriginal culture in which a group of women participate as women" (Mead 1932, 136). Imagine our surprise to discover in 1985 that women bearing the Mark of Honor were still alive and accorded considerable respect.

23. Maggie Johnson. Photograph by Jillian Ridington.

We were told that the Blue Spot indicated a woman's dedication to the care of orphans and needy children. Women bearing the mark were expected to live up to its honor through acts of compassion. We felt honored at being able to meet and speak to several of these women, among them Helen Grant Walker, Maggie Johnson, and Mabel Hamilton. Others still alive at that time were Margaret Saunsoci and Rachel Johnson. When we asked Mabel Hamilton about the name Hon'hewachi, the Night Blessed Society, she laughed as a way of acknowledging that there is sexual as well as a symbolic meaning that Fletcher and La Flesche neglected to report for their translation of the term as "rhythmic motions in the night."

In 1986 we talked with seventy-one-year-old Pauline Tindall, an administrator with the tribal health care center. She confirmed that some of the last tattoos had been done by a man named Silas Woods, whom she said was not considered to have the proper authority. The last properly authorized tattooer was named Morris. Pauline told us that the few remaining Blue Spot women will be the ones who must bring the tradition to an end:

> It's almost as if they're here to end the society. The White Christian attitude toward it was very negative, and consequently they just dropped it, and a lot of us that were growing up in that era that might have been marked, were not.
>
> I think they were recognized for their saintliness. They had to be good women and they were recognized for that. They were people who were supposed to be good to the poor and the sick, you know, and went about doing good deeds. They were an order that were recognized for that, and their character had to be above reproach.
>
> It's kind of interesting. As I look back over those years, those Blue Mark people, maybe with the exception of one or two, were never ever involved in any kind of immorality or anything like that. They probably carried that pretty much through.

During the years when Waxthe'xe, the Sacred Pole, was in the care and keeping of anthropologists, Xthexe', the Mark of Honor, remained a part of Omaha life. The last of these Blue Spot women were very old when the Pole finally returned to his people in 1989. They kept a blessing of the night alive for many years. Omaha women have kept the people together during hard times. They have maintained family life through years of poverty and discrimination. They have kept up the fundamentals of community life during those years when the Pole was away. Omaha women elders of honor have done their job and are ready for a rest. Now that the Pole has returned, the male side of Xthexe' can begin to restore a balance that was lost. When Jillian and I talked to Maggie Johnson about what it meant to her to carry the Blue Spot, she said:

> They told us, "If one need help, try and help some. If you orphan kids, pity them. That's what for," this one said. So I try that. All of them kids coming in, I just take them in, feed them, want sleep, well, I let them sleep. Stay here. Couple days, I let 'em stay.

Mabel Hamilton told us what it meant to her:

> I'm proud everybody respect me. They ask me, "What's you got that spot on you for?" "That's a church member," I said. "I'm supposed to be good to you orphan kids. When you see orphan child, take him in your house and feed him. Do good things to him. Talk to it when you see them," he says. That's what this spot is for.

The Sacred Pole and the Mark of Honor are complementary sides of a single reality. The empowering visionary experience of a young man who found "a tree that stands burning" many years ago, and of a young woman who receives the Mark of Honor, are night and day, male and female expressions of "a power by which all things are brought to pass." The young man receives his power through the blessing of the night, what Alice Fletcher called "the great mother force." The young woman receives hers from the sun in his highest place in the daytime sky. The Pole appeared as a vision beneath the pole star, the center of the night sky. The cosmic signs that empower a young woman become part of her body and spirit when the sun aligns the sky's center with that of the earth.

In times gone by, renewal came to the Omahas through formal ceremonies and rigorous initiations. Omahas now may learn from their past, but their renewal must be personal and individual before it can be of benefit to all. Each person carries a reed from his or her place in the circle to the center. Each person must find his direction in the forest alone, like the young man who found the Sacred Pole at a time when "a great council was being held to devise some means by which the bands of the tribe might be kept together and the tribe itself saved from extinction." Each person must come to the center from the place of his or her experience in the world. Each person is both a fragment and an entirety.

CHAPTER SIX

Whatever His Thoughts, Make Them Possible

This tree has been living, standing.
Whatever his thoughts, make them possible.
Make his good thoughts possible.
Eddie Cline (Cambridge, Massachusetts 1988)

Waxthe'xe xigithe, the ceremony of renewal, reached a solemn climax when the wife of the Pole's keeper shot seven sacred arrows through the Pole's wickerwork wrapping and into the earth altar, *uzhiṅ'eti*. She must have possessed great courage and great faith to go through with this ceremony, knowing that the tribe's very survival depended upon her success. The arrows had to reach their mark and stand firmly together within the sacred circle cut from prairie sod. They had to stand together in the same way that the seven chiefs stand together with the Earth people and Sky people in the buffalo hunt, or against a common enemy. When she had succeeded in her task and the seven arrows had found their way to earth for another year, young men of the tribe charged upon the camp as they would an enemy warrior. Their charge broke the solemn atmosphere and restored the tribe to a festive mood that would prevail in the He'dewachi ceremony to follow. A similar change from solemn to festive mood takes place after tribal elders have blessed the modern pow-wow arena with cedar smoke and prayers to Wakon'da at the beginning of the modern He'dewachi, or pow-wow ceremony.

Shooting the seven sacred arrows into the earth of *uzhiṅ'eti* called upon courage and faith in the tribe's unity of purpose. Renewing contact with the Sacred Pole after a hundred years in the keeping of anthropologists called upon a similar combination of courage and faith in the tribe. The Omahas who made contact with Umon'hon'ti in 1988 did so in the trust that people who make up the Omaha tribe are still capable of speaking with one voice. They came to the Sacred Pole with the hope that he would confer upon the tribe a blessing for a long time to come. They knew that the presence of the Pole had been "regarded at all times as of vital importance" and that "without it, the people might scatter." They also knew full well that in the past harm had come to people who made a mistake in the ritual order.

A century after Umon'hon'ti went to the great brick house, tribal leaders had to decide whether it was more respectful to leave the Sacred Pole in the Peabody Museum or to renew contact with him. Doing nothing would have brought little risk. For a century, most people had been content to leave matters where Fletcher and La Flesche had settled them with Yellow Smoke. Furthermore, for most of those years, there had been little chance that the museum would have entertained the thought of "deacquisitioning" such an important holding. Renewing contact was a riskier alternative. Since any possible relationship to Umon'hon'ti was different from the strict order of a traditional keeper's discipline, anyone making contact with him risked being accused of impropriety. They risked being blamed for whatever misfortunes should befall the tribe or individuals within it.

At the annual pow-wow following the visit of Doran and Eddie to Cambridge, the Sacred Pole was very much on Omaha minds. As recounted in chapter 1, Doran Morris invited me to speak to the tribe about the events to which Jillian and I had been witness. Doran asked that I pass on information I had obtained from my reading of Fletcher and La Flesche. (See chapter 1 for an excerpt from that talk.) Later that summer, the tribe collaborated with Nebraska Educational Television on a documentary about their annual He'dewachi ceremony. The film was called "Dancing To Give Thanks." It later won an award of excellence from the American Anthropological Association Society for Visual Anthropology. The pow-wow that summer was a time of familiarization with the idea of renewing contact with the Sacred Pole. The summer that followed brought the idea to fruition.

THE JOURNEY HOME

On July 12, 1989, an airplane landed at Eppley Airfield in Omaha. On board was Umon'hon'ti, the Sacred Pole of the Omaha tribe. Members of the tribe were waiting there to greet him. The moment was captured on film by Nebraska Educational Television and later used in another award-winning documentary, "The Return of the Sacred Pole." Lawrence Gilpin, his eyes brimming with tears, was among those who welcomed Umon'hon'ti home. It was a moment filled with joy and apprehension. The Venerable Man had been away for a length of time beyond living memory. What place could he occupy among a generation of Omahas whose parents and grandparents were unborn when he went away? No living person knew or had the authority to keep him in the old ways, or to perform any of the old ceremonies. How should they treat him? How would his presence enrich their lives? As of old, "the people thought." They thought about themselves as a tribe. They

24. Umon'hon'ti resting on a lawn chair at Omaha pow-wow, August 20, 1989. Photograph © Ilka Hartmann, 1997.

thought about their past and the ceremonies they once knew. They thought about this venerable man who was once again among them. They thought about a power of life and motion.

Omahas are in agreement that Umon'hon'ti is alive. He is a person. He is the Real Omaha. And in this reality, perhaps, lies the greatest ambivalence about how to relate to him. He both directs the tribe's moral authority and is directed by it. The nature of that authority has changed dramatically since the buffalo-hunting days of the nineteenth century. Omahas have embraced western education, they have become leaders in the Native American Church, they have gone through hard times, and they have abandoned ancient ceremonies. But they have also survived as a people, and have continued to come together in ceremonies like the He'dewachi, or tribal pow-wow. Clans and families continue to give away to one another.

Omaha singers and dancers maintain their tribal identity in the midst of a larger flowering of Plains traditions of music and dance. The Sacred Pole has returned to a dynamic and varied tribal culture. Differences of opinion exist now, as they did in the past. The tribe must come to some agreement about how to balance the Pole's power to direct their affairs with their own responsibility to uphold the ancient moral authority that he represents. The only consensus now seems to be that this balance can be realized only through the passage of time. The journey from Eppley Airfield to Macy was only the beginning of his new relationship to the tribe.

Dennis had arranged to bring Umon'hon'ti on the last leg of his journey from Omaha to Macy with an escort of tribal police cruisers. This was done both as a security measure and to indicate his importance as a returning elder. Following a ceremony in the tribal pow-wow arena, he would then be driven to Lincoln, where the Center for Great Plains Studies would house him in a secure place until such time as a proper home on the reservation could be found. (See chapter 7 for an account of events leading up to this arrangement.) Lawrence Gilpin took the role of master of ceremonies. He and other elders spoke and prayed. For the first time in more than a century, Umon'hon'ti heard the sound of Omaha music, sung by a group of singers led by Jacob Drum. Lawrence Gilpin spoke in English and prayed in Omaha. These are some of his words:

> Grandson [speaking to Doran Morris], they're going to sing four songs for you to present him to the people.
> The drum will sing four songs. Ladies and gentlemen, the Omaha version of our National Anthem.

Jacob Drum and his group of Omaha singers chanted the four songs, beginning with the "Flag Song" that is always sung to the warriors standing at attention at the beginning of the pow-wow after the grand entry:

> This flag you fought for
> Because of you, friend, I live,
> Because of you, friend.
> The flag is here.

Lawrence continued:

> Thank you, singers. The gentleman carrying the pole, Umon'-hon'ti, is a gentleman by the name of Joe Johns. He was the escort for our Sacred Pole. He brought it this far, back to the Omaha reservation and then sometime later here he will take it to Lincoln, where it will be placed in a museum until we provide a place for it here on the Omaha reservation and that will be soon.
>
> This is a great day amongst our Omaha people. Those of you that are here, that made the effort to witness this homecoming of our Sacred Pole, Umon'hon'ti, I want to say thank you to you that you brought your little ones here, little children, to witness this. They will remember this day in days to come, in years to come. Maybe they will relate this to their little ones, those that are coming, and it's a great day for our Omaha people.
>
> We have our Umon'hon'ti back on the reservation, that it will be good for us. That it will bring unity and good things to come, good things to happen, that we would listen to one another when we talk to one another. That we will be good Indians, good Omahas. All these things we think about with Umon'hon'ti back on our poor reservation.
>
> While the traditional songs of the Omaha are being chanted here in honor of Umon'hon'ti, you may be seated or you may remain standing if you wish. As soon as these four songs are completed, I will say a prayer with this fire, with this cedar, and with my feather. I was requested to do this by the Omaha tribal council, and I always try to do whatever people ask me to do, and I'm going to do this today in your presence. I try to say things; that God will make things good for us through this Sacred Pole.
>
> It belongs to you, each one, each Omaha that is here. You have an undivided interest in this Sacred Pole. It's been gone for many years. Myself, I feel real thankful. I say thank you to the Omaha tribal council for making the effort to bring Umon'hon'ti back home on the Omaha reservation where it belongs. It belongs to no one else but the Omaha people. It is yours, and it has come home.
>
> And I want to say thank you to those of you that made an effort to

welcome Umon'hon'ti back home here, and also might make it known to you that my son, Jacob Drum, was asked to come out here and bring his drum and again he was asked to walk with the tribal chairman, walk with him into this arena, being that he is the grandson of Yellow Smoke. I am speaking that you can understand this about them, that my son, Jacob Drum, is also a descendent of Yellow Smoke. I am speaking that you can hear this about us, about them.

The singers then sang "the Chief's Giveaway Song." Elsie Morris later translated the words for me:

It's difficult to be so poor; to have to sacrifice.
It's very difficult.
Sometimes you don't have anything to give.
And as we go on in life it is a thing difficult.
Giving is great,
Yet very difficult because I am poor.

Elsie Morris explained that they sing it for him, "like he was saying it." She said, "It's a sacrifice. The chiefs really never had anything. They had to take care of their people." Lawrence continued:

Four original Omaha traditional songs are being chanted here this afternoon in honor of Umon'hon'ti. Maybe Umon'hon'ti was amongst our people at the time these songs were composed, many many years ago. It is good to see Umon'hon'ti back on our reservation and I'm going to say something here to the Great Spirit.

Lawrence then prayed:

Aho! Umon'hon'ti!
Umon'hon'ti!
We're humble people the Omaha village
That you have come home to.
Today you have come home.
There's a few words I want to say to Wakon'da.
Umon'hon'ti,
You have come back to the Omaha camp.
I am very happy that you have come home.
Umon'hon'ti,
I am very happy that you have come home today
To our poor, humble reservation.
And towards Wakon'da, I'm going to say a few words.
Aho! Dadeho (Aho! my father).

Wakon'da, Most Holy Spirit above, you sit above us all.
Today is a day set aside. Today is a holy day.
The Omaha village is where we're living.
From way back that this has come.
Dadeho, Wakon'da Xube,
Father, Great Spirit, Most Sacred of All.

Throughout the prayer Lawrence repeats the phrase *"Dadeho, Wakon'da Xube,"* which Elsie translated as "My Father, Most Holy Spirit above." She reminded me that he uses the male speaking form of address. A woman would say *Aho! Dadeha.*

And today, we are just pitiful
    [Elsie says that pitiful here means loving and deserving of love.]
And yet today we are celebrating.
All the Omahas have come home together happy,
Feeling happy, good of heart.
And yet today, this is how things are.
Our relatives have gathered.
They have entered the doorway, the entry,
And we are seated together.
Dadeho, Wakon'da Xube.
God's son, Jesus, loving Jesus,
Good medicine, most sacred of all,
Healing medicine.
Today is Sunday, sacred.
Umon'hon'ti!
From way back, our forefathers, there was a tree.
There was a tree that grew from the earth.
Dadeho, Wakon'da Xube.
Whatever, how it was that he took it.
Somebody took it.
Through you, he received the tree from the earth.
From way back they used him for our lives.
It's been over a hundred years, past a hundred years,
In a strange place with strange people.
Dadeho, Wakon'da Xube.
Today the head of the people (the council),
Have brought him home,
Brought him home.
Dadeho, Wakon'da Xube.
Umon'hon'ti, they made him holy.

From way back in our camp he was the center,
Lived in the center of the people.
And whatever they did, how they lived,
They did it with him, through Wakon'da.
Wakon'da made life in that tree from the earth.
Dadeho, Wakon'da Xube.
From God's power (Wakon'da Xube) he gave that tree.
Father, you made that tree, you gave it life,
You gave it life from the earth.
And that was through your goodness,
Your power from the earth.
Dadeho, Wakon'da Xube.
You are the only one that has the power to do and give life.
It is yours.
Those, our elders, have brought him from way back,
And they have received nothing but good from him.
Whatever good that you have made, you have made for them.
Dadeho, Wakon'da Xube.
Wakon'da Xube Jesus.
Our people carried you from way back,
And good things came from you.
And whatever you have made, you have made everything good,
Dadeho, Wakon'da Xube.
Whatever thoughts that they have,
However they were able to live as beings,
Whatever good that God gave them,
From there on they were able to be living, to be the people.
Dadeho, Wakon'da Xube.
Today we are here, us Omaha people are here,
That Umon'hon'ti has come home.
Dadeho, Wakon'da Xube.
Whatever they have thought,
The good thoughts that we will benefit from,
Whatever good that we want and everything,
We will receive.
We are very pitiful people with hardly anything.
Dadeho, Wakon'da Xube.
Wakon'da Xube and Jesus.
Jesus, you stand as good medicine.
Today is the seventh day. Today is Sunday.
This town that we live, Omaha Reservation,

As you see us, pity us, have pity on us.
Dadeho, Wakon'da Xube.
Umon'hon'ti!
Umon'hon'ti has come back to the Omaha reservation.
Umon'hon'ti!
We benefit from him as we live.
There are times that we are grieving,
But today our grief has eased a little bit.
Maybe as we go on from this day we will be happy.
We won't be so heavily burdened with grief.
As we go from this day on we will benefit from the good.
Dadeho, Wakon'da Xube.
This is our prayer.
You know our needs.
You sit and you know our needs.
Dadeho, Wakon'da Xube, Most Holy Spirit, you sit.
You do everything right.
You never make any mistakes.
[Here Lawrence weeps as he speaks]
You are the only one that knows what our needs are.
Today is a holy day.
My humble prayer, I'm offering.
My humble prayer I'm offering.
Dadeho, Wakon'da Xube.
Father, Holy Spirit, Son of God, Jesus.

Lawrence placed cedar on a pan of coals and began to bless Umon'hon'ti with the smoke, spreading it toward him with an eagle feather fan. Elsie Morris explained that cedar is a symbol of life because it lives throughout the year. "There's no season for the cedar. It stays green year round. . . . Prayers are made to Grandpa Fire and the cedar so that people would walk in the protection of the smoke."

Aho! Umon'hon'ti!
We're humble people, the Omaha village
That you have come home to.
Today you have come home.
There's a few words I want to say to Wakon'da.
Umon'hon'ti,
You have come back to the Omaha camp.
I am very happy that you have come home.
Umon'hon'ti,

I am very happy that you have come home today
To our poor, humble reservation.
And towards Wakon'da, I'm going to say a few words.
Umon'hon'ti!
You are the one that gave Umon'hon'ti life.
As we face the future,
Those that are coming, those that are coming,
Have pity on them.
Father, the most Holy Spirit,
You are the loving God.
You made it sacred.
Everything you made sacred.
Grandpa fire is sacred.
You made the fire sacred.
Nobody to look forward to, to depend on,
Have pity on me.
Whatever their [the council's] wish is I tried to meet,
I tried to fulfill
In my humble words that I spoke with you,
God's son Jesus.
They made the fire sacred,
That we may get good from this from here on.
Aho you singers, you drummers, that was my prayer.

Lawrence continued in English:

All you people in the audience. It is my prayer that you be blessed by
what you have seen today. And now you can get your dishes out [for a
feast], right from the doorway around. The one that started all these
things is home. Umon'hon'ti. We'll start from the doorway and circle
around to the right. Go around this Pole.

    [in Omaha]
God is creator of all things,
Creator of all good.
He never makes any mistake.
Everything he creates is good.
It is us. We are only humans
And we are the ones that make the mistakes.
    [in English]
Try to believe those things that we see,
That it will be good for all of us
In days to come, in years to come

That our little ones, even those little ones coming
Be happy and be thankful to God for a good hunt
And all those things that go with life,
That they were successful with because of the Great Spirit.
It sounds good to hear these songs.
Those old people have gone back to Mother Earth
and yet their ways are still good
and we try to carry them on.
It was real good here this afternoon
to hear those different ones that came up here
To express themselves. It was real good.
Good words to hear, and I hope those things that were said
Will be strong for our people, for our young people.
We have many here this afternoon to witness this day,
an historical day in the days of our Omaha people here today.
I know this was of great significance,
Way back, over a hundred years ago.
Long, long time ago.
Umon'hon'ti became a reality to the Omaha people,
A symbol, something good from God.
He was gone. Today he has come home.
He's going to be with us. We have got to respect him.
It's going to be good for us.
I know that.
Whenever you respect something,
You do something good or say something or think good,
It's always going to be good.
You benefit from those thoughts.
And it's going to be that way for our Omaha people.
From this day on we're going to have a different feeling
About our whole lives.
We're going to be altogether different.
We're going to respect one another
And we're going to smile at one another
And put that hatred off on the side.
It's bad business. It's no good for us.
It's like a disease in an apple. It rots that apple
So that apple is no good no more.
I want to say thank you to the singers out there
For their fine efforts, for singing all those historical songs,
Those traditional Omaha songs.

I say thank you for your efforts
On behalf of the Omaha people.
On behalf of the Omaha tribal council,
I want to say thank you.

The return of Umon'hon'ti to his home on the Omaha reservation brought forth powerful emotions. People of all ages came forward to greet him and touch him with reverence. Many were unsure of how to make contact but others kissed him gently as they would a sacred relic. People bore witness to his return by placing their living hands upon his ancient body. They did so in a spirit of respect and welcome. Young and old alike came to him. Although the ancient ceremonies and keepers have passed on, Umon'hon'ti and his people remain. The people touched him in recognition of their common survival. They touched him as a respected elder. The touched him shyly but with confidence in his good will. Following this ceremony, Joe Johns carried him out of the arena to a waiting pickup truck. With police sirens blaring, he was taken to the University of Nebraska–Lincoln.

A few weeks after the tribe welcomed Umon'hon'ti home for the first time, he returned to Macy in ceremony for the 185th annual pow-wow, on August 20. Although the events of 1989 were in no way a revival of rites that were abandoned more than a century earlier, the sequence of renewal followed by pow-wow described an order that would have been familiar to Omahas of old. Those who participated in these events did so in a spirit of making their Venerable Man feel at home in the tribe as it now exists. The tribe first brought the Sacred Pole to the tribal arena on July 12, in Tehu'tan ike, "the moon when the buffaloes bellow." They next brought him back on the full moon, August 20, during the annual tribal pow-wow. Lawrence Gilpin spoke in English for the benefit of guests from the Peabody Museum:

> Well, Ladies and Gentlemen, at this time the tribal council has asked that I say something to the Great Spirit for the return of this Sacred Pole back to the Omaha tribe. Many years ago, our Omaha tribal people had this Pole. And they used it and believed in, that it was a good omen to the Omaha tribe. It was their belief, that God created man from this Mother Earth, and all things grow from Mother Earth. And he has caused this tree to grow from Mother Earth. That was God's doing. It is our belief.
>
> He made that tree to glow. Even the animals of the wilderness took a liking to this tree. At night it glowed. And so the Omahas took this tree. They give it a name, like a human, like a man. They called him Umon'hon'ti, "Real Omaha." And this Pole was used by the Omahas wherever they camped. It was in the midst, in the middle of their en-

campment, and they always walked around it clockwise in reverence to this Pole. It brought them good things because they believed. Because of their belief that it was a good omen. Because they believed in the Great Spirit. The Great Spirit caused this tree to grow from Mother Earth. It brought them good tidings. And if we believe here, today, if we believe in God today here, it will be the same for us. That is my belief. And I will say a prayer to the Great Spirit that all these things I've said will be possible for us. Thank you.

Lawrence then prayed for the blessing of Wakon'da as he had the month before. The Omahas presented Pendleton blankets to Peabody Museum officials invited to witness the homecoming and to me for speaking to the tribe about my interest in the Pole. Dr. Ian Brown, assistant curator of the Peabody Museum, spoke on behalf of the museum. Dr. Brown was obviously deeply moved by his participation in the Pole's return. He spoke for himself, for his institution, and for anthropologists generally. He spoke out of deep conviction and for the record. These are his words:

I usually don't like to read speeches, but I do want to make sure on this very important occasion that my words are clear and concise. And I also would like to keep it around five minutes. You're a very patient folk.

It is a great privilege and honor for me to be here today—to be included in your annual pow-wow. On behalf of the Peabody Museum and its director, Dr. Lamberg-Karlovsky, I appreciate very much your invitation. Today is truly a remarkable day. For it is the day that you, as a people, can finally pay homage to the Venerable Man, the Sacred Pole of the Omaha nation. A year ago during a ceremony at the Peabody Museum which was graced by the presence of Mr. Morris and Mr. Cline, I gave a short speech. In describing the Sacred Pole, I said that no object embodied so much of the soul of the Omaha. It represents the authority of their leaders, the unity between man and woman, and the binding element that has held the Omaha people together for centuries. In a recent article dealing with Indian policy and Indian religious freedom, Patrick Morse writes, I quote, "Collectively, sacred things tell us that life and spirit are continuous. They coexist and are not bound by immutable substance. Their sacredness comes from their inseparable unity with creation."

A little over a century ago the linkage between life and spirit appeared to be broken for the Omaha. Alice Fletcher, an anthropologist at the Peabody Museum who spent many years among the Omaha, was convinced that the tribe she loved would soon cease to exist. Eventually, she thought, the Omaha would dissolve into the great American melting pot. They would become indistinguishable from anyone else. And their religion, their spirit, would be lost in the march of time. There was no doubt in her mind that this would happen, and she herself even played a role in making it happen in her support of the infamous Dawes Act, an act whose main purpose it turns out was to separate the Indians from their land.

Indian culture, religion, beliefs, languages would soon be dead, or at least this was the thought of anthropologists, missionaries, and government officials of the late nineteenth century. Fletcher certainly was no exception to this belief, but she did feel that something, something could be preserved for the future to teach later generations of the once rich life of the Omaha. If not the people, at least the sacred materials of the Omaha could be saved. And this objective was eventually fulfilled through the agency of her Omaha Indian colleague, Francis La Flesche.

In the 1880s many sacred materials of the Omaha came to the "great brick house" in the East which I represent today. The Sacred Pole was one of those items. Since 1888 it has rested in the Peabody Museum, protected from the ravages of time, studied by several generations of anthropologists, but certainly, certainly not revered. Its sacred nature continued, however, because the Omaha themselves continued. Fletcher was wrong. The missionaries were wrong. And the government bureaucrats were dead wrong.

George P. Horse Capture recently wrote in the preface to his book, *Sacred Materials*, that (I quote), "Indians are special and unique. Despite their turbulent history they have managed to survive, keeping relatively intact many of their traditional ways. One of the major cultural traits that holds these people together and is least understood by non-Indians is sacredness."

Over the past year, during the long period of negotiations concerning the return of the Sacred Pole and the remainder of your sacred materials, a number of us at the Peabody Museum received letters from various individuals asking for a speedy return of the objects. I would like to read portions of two of these letters. The first letter is from Robert Wolfe, who, at the time of his writing, was thirteen years old and attending the Lincoln Lutheran junior high. In his letter he says (I quote), "My reason for writing to you is to try and persuade you to let my people, the Omahas, have their Sacred Pole back. I feel that the Omahas have a strong young generation." He continues, "They are proud of their heritage and are learning the old ways. If you give us back our Pole, I think it would bring our people together and unite us more as a family. It is a part of us as [is] any family member. It will let the Omaha touch the past and reunite with their ancestors."

In a similar vein, Cary Alice Wolfe writes, (I quote) "My Indian name is Pakason. I am a future adult member of the Omaha tribe." Listen to that phrase: "I am a future adult member of the Omaha tribe." It's a profound statement for one so young, and demonstrates most emphatically the continuity of the Omaha and their beliefs. She continues, "My grandmother, Elizabeth Stabler, wrote two books on the Omaha language and I am learning the old ways of my fathers and my people. Our young generation of Omahas do cherish the sacred ways. We will take care of and keep the Sacred Pole for our future children. Just as our elders have kept and are teaching us the ways now, we will teach the future Omahas."

Fletcher clearly was wrong. As revealed through the words of the children, the Omahas are here to stay. Indians are here to stay. And we at the Peabody Museum are proud to have returned to you what we have held in trust for you for this last century. The Sacred Pole is here now and the remainder of your sacred materials will be returned by the end of this year. At the ceremony held at the Peabody Museum last year, I ended my speech with a statement, and I would like to repeat this statement now.

Over this past century the Sacred Pole has failed to play the role it was meant to serve among the Omaha, but it should be emphasized that this sacred symbol of the Omaha has still survived. It is our hope that the ceremony which has occurred here today will once again be an annual event and that someday in the not-too-distant future this ceremony will be held where it should be held, among the Omaha themselves.

And now, a year later, the dream has come true. I myself am proud to have played a role in returning these materials to you. Our role was a small one compared to that played by your tribal chairman, Doran Morris, and your tribal historian, Dennis Hastings. Over the past year we have developed a friendship and trust. This trust has been based on communication. Communication. The channels have always been open. We have always been talking. From this I anticipate and hope that the linkages between the Peabody Museum and the Omaha tribe will remain forever strong. Again, I thank you for your invitation to be here today at this very, very great occasion. I thank you for the opportunity to share my thoughts with you. And I thank you for the honor of once again paying my respects to the Venerable Man.

Doran then asked me to speak. In the past, I had spoken about the Sacred Pole while facing the tribe. This time, I spoke to them facing Umon'hon'ti himself. I was only a few feet away from where he rested. It was indeed a memorable experience to give voice to the words that Yellow Smoke had spoken just over a century before and to do so in the very presence of the Venerable Man himself. This is what I said:

Thank you, Doran. Thank you members of the tribal council and everyone. Today is a very special occasion for me personally, as I know it is for you, Inshta'thunda, you Hon'gashenu, you people who together are the Omaha tribe. Twenty-seven years ago I first laid eyes on Umon'hon'ti, the real Omaha who is your Sacred Pole. He was resting in a glass case in the Peabody Museum at Harvard University. He was motionless physically, but when I was in his presence I could feel a power of life, a power of motion within me and all around me, and extending out to wherever it was that his people, you people, were living. At that time I didn't know where the Omaha people were or how they were living. I began to study their traditions from what was written down by James Dorsey and Alice Fletcher and Francis La Flesche, who was the first Native American anthropologist.

I began to study those writings and as I was doing that I also discovered that your tribal historian, Dennis Hastings, was studying these same documents. So I sent him a copy of what I had been writing and he called me up and he said, "You can't be studying about the Omahas until you've come to Macy; come to a pow-wow and see us in person." So I did. That was in 1985, that was my first pow-wow. I've been to several others since then. And I've also continued my studies about the Sacred Pole. And I'd like to share with you some of my thoughts of what I have learned.

Although he has been away from you physically, the spirit of the Sacred Pole has never left you. The people who went before you would be proud of this moment in the ongoing history of the Omaha tribe. They would be proud to share the Pole's blessing with you just as you will be proud to pass on blessings that you are receiving today and have been receiving from your Sacred Pole now and in the times to come.

The Pole stands for the authority of your ancestral ways. The spirit of these ways remains strong within you. That spirit does not depend upon particular material things from the past like hunting buffalo or living in earth lodges as your ancestors did. It lives on in the generosity with which you live your lives. It lives in the help and respect that you give to one another. It lives in the blessings you pass on to those who come after you. In the old days, the chiefs told people:

Whenever we meet with troubles
We shall bring all our troubles to him, Umon'hon'ti.
We shall make offerings and requests.
And all our prayers must be accompanied by gifts.

   The chiefs said that the Pole belongs to all the people. The Pole and his teachings are gifts they have passed on to people of the present generation, to you. Your responsibility is to make these teachings your own and to pass them on with your prayers to those who come after you. Some of the teachings about the Pole are contained in a story of its origin that Yellow Smoke told to Alice Fletcher and Francis La Flesche in 1888. And I'll just give you a few excerpts from that story. Many of you already know the details of it. It's part of tribal history. It says:

A long time ago, there was a young man, the son of a chief, who went out hunting during a time when the elders of the tribe, the chiefs, were in council trying to deal with a problem just like the problems that the tribe has today and it's always had, that is, to keep itself together, to keep you together, to keep your traditions and your families together, living in the proper way. And this young man got lost when he was out at night. And for a moment he didn't know his direction. And then he remembered there is one star, the motionless star, right up there. You'll see it tonight if it's clear. And he found that star, the star around which all the other stars of the heavens turn. That star is the north star. It gave him his direction. And then he looked down from beneath that star, and I'm going to read you the description of what he saw.

He saw a light.
He saw that it was a tree that sent forth light.
He went up to it
And found that the whole tree,
Its trunk, branches, and leaves, were alight,
Yet remained unconsumed.
The young man watched
Until with the rising of the sun
The tree with its foliage
Resumed its natural appearance.
He remained by it throughout the day.
As twilight came on it began to be luminous
And continued so until the sun rose again.
When the young man returned home
He told his father of the wonder.

Together they went to see the tree.
They saw it as it was before,
But the father observed something
That had escaped the notice of the young man.
This was that four animal paths led to it.
These paths were well beaten
And as the two men examined the paths and the tree,
It was clear to them that the animals came to the tree
And had rubbed against it
And polished its bark by doing so.
The young man and his father returned to where the chiefs were still in council. The father explained to them and to his son the meaning of what the young man had seen, this visionary experience. He told the chiefs:
My son
Has seen a wonderful tree.
The Thunder birds come and go upon this tree,
Making a trail of fire
That leaves four paths on the burnt grass
That stretch toward the Four Winds.
When the Thunder birds alight on the tree
It bursts into flame
And the fire mounts to the top.
But the tree stands burning,
And no one can see the fire except at night.
 The men of the tribe returned to the tree. They painted themselves. They put on their regalia.
They ran as in a race
To attack the tree
As if it were an enemy warrior.
 The first to reach the tree struck it and then they cut down the tree.
And four men, walking in a line
Carried it on their shoulders
To the village.
The chiefs worked upon the tree.
They trimmed it
And called it a human being.
They made a basketwork receptacle of twigs and feathers
And tied it in the middle.
 They made a tent for the tree and set it up within the circle of

lodges. They placed a large scalp lock on top of the Pole for hair.
And then they painted the Pole
And set it up before the tent,
Leaning it on a crotched stick [just as you see today]
Which they called "*imongthe*" (a staff).

   When the people were gathered, the chiefs stood up and said:
You now see before you a mystery.
Whenever we meet with troubles
We shall bring all our troubles to him.
This belongs to all the people.
And when all was finished, the people said:
Let us appoint a time
When we shall again paint him
And act before him
The battles we have fought.

   This was the beginning of the ceremony called Waxthe'xe xigithe, which means "to paint, to anoint, to grease the Sacred Pole with red." Although that old ceremony of renewal was part of your buffalo-hunting way of life and is no longer practiced, the spirit of renewal remains very much alive among you today. The old renewal ceremony took place in a Sacred Lodge made from tipi poles contributed by each family of the tribe. Today's renewal of your Sacred Pole is possible because each family and each clan continues to contribute its spiritual gifts to the tribe as a whole. The Pole is a person who stands for all of you together. His return to you today is a celebration of your survival during the past century, and a promise that you will continue to honor the spirit of your traditions throughout the centuries to come.

   I thank you for allowing me to speak to you. I thank you for allowing me to stand before Umon'hon'ti, your Sacred Pole. I thank you all. All my relations.

While the events of that day were deeply moving to all concerned, there were also unplanned moments that brought to mind the episode with the Peabody elevator the year before. Eddie Cline had prepared a forked stick on which to lean the Pole, but when Doran tried to drive it into the ground of the pow-wow arena, he was unable to penetrate the hard earth that had been packed down by the feet of many dancers. Amid the rustle of feathers and the gentle music of the dancers' bells and rattles, Doran and the lead dancers talked about what to do. One of the dancers produced a knife from his regalia and they attempted to dig a small hole for the forked stick. Although the base of it did go into the hole, the arrangement was still not secure. Then somebody called out, "Get a lawn chair." At every Omaha pow-wow, elders and members of families who will be sponsoring "specials," or public giveaways, sit in folding lawn chairs in front of the bleachers. Quickly, one of the lawn chairs was produced and the Pole was secured with the forked stick propped against it (see photograph). It was only after the ceremony was over that people thought about what had happened. In retrospect, they said, it made perfect sense that Umon'hon'ti, like any other returning elder, be given his own seat of honor in the form of a lawn chair.

The Venerable Man's return in ceremony that day was very beautiful. It brought to mind the suffering and repression that Omahas have endured during the past century, as well as their individual triumphs and the ultimate triumph of their survival as a people. The Pole's return also brought to mind, for some Omahas, the feelings of fear and apprehension that Fletcher and La Flesche reported among Omahas in the 1880s. An account of his return would not be complete without some mention of the differences of opinion that emerged and are now being worked out among tribal members.

SOMEBODY'S THROWING GOSSIP OUT THERE
While the Pole's return in 1989 was genuinely celebrated by the majority of Omahas, an undercurrent of fear and apprehension remained, almost as it had more than a century before, following the collapse of buffalo hunting in 1875. Then, people came to fear the Pole because they recognized that a permanent and irrevocable break in the ceremonial order had come upon them. Some were also under the influence of missionaries and Indian agents, who viewed any Indian ceremonies as relics of a "savage and barbarian" past. Omahas knew that the old renewal ceremony of *Waxthe'xe xigithe* was possible only during the annual buffalo hunt. That ritual order was already gone when Yellow Smoke told Fletcher and La Flesche the Sacred Legend in 1888. It was common knowledge then that the tribe had tried to revive the ceremony and had not been successful. Some Omahas came to fear that bringing the Pole back to Nebraska would also be unsuccessful and dangerous.

In the year between the 185th and 186th tribal pow-wows of 1989 and 1990, a feeling like that described by Fletcher and La Flesche began to surface among some people within the tribe. Despite this development, and perhaps even as a challenge to it, the tribal council decided to bring Umon'hon'ti into the arena again for the 1990 pow-wow. They wished to use the occasion to explain the success of their collaboration with the University of Nebraska in studying the remains of Omahas from Ton'wontonga prior to their reburial. The decision to bring the Pole back again, though, was not made without opposition. A prominent elder who had been educated at the Carlisle Indian School is reported to have told some council members that the Pole should go back to where he came from and should not come back to the reservation again. The head of a prominent family who conducts one of the Sioux-style sweat lodges on the reservation told me that the Pole is "too sacred" (*waxube*) and should be taken care of only by people who had made significant spiritual sacrifices in preparation for that role.

During the year after the Pole's return home, an atmosphere of fear and apprehension about him as "a thing that was powerful for harm" seems to have grown in the episodes of gossip and factional dispute that are inevitable within any small community of closely related people. Some people felt that it was impossible for contemporary Omahas to pay him the proper respect. Others probably feared him more out of ignorance than any real understanding of the complex issues of respect related to a ceremonial order that had nearly faded from memory. As Doran Morris later told me, one person even attributed a highly publicized plane crash in Sioux City to the Pole's return: "Two, three weeks after I brought the Sacred Pole home they had a big plane crash here, killed hundred and some people. One guy, he went and told around the community that because Doran Morris brought the Sacred Pole home, they killed a lot of people up here."

The dread that was growing became more focused when Lawrence Gilpin, like many Omahas a diabetic, suffered a stroke that left him with some difficulty walking and a minor speech impediment. Despite his condition, Lawrence was able to share with Clifford Wolfe Sr. the role of master of ceremonies that summer. There, he found himself in a position of dealing with public fear and apprehension directly and in relation to his own life. He was well aware that gossip was going around linking his contact with the Pole to his stroke. He had been the first person to touch the Pole the year before. There was clearly an air of tension and apprehension on August 12, 1990, when it came time for the host drum to begin the Flag Song welcoming Umon'hon'ti back to the arena. Singers and drummers were reluctant to begin. Lawrence confronted their fear directly and in public. He spoke directly to the singers and dancers:

> The Omaha tribe had this Sacred Pole in the center of where they lived, and it was a good omen. They went to this Pole on their way out to a hunt, on an expedition, or something that was good for them. It's a God-given thing. God give it to the Omahas for that purpose. And you believe in it that way it's going to be that way. It's gonna be good for you.
>
> I hear somebody's afraid of it. They're not afraid of alcohol. They're not afraid of whiskey. They're not afraid of bad things. But this omen is a good thing. It'd be good for your everyday life. You should not be afraid of it. It'd be good for you. The more you believe in it, it be better for you. That where they fall wrong.

Somebody's throwing gossip out there. That's no good. They should know what they're talking about. The old people didn't tell them. Maybe they weren't raised here, that's why. Amongst the Omahas. That is one reason that we make many mistakes. We make errors and that's where you are *wrong* and I can say that with authority. That sacred wood is good for you. The old people believed in it. They had it in their camp wherever they camped. And they walked around it on the way out of that camp and it brought them good luck. And that is why we call it sacred. It was good medicine. Here we are, trying to condemn it. We're trying to say things that we don't know anything about. Try to learn the good things. And I know it'd be good for you. Be good for your everyday life. It'll bring you good health. It'll bring you good luck. Maybe you won't grow rich, but you'll have the things that you need to live, and that is good.

The old people had this. They had it in their camp. And they thanked the creator for this. And they walked around it in camp where they could see it, where everybody could be amongst it. It was good for them. That's why they called it the Sacred Pole and they had it put away and they could not take it with them and they left it and we have it today. The Sacred Pole. It is good for us as Indian people. You believe in it and it's gonna be that way.

You believe in bingo. You believe in card games. You believe in gambling, trying to win more money. Them things you believe in. You should believe in the good things too, and the Sacred Pole is good. It's good for your everyday life. It'd be a betterment for your life. You believe in it's gonna be good medicine. And that's why the Omahas had it. It was Omahas that had it, not some other tribe. The Omahas had it and if you think you're an Omaha you should believe in it and live by it and it's going to be good for you. And that's my belief.

I believe in God. I believe in all the things that he does and all those things that he created for the humans and that still exist. And we believe in God. We believe in his ways. It's going to be good for us. And this is one of the things that God created. And he put it there for the Indian, the Omaha.

An Omaha boy found this Sacred Pole. It was a tree. The tree lit up at night. It made light. And the next night this boy went back and the same thing happened. That tree was lit, making light like electricity. That was way before electricity was thought of, and it made light. And he went home and told his people, the Omahas, and they went over there and discovered their Sacred Pole. It wasn't a pole then. It was a tree that was lighting at night. That was something. They didn't know where that light came from. A God-given thing. So they took that tree and they made it sacred and they put it in front of the camp. It brought them good luck. They had good luck at their hunt. They were able to do those things they needed to do easily. That's why they called it the Sacred Pole, because it brought them good luck.

Maybe we do that today, it will bring us better luck. Maybe we'll live better than we live. Maybe we'll own our own home instead of living in government homes. All these things are possible. Through your belief you can make it that way. You can make anything possible through your belief. I hope that we believe and we're going to bring the Sacred Pole here today for you to see. You can even go up and bless yourself with it, touch it. And that's how strong my belief is in those good things that happen.

And I believe in the sacred medicine, the peyote. I believe that God gave us this medicine so that we could use it. And we still use it. We believe in that. All those good things that God gave us, we want to believe. If you don't believe well you're just wasting your time. Wasting your mind on something else. Believe in the good things that God created, that God gave us. It'll be good for you. Good for your everyday life. I know.

All you dancers and all you singers. Make your way to the arena. The time is getting close. Quarter till two. We're fifteen minutes past. I thought we were supposed to start at one-thirty. Here it is, quarter to two. All you dancers and all you singers. The head singer's sitting around here all by his lonesome. Come on out and help him.

Somebody said you were scared of the Pole. You're not scared of alcohol. That's worse than anything. I know. Here we have something of our own. Good medicine and you're afraid of it. If you knew something about it it'd be different. But you don't. Only what somebody else is gossiping about. That's what you heard. But I'm gossiping too. It's good. It's good medicine for you. It was good for our people and it's going to be good for you today. You believe in it. You believe in God. This is God-given thing. God gave it to the Omahas so it would be good for them. We're a chosen people by God.

All you singers and all you dancers. Make your way to the arena.

Don't believe in things you don't know nothing about. This is something that's good. Our old people had this and it was good for them. That's why they took good care of him. They carried him along with them wherever they camped. Good medicine. And here we are, we're scared of it. We're not scared of alcohol. We're not scared of bad medicine. Here it is, we've got something good and you're scared of it.

I don't understand. That's what I hear, here this morning. That's too bad. You as Omahas should believe in him. It was given to the Omahas by Almighty God. God made this possible for us, that would bring good omen for us. It would bring good luck to us. Here we are, scared of it. There's a lot worse things you're not scared of. I know. Because I used to be one of you.

The head singer is here and he is waiting. Where is all the helpers? All you singers. Act like a good Omaha and come up here and help the head singer. There's a lot of worse things that you're not scared of. This is good medicine. Here you are, scared of it, I understand.

Finally the singers assembled and began their entry song. Lawrence finished his prayer and asked Eddie Cline to speak:

Ladies and gentlemen. The Chairman asked me to say a few words about the Pole so dancers, your cooperation is needed and certainly we're grateful that the Pole will be taken out as soon as I get through talking. And I hope that I don't talk too long. I know that you're tired. Some of you have heard the story about the Pole and the history that is written. The white people wrote a history talking to members of the tribe about the Pole. It's a great and wonderful history.

The Pole was the center of our tribe and the historical days. The Pole had been gone for a hundred years and after one hundred years he finally came home. And I would wish that we would look upon the Pole as something good for us.

THERE'S BEEN GOOD THINGS HAPPENING

Since August 12, 1990, Umon'hon'ti has rested at the University of Nebraska in Lincoln under the curatorial care of Dr. Thomas Myers. On September 20 of the same year, the Peabody returned 280 other sacred objects, including birds wrapped in bladder skins, elk fetal skins, perfume bottles, shells, fabric and matting fragments, lacquer boxes, beaver trunks, scalps, sweet grass, arrows, sinew cord, brushes, rattlesnake fangs used in tattooing, a wolf skin, mica, and a human effigy made of skin that held medicinal and poisonous substances. They and the Sacred Pole are now in the same room as Tethno'ha, the Sacred White Buffalo Hide, and the objects that were buried with the people of Ton'wontonga. I will tell the story of how this came to be and what it meant to Omaha observers in the last chapter, All My Relations.

On the last day of the 1994 Omaha pow-wow, Doran Morris and his wife, Vivian, took me out to dinner in Sioux City. We discussed the book I was writing, and the different ways Omahas had reacted to the Pole's return since 1989. Several of the elders who had greeted the Pole then had since passed

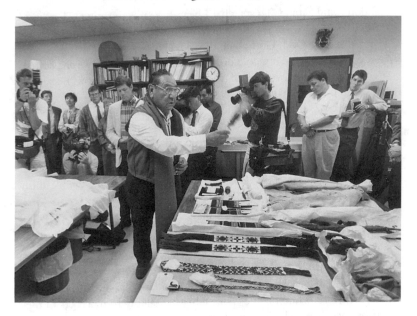

25. *Clifford Wolfe Sr. blessing the returned artifacts at the University of Nebraska–Lincoln. Photograph by Robert Becker. Copyright* Lincoln Journal-Star, *September 20, 1990.*

away, including Lawrence Gilpin, his brother Alfred (Uncle Buddy) Gilpin, and Clifford Wolfe Sr. Doran was concerned that some people thought these deaths were because of the Pole's return. They were his relations, he said, and they had greeted Umon'hon'ti with the respect due a returning elder of the tribe. He told me:

> You know, a lot of our older people are really superstitious. They say if you do some things this way, something bad will happen to you or your family. I don't believe that. I think we ought to try to get rid of those things. It really hinders trying to go ahead, you know.

Doran repeated his confidence that the Sacred Pole is a force for good in the community.

> I would like to say, ever since the Sacred Pole came home, there's been good things happening. Of course there's been bad things that happen between, but overall, I think really good things happened to the Omaha tribe that never happened before. Not because I was the leader of the tribe, but because the Sacred Pole came home.

That dread of the Pole as "a thing that was powerful for harm" is still pres-

ent among some people on the Omaha reservation, even though no one has
suggested that the tribe attempt to conduct traditional ceremonies about
which they have insufficient knowledge and authority. The fundamental difference of opinion that divides Omahas is whether Umon'hon'ti is to be "a
blessing for a long time to come" or "a thing that [is] powerful for harm."
Doran Morris expressed the hope that a younger generation will come to appreciate Umon'hon'ti as a blessing rather than a danger:

> Well, I think through education we'll be able to overcome a lot of that
> with your book. Like I said, a lot of our elders are really superstitious,
> not so well educated. It's like, the other night I stayed at the Native
> American Church and one elder got up and said that when the Pole
> came back, that killed my grandfather. Caused him to have cancer and
> killed him. See, those things, it's not true.

I suggested to Doran it must be hard on him to have people say things like
that. He replied that it is was hard, "but you cannot not speak out." He went
on:

> Well, in the next Native American Church I got up and said, "I believe
> that we have a lot of superstition that we need to get rid of. But I be-
> lieve this way, the churches have different theories, the philosophy that
> if you do something God's going to punish you. Might be true in other
> ways, but myself, I believe this way; that a person gets killed, that car
> does that; a person dies, has cancer, the cancer does that. God does not
> punish people that way, kill them. He's so loving. He gave his own son
> out for our sins."

We talked about how Omahas today are coming to use the expression "all my
relations." Doran said that it reminds him of the way the tribe used to be held
together by ties of kinship:

> The people were together back there. I did not call your English name
> or your first name. I called you by my relationship. You were my uncle,
> I'd say "uncle" and then your Indian name. And that happened clear up
> to probably twenty-five years ago. We addressed each other by rela-
> tionship. The reason for that was that we had respect for one another,
> so that happened. But the time the Pole left the reservation and it came
> back, we see those terrible things, problems amongst our people. The
> alcohol, the hatred of how they carry on politics. You can see that to-
> day. So you see the variance. When the Pole was here and when it
> wasn't here.

I asked Doran if he had thought about being criticized in this way when he began negotiations for the Pole's return. He replied:

> Oh, yeah. That's the main reason I went out and brought the Sacred Pole home. 'Cause I know nobody's going to do it. Then if it was true what they're saying that the Sacred things will kill you if you don't handle or do things right, so I let it be me. I'll do it. So that's what happened. But they're saying that since the Pole came home, it's killing this one, it's killing that one. It's not true. I know that.

Doran's confidence in his decision to bring the Pole back home makes particular sense in light of his awareness of the repressive atmosphere that prevailed in the 1880s. When I discussed my writing with him, Doran asked me to be sure to explain the coercive pressures Yellow Smoke and others were experiencing at the time of the Pole's departure. He repeated what I had heard often before, that the Pole was stolen from them. Many Omahas, and particularly those of an older generation, he suggested, have deeply internalized the assimilationist pressure that Fletcher and the "Friends of the Indian" represented.

While the reformers largely failed in their attempt to eradicate Indianness, they did create a sense of ambivalence and conflict among many Native Americans, particularly those who attended Indian schools like Carlisle in Pennsylvania. It is no wonder that some people fear the Sacred Pole; they associate him with the "Indian religious rites and practices" abandoned long ago. On the other hand, the newer but distinctively Indian ceremonies of the Native American Church have been part of Omaha culture and experience for most of this century. Lawrence Gilpin was a national past president of the church. According to the late Victor Robinson of the Hon'ga clan:

> Presently, peyotism is considered the religion of the Native Americans. To protect the religion from various attacks from religious and political antagonists, members of the peyote religion have joined together to have themselves legally incorporated as the Native American Church. The church presently has chartered national and local chapters.
>
> The purpose of this corporation is to foster and promote religious beliefs in Almighty God, and to continue the culture of Indian tribes in the United States, in their worship of a heavenly father. The church promotes morality, sobriety, industry, charity, and "right" living. Peyote is used as a sacrament to cultivate a spirit of self-respect, brotherly love, and union among members of different tribes.
>
> The beginning and growth of the Native American religion started when Indians were placed within the restrictive reservation system. On the reservation, disintegration was encouraged, and it destroyed estab-

lished economic and political structures. The reservation system served to spiritually demythologize the Indian, stripping him of his heritage, his hope, and his spiritual identity. The Peyote serves as a re-awakening agent for the Indian and his mystique. It awakens the knowledge that the spirit of God has come close to strengthen and comfort him. (Robinson 1982,148–49)

The Native American Church is not incompatible with a reverence and respect for more ancient tribal religious symbols. In the months and years since *Umon'hon'ti* returned to Nebraska, religious leaders within the Church have begun to think and pray for his well-being and that of the tribe. Meanwhile, he is being kept safely and away from public view for the tribe by the University of Nebraska. In 1995 Doran did a sweat with spiritual leaders from the Native American Church, who told him that Umon'hon'ti was unhappy being confined in the long coffinlike case the Peabody had constructed to transport him in. They said it was like being in prison. Accordingly, Doran visited Umon'hon'ti and removed him from the box. He is now comfortably under cover on top of one of the cabinets, aligned in a north-south direction. As in times past, he stands out above the others as a dark object, Washa'begle.

AN UNDIVIDED INTEREST

Umon'hon'ti is the Real Omaha, a part of the tribe who stands for its entirety. He is the person in whom Omahas have, in Lawrence Gilpin's words, "an undivided interest." A young man who lost his way came upon "a tree that stands burning" beneath the "motionless star," the center of the night sky. He was lost as an individual at a time when the tribe was lost as a collectivity. The Sacred Legend reports that "a great council was being held to devise some means by which the bands of the tribe might be kept together and the tribe itself saved from extinction."

The young man experienced the "tree that stands burning" as a mystery. His father, a chief of the tribe, read his son's experience as an encounter with the power of Wakon'da, an "invisible and continuous life" that "permeates all things, seen and unseen." His father knew that the tree represents the world's center by "the four animal paths that led to it," just as his son knew to take his direction from the motionless star that is the center of the night sky. By night, the wonderful tree that became Umon'hon'ti pointed north to that center. By day, it stood at the world's center and pointed to the zenith. The young man's father recognized it as a place where the four directions converge in the form of animal trails. The young man's vision connects "a fragment of anything to its entirety." He is a part; the tribe is a whole. The "wonderful tree" he discovered became Umon'hon'ti, the Real Omaha, another part that stands for the whole.

The young man receives his vision at the center of the night sky through what Fletcher and La Flesche called "the great mother force," a blessing of the night. In a complementary vision, a young woman receives the Mark of Honor, whose name is the same as that of the Pole, when the sun reaches the center of the day sky. Her empowerment comes as the culmination of her father's initiation into the Hon'hewachi, the Night Blessed Society.

The annual renewal ceremony works out a similar language. A reed represents each man of the tribe, and through patrilineal kinship, each family. Reed stands for man stands for family. Similarly, the ceremonial tent in which the ceremony is conducted is constructed of single poles taken from each of the lodges represented by the bundle of reeds. Expanding the bundle creates the renewal lodge. Contracting the *hu'thuga* similarly creates *uzhin'eti*, the sacred earth altar.

Omahas today carry with them a legacy of oppression as well as one of survival. The experience of being told that Indian culture is bad is as much a part of Omaha history as are the music and dance of pow-wow. Every person's experience is a reed that he or she carries to a common center. Every experience must be acknowledged in order to make up the whole. At the time of pow-wow, tribal members bring a variety of experiences both on and off the reservation to a common center. They come together there for a common experience of renewal. Now, the Venerable Man has come back to join them. His experience spans generations beyond the memory of living people. In time, he will assume a comfortable place in the tribal circle, and will return to an honored place at the center of Omaha conversation. In time, he will certainly fulfill the spirit of Eddie Cline's prayer:

> This tree has been living, standing.
> Whatever his thoughts, make them possible.
> Make his good thoughts possible.

CHAPTER SEVEN

All My Relations

For the last three years I constantly have heard people crying in my
ears, and lately it's never been happening. It doesn't bother me any
more.

> Dennis Hastings (August 17, 1989, following the
> Sacred Pole's return)

We're going to be here forever.
Doran Morris (October 3, 1991)

Between 1775 and 1819, Omahas lived at Ton'wontonga, their "Big Village"
beside the Missouri River near the present town of Homer, Nebraska
(O'Shea and Ludwickson 1992, 23). They were prosperous for much of the
time they lived there, but they also suffered enormously from epidemics of
smallpox. Umon'hon'ti, the Sacred Pole, and Tethon'ha, the Sacred White
Buffalo Hide, with their respective remarkable catlinite pipes, were with the
people at Ton'wontonga and accompanied the tribe on its buffalo hunt each
summer in "the moon when the buffaloes bellow." Like the two tribal pipes
that were always kept together, Umon'hon'ti and Tethon'ha were inseparable at that time. When the Omahas finally abandoned the village in 1819,
they took their sacred objects with them but left behind the graves of many
who had died there.

Some of the elders buried at Ton'wontonga might, as young people, have
known the chief's son who first encountered a "wonderful tree," had he lived
to an old age. Certainly, the elders that these people of Ton'wontonga knew
when they were young were among the Omahas who first knew
Umon'hon'ti. We have very little information beyond what archaeology,
physical anthropology, and ethnohistory can tell us about particular individuals buried at Ton'wontonga, but it is quite likely that some of them were the
keepers of sacred objects. From the grave goods we know that one of them
was a gunsmith and was probably the person Edwin James referred to in 1819

26. Return of the Sacred White Buffalo Hide, August 4, 1991. Photograph courtesy of the Omaha World Herald.

as "an individual of this nation, who is no more, without acquiring any knowledge of white people, as far as we could learn, mended the guns and traps of his countrymen, when not too seriously injured" (James 1823, 286). It is not impossible that former keepers of Umon'hon'ti and Tethon'ha could have been among those buried at Ton'wontonga. What we do know is that the remains of more than a hundred Omahas buried there were being held by the University of Nebraska at the time the tribe began its negotiations for the return of Umon'hon'ti.

As in that long-ago time when the tribe was in council "to devise some means by which the bands of the tribe might be kept together and the tribe itself saved from extinction," the Omaha tribal council in 1988 and 1989 was committed to paying respect to tribal elders being held by non-Indian institutions. Umon'hon'ti was the most venerable of these, and bringing him home was their highest priority. Liberating Tethon'ha, who had been stolen from the tent of her keeper, Wakon'monthin, in 1898, was another goal of the tribe. The people of Ton'wontonga also needed to come home. Thus, two hundred years after the time when Ton'wontonga was most prosperous, the Omaha tribe was engaged in two important but seemingly separate projects. One was negotiation with the Peabody Museum of Harvard University for the return of Umon'hon'ti. The other was a challenge to the Nebraska State Historical Society, which had strongly opposed legislation that would require repatriation of bones and burial goods being held by academic institutions. At one point, Dennis Hastings even ran for the society's board, hoping, as he told me later, "to get in there and be at least in the institution to try to make some change." While he did not win the position, he did make contact with sympathetic individuals, including archivist Anne Diffendal.

The tribe's position at the time it was challenging the historical society was that all Native American remains being held by institutions should be reburied and that interested scientists should be given a deadline for completing their work. Initially, the tribe worked on the repatriation issue with the Native American Rights Fund. Later it took its own direction to focus its particular interest on the Omaha remains that the University of Nebraska–Lincoln had been holding for fifty years, following excavations it had conducted between 1937 and 1941 (Reinhard 1994, 4). The collection of bones being held in Lincoln represented a cross section of the people who had lived and died at Ton'wontonga.

NEGOTIATIONS WITH THE PEABODY

Negotiations with the Peabody were not going well in the fall of 1988, despite the good beginning made during Doran and Eddie's visit there the previous summer. Doran had written Associate Curator Ian Brown on July 25 thanking him for the Peabody's hospitality in June. He went on to say:

> I need to tell you that the moment Mr. Cayoin [Joseph Johns] brought the Sacred Pole out of the Peabody Museum, I felt a sensation that came close to being next to my Great-Great-Grandfather and to the old days of our old ways. It was a very powerful moment and moving experience for both Ed Cline and myself.

His letter concluded by informing the museum that

> Shortly, we will be writing a formal letter requesting our Sacred Pole back and also assuring the Peabody Board, that will be meeting October, 1988, that care will be taken to preserve something that is so precious and dear to the Omaha people.

At this point, there appears to have been a serious breakdown in communication. Doran sent a formal letter on August 8 requesting the Pole's return. To the letter he attached the Peabody's list of its Omaha holdings. The idea of any sort of repatriation was still quite radical in 1988, and Director Lamberg-Karlovsky apparently interpreted Doran's letter as a serious attempt on the tribe's part to set a precedent that would empower other tribes to request the return of anything that had originated with them, no matter how it had been acquired. The Peabody was undoubtedly afraid of setting a precedent that other institutions would be unwilling to follow. In 1976, the Smithsonian had told Zunis requesting return of their sacred Ahayu:da, "War Gods," that the institution "had a trust responsibility to preserve these collections for all people" (Merrill, Ladd, and Ferguson 1993, 532). As of 1986, it had agreed to return the Ahayu:da but not other Zuni holdings.

It is in the context of this apprehension that Lamberg-Karlovsky replied with a letter on September 9 that Doran interpreted as rejecting the tribe's claim to the Sacred Pole. Doran informed me of what appeared to be bad news and repeated an opinion that is widely held on the reservation, that Fletcher and La Flesche had simply taken the Pole from Yellow Smoke's tent without his consent. I was unaware of the reason for the director's change in tone but I wrote Doran on November 22 with the following advice:

> I was sorry to hear that Dr. Lamberg-Karlovsky appears unwilling to recognize the Omaha tribe's right to the Sacred Pole which the Peabody has been holding for safekeeping during the last century. I hope that a direct appeal to the museum's board of directors will resolve the problem and avoid legal action.

I went on to say:

> As you pointed out, La Flesche may have taken the Pole without Yellow Smoke's full consent. However, I would suggest that an argument based on that claim might be used against you by an opposing lawyer on the grounds that it brought into question any account of what is reported to have happened. I think it is enough to point out that La Flesche stated in writing that Yellow Smoke transferred the Pole to him so that "it could dwell in a great brick house instead of a ragged tent," and that he and Fletcher referred to securing the Pole for "safekeeping."

I concluded my letter by stating my own feeling that it made sense to accept that the Pole himself continued to exert an authority over events.

> I am confident that the Pole is exerting an authority we can understand and follow if we come to it in a respectful state of mind. (Ridington to Morris, November 22, 1988)

Both Lamberg-Karlovsky and Doran Morris were aware that the Omahas had requested the Sacred Pole's return on several previous occasions. Their requests had always been turned down. The director's unease with Doran's request reflected that history as well as internal politics, both within Harvard

University and among museum professionals nationally. Lamberg-Karlovsky, whose term as director was nearly over, did not want his twelve years in the position to end in what his peers might view as a disaster. On January 3, 1989, he proposed to Doran Morris that instead of making a legal transfer of the Pole and other sacred objects collected by Alice Fletcher, the Peabody make "a long-term loan to a nearby well-established museum like the Joslyn Art Museum [in Omaha, Nebraska]." Dennis Hastings had already established contact with staff at the Joslyn. He hoped that the museum might help mediate between the tribe and the Peabody and provide temporary storage for the Pole. Lamberg-Karlovsky's letter defined long term as "a five-year loan with renewal for further defined periods," but also went on to say:

> At the end of three years we can begin the process of transferring legal title of the Fletcher collection to the Omaha tribe. Three years should give you ample time to document the permanency of your own custody with regard to the building the collection is to be stored in, how it is to be cared for (curatorial staff and conservation) etc. (Lamberg-Karlovsky to Morris, January 23, 1989)

At the end of the letter he listed a few conditions regarding expenses. His words turned out to be a momentous fulcrum in the eventual turn of events. While agreeing to "absorb all conservation and packing costs" and, without any evident awareness of irony, agreeing "to waive all loan fees," he also stipulated that "the shipping expenses will have to be absorbed by the Joslyn."

At this point, the tribe seems to have had two options. One would have been to break off negotiations with the Peabody and pursue legal action, an option warranted by the widespread belief among Omahas that the Pole was stolen from Yellow Smoke. Some members of the council advocated this course of action. The tribe's other option was to agree to the museum's proposal for the time being, but also to present their case directly to the Peabody faculty. They chose the latter option and accordingly, on February 8, 1989, Doran Morris returned to Cambridge and met with the museum director, Peabody faculty members, and Derek Bok, the president of Harvard University. Doran showed a five-minute video of the talk I had given at the 1988 pow-wow and said that it was the tribe's priority to have the Pole returned to Macy for the pow-wow in August 1989.

The Peabody faculty were apparently impressed with Doran's determination to bring the Pole to Macy for that summer's pow-wow, but they repeated their request for assurances about the tribe's ability to provide custodial care. They seem to have been particularly concerned that they not be held legally or morally responsible should any harm come to the Pole. Accordingly, Ian Brown wrote Doran Morris a letter on May 15, 1989, requesting that he transfer to Omaha stationery and sign the text of a letter "that he [Dr. Lamberg-Karlovsky] needs from you to protect the interests of the university." The letter Lamberg-Karlovsky said he needed from Doran was detailed, and moved between adaptations of passages from letters Doran had written previously and text attending to details of particular concern to a museum administrator and the university's legal counsel. It gave the dimensions of a display case for the Pole and stated that "until we [the tribe] construct an adequate facility, we have an arrangement with the Joslyn Art Museum whereby they will house our materials. They do have the necessary space as well as the conservation staff to care for these relics until the appropriate time when they can be returned to our land." The letter went on to repeat Lamberg-Karlovsky's condition that "we (through the Joslyn Art Museum) will pay for the shipping costs via a standard carrier of museum objects."

While Doran sent the letter the Peabody had requested, it overstated the tribe's agreement with the Joslyn. Nothing had gone beyond the stage of telephone calls between Dennis and his contacts on the museum staff. The Joslyn itself was undergoing an internal struggle about whether to continue its involvement with Great Plains history or to become mainly an art museum. As it turned out, the art side of the museum carried the day and staff sympathetic to the Omahas eventually left the institution. While this struggle was going on, the Joslyn evaded commitment by suggesting that the tribe engage a designer who often worked for them to construct a case in which the Pole could be housed in the tribal building in Macy.

Meanwhile, Michael Farrell, the Nebraska Educational Television producer of the award-winning *Dancing to Give Thanks*, had received the go-ahead from his institution to film the Pole's return, from locations in Cambridge, Eppley Airfield in Omaha, and Macy. With less than a week to go before filming was to start in Cambridge and only a month before the transfer itself was to take place, the Peabody required an assurance of the Joslyn's institutional support and willingness to provide temporary storage. In May the tribe had been distressed to receive a quote of seventeen thousand dollars to construct a case by the Joslyn's exhibit designer. When they questioned this figure, on the advice of Ian Brown at the Peabody, the designer responded that he would not even draw preliminary sketches unless they paid him one thousand dollars up front. The tribe concluded that he was being unreasonable and declined his offer. So matters rested as of the middle of June.

I was in Macy in June and was party to some of the phone calls between Macy, Cambridge, Omaha, and later, the University of Nebraska–Lincoln. Only the determined commitments of Ian Brown and Dennis Hastings kept communications open. While the two did not meet in person until the ceremony on August 20, 1989, they had come to respect and understand one another as they negotiated the delicate issues to be resolved between the two cultures. On August 18, 1989, two days before the Pole returned to Macy for the 185th tribal pow-wow, Ian Brown wrote the following letter expressing his admiration for the work Dennis had been doing to accomplish the return successfully:

> To Whom it May Concern:
> This letter is written with regard to Mr. Dennis Hastings, Tribal Historian of the Omaha Indian Nation. Over the past year I have been deeply involved in the process of returning the Sacred Pole of the Omaha to its original home. This sacred object is synonymous with the Omaha people. It represents the authority of their chiefs, the unity between man and woman, and the binding element that has held the Omaha people together for centuries. The last hundred years it has resided at the Peabody Museum. My role in the endeavor of returning the Sacred Pole to the Omaha has largely occurred behind the scenes at the Peabody Museum. My principal task was to make sure that things ran smoothly on this end. Dennis Hastings has been my counterpart in Nebraska. It is no exaggeration to state that without his constant work, encouragement, and positive attitude, this project of returning the Sacred Pole probably would never have come to its successful completion.
> Sincerely,
> Ian W. Brown
> Assistant Director and Associate Curator of North American Colls.
> (Brown, August 18, 1989)

In a conversation with Dennis I recorded on August 17, 1989, Dennis described the responsibility he had been feeling toward the Pole and its return.

> My feeling was that I had a tremendous burden on me to follow through and make sure things happened. I didn't have time, but then again, I always knew the presence of it. It was sort of like I was a servant, at the point to where I couldn't have time—I had to do other things for it. I didn't have time to be a part of it, and if I didn't do it, then there's a lot of things that wouldn't happen, 'cause a lot of people there was, sort of didn't know what to do or what was going to happen, since it's been such a loss, you know. They weren't sure of themselves and I had to kind of be a reassurance—make sure that the case got out of the truck, and make sure it was set down, make sure the box was open, you know, it was just sort of like following through.

During May and June 1989, Dennis put to use all his contacts with academics, museum people, and the media to keep the process going. In my fieldnotes I wrote:

When Dennis and I arrived at the tribal building on Monday [June 12, 1989] things were pretty much at a standstill. After talking to Doran and other council members, we began to make phone calls. Between Monday and Tuesday we called Carl Lamberg-Karlovsky, Ian Brown, Roger Welsch's answering machine, Bodner the designer, Dr. Paul Olson who teaches English at the U of N, and Mike Farrell of Nebraska ETV.

On June 15 matters reached a critical point. Marsha Gallagher, a representative of the Joslyn, finally told Doran directly that the museum would not be able to accept any of the sacred objects, even on a temporary basis. It seems likely in retrospect that the Joslyn backed out because of issues having to do with money, as well as its internal turmoil. Museum officials were undoubtedly disturbed at Lamberg-Karlovsky's condition implying that the museum might have to "pay for the shipping costs via a standard carrier of museum objects." They were probably also put out that the tribe was unwilling to pay their designer's fee for constructing a case. Whatever their reasons, by June 15 it was clear that they were out of the picture and that without a secure temporary storage facility the transfer could not happen.

Just as the Joslyn was pulling out of the project, the NETV film crew was finalizing plans to begin filming in Cambridge on June 20. While Dennis wracked his brain for a possible way out of the dilemma, Ian Brown attempted to dissuade Lamberg-Karlovsky from simply cancelling the entire project. Such was the state of affairs when, at the suggestion of archivist Anne Diffendal, Dennis called Dr. Paul Olson, a professor of English and one of the founders of the Center for Great Plains Studies at the University of Nebraska. Dr. Olson, in turn, suggested that Dennis call Dr. John Wunder, who had come to the university to direct the center the previous fall. To Dennis's delight, Dr. Wunder told him that the university would be honored to provide safe storage for the Sacred Pole. Dr. Wunder later told me:

Dennis called and told me about the Sacred Pole, how things had fallen apart with the Joslyn. I allowed that that was not surprising, how he really couldn't deal with the historical society, which was true. Dennis explained how he didn't wish to work with the museum at the university which held the remains of the Omahas, and he asked if he might have a secure place to store the Sacred Pole. I said we'd be happy to help out, but only with one stipulation, that we would not let anyone see the Sacred Pole without the express permission of the tribal chair, Dennis the tribal historian, or the tribal council. I told Dennis that if the Sacred Pole were to be in our art collection we would not display it nor let anyone else see it without the Omahas' permission. And we would not want a fee or have any charges. I told Dennis I was familiar with repatriation issues, that I believed we should help out the Omahas if we could. Above all, the Sacred Pole in my mind was the Omaha people's sacred trust, and I believed that we would do what the Omahas wished. I made this decision on the authority of being the director of the Center for Great Plains Studies, nothing more, nothing less. (Wunder to Ridington April 19, 1996)

After the struggle and frustration of trying to house the Pole in Omaha, the plan for him to go to Lincoln fell into place effortlessly. Everyone involved breathed a sigh of relief. It was not until after the immediate crisis was over that Dennis and Doran and members of the tribal council began to understand that something momentous had taken place. Rather than continuing to be apart from the ancient ones from Ton'wontonga, the Pole would be coming to the very university in which they were being held. Furthermore, he seemed to be coming there on a mission of responsibility to the people who had once cared for him. The university's offer to house the Sacred Pole, in fact, began a process that resulted in collaboration between the tribe and the university to study how the Ton'wontonga people had lived, prior to giving them a respectful reburial on the Omaha reservation.

John Wunder described how the Pole's return and the reburial issue came together. In the process of making arrangements for the Sacred Pole's arrival, Dennis and John Wunder had talked to one another on a daily basis, during which time a feeling of mutual trust and respect developed. John later described how their relationship grew:

In the process of these conversations, I allowed that we should do more than what we were doing, that we could both be in a position to help each other's constituencies out. We then started to discuss the Omaha burial remains. At this time the debate in Nebraska had reached a fever pitch. The legislature was incensed with the historical society's treatment of this issue, and it was considering the most stringent of legislation (LB 340: Nebraska Unmarked Burial Sites and Skeletal Remains Protection Act). There was a great deal of publicity over the repatriation issue, and the historical society and its director looked very bad in the press. I knew the university would not want the same kind of situation to develop, and I knew that it was most likely that the legislation would pass. So it was an opportune time for action, and Dennis and I were the actors.

Both Dennis and John Wunder told me about a meeting that took place in Anne Diffendal's kitchen. Dennis told me:

> I hypothetically put the situation to John Wunder and I said, "What would it be like if the university made the first approach to the tribe and says, 'Basically we're sorry this happened and we want to look at a positive relationship and return the skeletal remains, and this won't happen again without the authority of the tribe.'" And he said, he didn't know but let him throw it around a little bit with John Yost [dean of graduate studies] and then Martin Massengale [the chancellor at the time].

John described the meeting in Anne's kitchen as follows:

> Anne prepared sandwiches while we talked and met for the first time. We had instantaneous rapport. We came away from the meeting with a strategy. I said that I needed to go see the chancellor of the university to talk with him about what the center had done, my conversations with Dennis, and the role the university should play in repatriation. I would then contact Dennis after that meeting and suggest the next strategy.

John then met with Chancellor Massengale and explained how important the issue was for both the university and the tribe.

> I told him it was an opportunity for the university to put its best foot forward. It needed to repatriate the Omaha remains. Here we could take the initiative and the obvious comparisons would place the university in the right public position. Moreover, it was the right thing to do. Martin told me to draft a letter that made the appropriate promises. The most important parts involved a public apology, a promise to return the Omaha remains, and a promise to meet further and develop a more long-range relationship with the Omahas. Some on Massengale's staff resisted offering the apology and after I was contacted about this, I called Dennis. Dennis insisted on the apology. He said that without it, the rest might be perceived as gratuitous. I agreed with him and told the staff that the apology had to stay or the situation would be out of our hands. Evidently, Chancellor Massengale's initial views prevailed. As you can tell, the meeting at Anne Diffendal's kitchen table was important. (Wunder to Ridington April 19, 1996)

A few weeks later, John Wunder spoke publicly to the entire tribe and to Umon'hon'ti himself, conveying the university's regret at having held Omaha remains for so long and looking forward to a new relationship to the Omaha people and their heritage:

In July we were able to come once again to Macy and it was an honor to be here at that time. Since then, the Sacred Pole has rested comfortably in Lincoln at the Center for Great Plains Studies. And that has worked out very well and I am glad that we were able to come up once again to return him to you. This is a very positive day, a very good day, and on behalf of the university I wish to bring you the greetings of the chancellor and all the rest of the persons at the university. This week, the chancellor sent a letter to the tribal chairman, the tribal council, and the Omaha people. Very important things were said in the letter. The most important thing in the letter was that the chancellor regretted the university having had burial remains of the Omaha people for so long and he hopes very soon that those will be returned. Very quickly, in September, the leaders of the Omaha people and the leaders of the university will meet and very soon the Ancient Ones will return. In addition to that, other important matters will be discussed at that meeting in September. And the university looks forward to working with the Omaha people on all of these things. I thank you for allowing us to be here with you today. I wish you well in your pow-wow and I am proud of the university for the way in which it has responded at this particular time. Thank you. (John Wunder at Omaha Pow-wow in Macy, Nebraska, August 20, 1989)

On that same pow-wow weekend, after the Pole was formally returned to the Omaha people, Dennis Hastings went out to dinner in Sioux City with me, photographer Ilka Hartmann, and Jillian Ridington. Over Chinese food, he told us about his very personal and spiritual connection with the people from Ton'wontonga. He explained that throughout the time he had been working on the Pole's return, he was aware of the sound of people crying:

But I think my reward was that the burial skeletal remains will be returned, 'cause the first thing I said when the Pole was put in the university, I said, "It's with those original people." I was telling Uncle Buddy [Alfred Gilpin], I says, "Geez, I'd like to be there in that meeting, look at what's going on there." And if I can go into spirit form and see that meeting. And then when the meeting was done, they're going to come home.

The biggest burden to me though, is that, you know, I told a few people this, two years ago, three years ago—burial issue, was that I constantly have heard people crying in my ears, and lately it's never been happening. It's not, you know, it doesn't bother me any more.

I never physically heard them, it was, but I heard them. It was like loud. It was spiritually I heard them. It was real eerie and very sad. And that bothered me for almost three years. In a sense, I think it won't bother me no more, so that might be the reward, I guess. But I don't look at that as any great spiritual outlook, other than the fact, you know, I don't like it. It bothers me when that kind of thing happens. It really takes its toll on my sleep. (Recorded by Jillian and Robin Ridington, August 17, 1989)

THE PEOPLE OF TON'WONTONGA

Prior to 1989 the tribe had been concerned largely with supporting state legislation mandating the return of human remains to tribal control for reburial. They had not made any request for return of the bones to the University of Nebraska but had made their position known to the Nebraska State Historical Society. They were aware that some scholars were of the opinion then that Native American remains belonged exclusively to science rather than to their living descendants. Others wished to find a way of making scientific findings known to contemporary tribal people prior to return and reburial. The Pawnees of Nebraska had become involved in a bitter struggle with the state historical society. Perhaps because of this example, the Omahas were hoping to resolve outstanding issues through cooperation rather than litigation. However, they were upset that associates of the historical society, John O'Shea and John Ludwickson, had been studying the remains and grave goods without consulting the tribe about its interest in the remains of its ancestors.

In mid-September 1989, Chancellor Massengale and other members of the university community met with Dennis, Doran, tribal council members, and Omaha tribal attorneys. Dean Yost chaired the meeting. By this time, opposition to returning the bones had been silenced within the university. John Wunder describes the meeting:

It was an interesting event. It began with Doran giving an address of some length with praise to Chancellor Massengale and the university. The chancellor responded in kind with his praise and respect for Doran. Then he asked if the Omahas would formally request the return of burial remains, so that the Nebraska law could officially be invoked.

John Wunder went on to describe how, once the tribe had made its request, the chancellor offered "to bring the full assistance of the university to the Omahas." His offer began with offering the services of the school of architecture (which had a representative at the meeting) to design a cultural center and museum in which to house the sacred objects. It ended with offering the Omahas free tickets to a Nebraska Cornhuskers football game in the fall and an invitation to a pregame luncheon as his guests. They took him up on both offers. In between discussions of architecture and football, Massengale proposed to provide an agricultural extension agent to serve the needs of the Omahas. Then the Omahas made an offer that surprised the chancellor. They formally requested that scientific information be obtained from the skeletal remains prior to reburial.

On the strength of the agreements achieved at this meeting, the Department of Anthropology assigned a new faculty member specializing in bioarchaeology, Dr. Carl J. Reinhard, the task of assembling a team of experts to conduct a multidisciplinary study of the Ton'wontonga remains. Department chair Jim Gibson also offered a fellowship to any qualified Omaha to study in anthropology.

In the fall of 1989 Dr. Reinhard and his team began meeting with Dennis and members of the tribal council to define research objectives that would be of mutual interest to the tribe and the university, and to develop a schedule for repatriation. Dr. Reinhard summarized the terms of these discussions as follows:

> Physical anthropologists have established guidelines and goals for the analysis of skeletons slated for reburial. These goals and guidelines address the following needs: 1) that the complete and responsible analysis of skeletal remains be accomplished before reburial, 2) that uniformity in data collection and storage techniques between laboratories and researchers be established, 3) that the maximum scientific data be recovered from skeletons prior to reburial, 4) that complete reconstructions of ancestral diseases and health are provided to living descendants of skeletal populations. . . . As much as possible it was my intent to follow these guidelines to insure that as much information as possible would be gained for the Omaha tribe and that the University of Nebraska reburial analysis policy would be a model for other universities faced with the reburial issue.
>
> It should be noted that the reburial analysis policy followed thus far at the University of Nebraska is one of the most progressive policies followed by any academic institution. The progressive nature of this policy incorporates responsible analysis of skeletal remains in conjunction with and in response to the desires of Native Americans, specifically the Omaha tribe. The progressive nature of the university policy is ultimately a reflection of the desire of the tribe's to learn about its ancestors. Thus, the policy carried out by the University of Nebraska is a union of the concern of the tribe with the ancestral past, and the scientific responsibility on the part of the university. I cannot credit enough the Omaha Tribal Council, the director of the Omaha Tribal Historical

Project, and interested members of the tribe for their openness, interest, and guidance of the analysis (Reinhard 1994, 2).

At the 186th Omaha pow-wow in 1990, Dennis Hastings introduced Dr. Tom Myers, representing the University of Nebraska State Museum, who spoke to the tribe about what Dr. Reinhard and his team had learned about the people from Ton'wontonga.

It's a great pleasure for me, an honor for me, to be able to come and talk to the people today and to begin to communicate some of the things that your ancestors are communicating to us about the way the Omaha were in the past. Two hundred years ago when the people who are now at the University of Nebraska lived along the Missouri River here, it was a very different time. Some of them were alive before the first white men came into this area. And then traders came, bringing kettles, iron axes, steel knives, guns, and a whole variety of things that the Omaha had never seen before and which made life very different for them.

The life for these Omaha was very hard. You find that in the bones there are many kinds of breaks, stresses, fractures, and the people worked very, very hard. One of the things that we find is that all of the men worked very hard; the women worked even harder. There are more breaks in the bones and stress indicating breaks from work. With the new things that the Omaha were getting from the whites in exchange for their furs were the guns, the knives, and one of the things that we have found that we were very much surprised to find was that one of your ancestors was a gunsmith. He had hammers and locks and flints and all the rest of the paraphenalia necessary to be a gunsmith on the frontier of the United States in those days, working here on the Missouri River and working for the people.

Life was hard. One of the things that we find with these bones was that the teeth were very much worn, and we think that that has to do with the stress these people were putting on their teeth from preparing skins in exchange for the knives and the guns and to lead their lives in some other way. We find that the Omaha were wealthy people at that time. There were many silver ornaments. Some of those silver ornaments were made in the United States and shipped up the Missouri River by the traders in St. Louis. And other silver ornaments were made in Montreal, Canada, French Canada, and probably traded to the Omaha people by the Sioux, who at that time lived west of Lake Superior and traded things across country to the Omaha people.

And with the Omaha people living and working hard here on the banks of the Missouri, burying their dead, honoring their dead as they always had, we find that suddenly great numbers of Omaha died. They died quickly, and men died and women died and children died, and they all put them together into a common grave. They were dying of smallpox, a new white man's disease that the Omaha didn't know; that they had no natural protection against, such as the people who came from Europe, who came from Africa, who came from Asia. The Indians didn't have any familiarity with smallpox. They didn't have any natural immunity. And tens of thousands of Indians died; here in Nebraska and all over the United States, all over Canada, all over South America. Tens of thousands, millions of Indians died from these white diseases.

They were all buried together. We're learning that your ancestors suffered from many diseases; from stress, from osteoporosis, a variety of other diseases. The next things that we're going to be looking at and finding out about are the kinds of things they were eating, the kinds of stresses, the kinds of dietary stresses that were taking place, the seasons, whether they suffered famines, things like that. That's all going to come from the next year's study. We at the university museum are very pleased to be able to participate and help the Omaha learn about themselves and we look forward to participating and helping to learn more about you over the next upcoming years.
Thank you.

Dennis then thanked the chairman and the tribe for supporting his work as tribal historian and co-ordinator of the Omaha Tribal Historical Project.

THE ANCIENT ONES TELL THEIR STORY
Dr. Reinhard's research did, indeed, turn out to be of considerable interest to the Omahas. From the otherwise mute bones, he and his associates were able to look closely at how the people who were Umon'hon'ti's companions had lived a century before he went into the Peabody Museum for safekeeping. Some of these people were at Ton'wontonga during Blackbird's time and before. Others may have died in the smallpox epidemic that carried him away. Still others were survivors, to whom fell the task of putting their life as a tribe back together. Umon'hon'ti must have been immensely important to them at that time, and it is likely that the ceremonies Fletcher and La Flesche report from later in the nineteenth century contributed to the healing.

The remains that were held by the University of Nebraska come from two separate cemeteries, designated as sites 25DK10 and 25DK2a, which were excavated as part of a larger archaeological project funded by the federal government to provide employment in the late 1930s and early 1940s. Site 25DK2a was excavated in 1939 by Stanley Bartos Jr. Site 25DK10 was excavated in 1940 under the direction of John L. Champe (Reinhard 1994, 7). The two cemeteries were probably used at different times and represent people living under somewhat different conditions. Based on brass wire bracelets and other artifacts found at 25DK10, Reinhard suggests that "the individuals buried there lived between 1780 and 1800." Materials from the other site, 25DK2a, are more likely to be utilitarian, suggesting a later trading period that began after 1800 (Reinhard 1994, 3).

The trade journals of Truteau and MacKay, written between 1794 and 1796, shed light on what might have been expected to be found at the earlier site. Truteau complained bitterly in the winter of 1794–95 that Blackbird:

> freely takes a third at least of all the merchandise which comes to his village. Upon the arrival of the French at his villages he causes an exhibition of the goods to be made and then carries off and appropriates whatever is pleasing to him. . . . As to the common people the trade is carried on with much profit, but the loss which this chief and his followers bring to the traders which takes from them the better or greater part of their effects at a low price, places them in a condition to make no gain. This Omaha post is about the most disadvantageous on the whole river at the present time as much through the great knowledge they have of trading through the English on the Mississippi, as through the evil disposition of this nation and of their chiefs in our regard. (Nasatir 1952, 383–84)

Blackbird and his followers clearly benefited from playing off one trading nation against another. While the Spanish nominally controlled the Missouri River through the Company of the Missouri, many of their traders were French. English traders from Montreal were in competition with them and were often able to supply better goods at lower prices. In 1795 James MacKay set up a trading house adjacent to Ton'wontonga for the Company of the Missouri. He quickly established friendly relations with Blackbird, calling him "the soul of the village" and "my sincere friend." While stating that "he is more despotic than any European prince," Mackay called him "courteous and of great talent." Still, Mackay reports that when he presented Blackbird with a "famous medal and *patentes* which pleased him greatly . . . he was surprised at not finding in it a large flag, telling me that the English always gave one with the medal" (Nasatir 1952, 359).

MacKay reported to his company director that Ton'wontonga contained seven hundred warriors and that he had promised them two hundred muskets for the coming year. "They care," he said, "for only the English guns and not the French ones which burst in their hands, and good powder, for bad powder is regularly sent to them, which is of the greatest consequence for the hunt." The wealth of trade goods buried at Ton'wontonga provide a fascinating complement to these historical accounts of European trading. During the time the earlier site was used, the Omaha traded primarily for ornaments. Reinhard reports that "these ornaments became markers for a multi-tiered social organization focusing on men during the time of Chief Blackbird" (1994, 4).

Both men and women from the period before 1800 seem to have lived extraordinarily active lives. Reinhard found a number of fractures that he feels were related to the hazards of horseback riding. The bones of both men and women show evidence of having ridden extensively. He also found that "most of these fractures were well healed," indicating that Omahas had developed expertise in the treatment of bone injuries (1994, 3). The level of physical activity among women, he suggests, was sufficient to have significantly delayed the age of first menstruation:

> I feel that the typical Omaha woman activity pattern was equivalent to that of modern female athletes. It would appear that the advent of Euroamerican contact, and especially the fur trade, increased the physical demands on women. This resulted from the development of at least a partially nomadic lifestyle and the responsibility of preparing hides for trade. We also know that girls were trained in these tasks from the preteens and early teens onward. Therefore, the onset of this rigorous lifestyle preceded puberty and continued through adolescence. (1994, 4–8)

In the years when the later site was used, during the time of Lewis and Clark and after, Blackbird was dead and the Omahas no longer enjoyed a controlling influence on Missouri River trade. At this time, Reinhard says, "the trade focussed on acquiring more of the technology of the Euroamericans." This resulted, he reports, "in the emergence of new roles for the Omaha such as gun repairing for Individual 1 and clothing manufacture as represented by the shears, textiles, and button found in the trunk of Individual 28. The shift to trade with the Americans also seems to have brought about new roles and higher status for women, as seen in the amount and variety of high-status ornaments buried with them."

Lewis and Clark camped near Ton'wontonga August 12–20, 1804, but found the village empty. Their journal entry for August 14 reads:

> At about 12 oClock the Party returned and informd. us that they Could not find the Indians, nor any fresh Sign, those people have not returned from their Buffalow hunt. Those people haveing no houses no Corn or anything more than the graves of their ansesters to attach them to the old Village, Continue in perseute of the Buffalow longer than others who has greater attachments to their native village. The

ravages of the Small Pox (which Swept off 400 men & Women & children in perpopotion) has reduced this nation not exceeding 300 men and left them to the insults of their weaker neighbors, which before was glad to be on friendly turms with them. I am told when this fatal malady was among them they Carried their franzey to very extraordinary length, not only of burning their Village, but they put their *wives* & children to *Death* with a view of their all going together to some better Countrey. they burry their Dead on the top of high hills and rais Mounds on the top of them. The cause or way those people took the Small Pox is uncertain, the most Probable, from Some other nation by means of a warparty. (Moulton 1986, vol. 2, 479)

After trying in vain to contact the Omahas by means of setting fire to a section of prairie, Lewis and Clark continued upriver. On their return voyage, they passed by Ton'wontonga on September 5, 1806. They record that the tribe had just recently returned from the buffalo hunt:

the report of the guns which was heard must have been the Mahars who most probably have just arrived at their village from hunting the buffalow. this is a season they usialy return to their village to secure their crops of corn Beens punkins &c &c. (Moulton 1986, vol. 8, 350)

Reinhard notes that while there is substantial documentation of certain aspects of Omaha culture from the traders' perspective, "there is relatively little evidence of what daily life was like for Omaha during this period." He points out that "the remains of Omaha ancestors hold that information" (1994, 7). "The presence of both articulated and disarticulated bodies in the cemeteries," for instance, indicates that the Omaha often placed their dead "on a scaffold above the ground for a time" and then transferred the remains to a burial pit. Often, disarticulated bones from above-ground burials were placed with the bodies of individuals, suggesting an intention to reunite the remains of family members.

Unlike the study by O'Shea and Ludwickson (1992) claiming that many of the buried individuals were war victims or even "trophy heads," Reinhard's study found little or no evidence of such traumas or practices. O'Shea and Ludwickson argue that warfare contributed to Omaha population decline in the early 1800s more than disease. Reinhard does not support their contention. Although he did identify one individual with a well-healed bullet wound to his upper left arm, the remarkable aspect of this wound, he says, is that it healed well because "the bone was properly reoriented, braced, and bound" (1994, 71). Omahas of the early 1800s were clearly able to perform successful medical procedures.

Reinhard argues that epidemics do not necessarily "lead to the demolition

27. *Dennis Hastings (on the right) and Dennis Turner. Photograph by Robin Ridington.*

of social and political structure as indicated by O'Shea and Ludwickson" (1994, 7). Rather, he says, social and political systems survive and adjust to the loss. Among the adjustments for which the human remains provide evidence is "the differentiation of subsistence activities between the sexes after

1800 and increased social standing for women." Overall health probably deteriorated as Omahas became more involved with trading for utilitarian objects. While the people of Ton'wontonga continued to have a well-developed and reliable subsistence base, infectious diseases may have increased mortality among women and children (1994, 9–10).

Carl Reinhard and his team completed their studies by the fall of 1991. On October 3, 1991, the bones came home to the Omaha reservation. They were reburied on a rolling hillside not far from the Missouri River. Carl Reinhard, Dennis Hastings, Thomas Myers, Robin Ridington, Doran Morris, Edward Cline, Clifford Wolfe Jr., Wynema Morris, and spiritual leader Dennis Turner were among those present on that rainy morning. It was a moving occasion for all concerned. More than anyone else present, the scientists seemed to experience the reburial as a loss of people they had come to know and respect. For Dennis it was the completion of something that had consumed his energies for nearly five years. For Doran it was also a moment of completion. After Dennis Turner prayed over the bones and blessed them with cedar, Doran spoke:

> The Omaha tribal council cedared relatives here that are laying here this morning. I'll briefly explain that we use cedar. Cedar is considered sacred amongst the Omaha tribe. Cedar represents everlasting life. As you see, evergreen trees, they survive year-round even though we have harsh winters, rain. It survives, so the Omaha consider the cedar sacred and as I said before, it has everlasting life. So my grandfather, Dennis Turner, did that for the relatives lying here this morning. All that was present here was our treasurer of the Omaha tribal council, Cliff Wolfe Jr., as I mentioned Dennis Turner, a member of the Omaha tribal council, and the former tribal chairman of the Omaha tribe, Eddie Cline, was here, and myself. My name is Doran L. Morris, chairman of the Omaha tribe.
>
> As I mentioned this morning, these relatives that are laying here this morning met Lewis and Clark when they came up the Missouri River in 1806. And at that time, our Sacred Pole, and just recently we brought home the Sacred White Buffalo Hide that was together with the Sacred Pole and at that time they were with our relatives. And thereafter, they separated. That was not appropriate. People stole our relics, they stole the Sacred Pole, they stole the Sacred White Buffalo Hide. And just the last few years, we were able to bring those home, and just recently, we brought the Sacred White Buffalo Hide home. So they're all together back home here on the Omaha reservation where they belong.
>
> So on behalf of the Omaha tribe I'm happy this morning that this

could happen. As where the Omaha is the people of this land here, we call it "The Omaha Land." My people were here before the State of Nebraska became a state, and we're still here and we're going to [Doran weeps and says, "Excuse me."]

We're going to be here forever. I like to tell my people that because at one time our relatives were one people and they got along, and someday I'd like to see my people in that way. I try to preach that to my people today. We need to get back together, getting along with one another. That was the teachings of our Omaha relatives who are lying here this morning. We want to proceed to cover the grave here this morning and thereafter we're putting up a feed which is our tradition. We put up food to have God witness the Omaha people. God has given his greatest gift to people, his food, so we do that in honor of our people. Back down to the community we're going to have a little feast and some prayers that will be done, and we'll take questions from each one of you if you wish. We're going to proceed back to the community, to the community building. We're going to have dinner. You're all welcome to join us in this noonday meal. Thank you.

TO COMPLETE THE MOST SACRED CIRCLE:
TETHON'HA COMES HOME

In 1897 Francis La Flesche visited Wakon'monthin (Mystery Walking or James Robinson), the last keeper of Tethon'ha, the Sacred White Buffalo Hide. He recorded the ritual songs belonging to the Hide and obtained the keeper's agreement to have the Hide and its Sacred Pipe later join the Sacred Pole at the Peabody Museum in order that, as an elder expressed it to Peabody Museum Director F. W. Putnam, "their children should be able in future times to see and understand the methods and thought of their fathers" (Putnam 1900, 2) Sadly, the Hide and Pipe were stolen from Wakon'monthin in February 1898. The old man was devastated at the loss and told La Flesche:

All that gave me comfort in this lonely travel was the possession and care of the Sacred Buffalo, one of the consecrated objects that once kept our people firmly united; but, as though to add to my sadness, rude hands have taken from me, by stealth, this one solace, and I now sit empty-handed, awaiting the call of those who have gone before me. For a while I wept for this loss, morning and evening, as though for the death of a relative dear to me, but as time passed the tears ceased to flow and I can now speak with composure. (1911, 250)

In October 1898 Fletcher received a letter from Elmer C. Griffith, director of the Warren Academy of Beloit College in Warren, Illinois, claiming to know the Hide's whereabouts and offering to sell Fletcher a photograph of it. He also told her that "the hide is now unobtainable" because of "parties frightened by detectives." He then put her in contact with Preston T. Hicks of the *Warren Leader* newspaper, who offered to act as a go-between for a Mr. E. O. Smith, who was said to possess the Hide and would return it for "quite a sum of money." Fletcher wrote Peabody Museum Director Putnam in November 1898, describing her negotiations with Mr. Hicks. (Copies of this letter and all other correspondence regarding the theft and return of the White Buffalo Hide were made available to me and Dennis by the National Museum of the American Indian upon the occasion of the Hide's return to the tribe):

> I do not think that I was as judicious in my talk with this man as I should have been, for I betrayed to him the knowledge of a ritual connected with the Hide, and said I would never publish it until the Hide was restored to me, and without the ritual the thing was worthless even to ethnologists.

Putnam then authorized the sum of $100 to be paid to Smith on receipt of the Hide, but before the deal could be completed, Hicks reported that Smith had sold the Hide to another party for $250. In June 1899, Fletcher obtained the assistance of Mr. E. J. DeBell, a "Licensed Indian Trader" in Valentine, Nebraska, in locating the Hide. DeBell, who seems to have been an honest and forthright man, met in Warren with Hicks, who told him:

> A man by the name of Mark Flowers came there with this robe and some other curios, which are now all in the Warren Academy with the exception of the white buffalo robe. The Hide, he told DeBell, was now in the possession of a "party in Chicago" whose name he would not reveal. A few days later, DeBell positively identified Mark Flowers as a man living near Sioux City and wrote that, "There is no question now about his being the thief." He suggested that, "by threatening him with arrest [I] can frighten him and so find out all I want to know about the matter." He reported the more promising information that:
>
> I have also written to Chicago where the robe was sold, and hope to be able to locate it there. If Mr. Hicks gave me the proper name of the Chicago man, as he did of the fellow who brought the robe there, I think we will have no trouble in locating it. I will keep you advised but don't write to any one yourself about it.

On August 12 he informed Fletcher that he had located the robe:

I have located the robe at Chicago but too late to give Mr. La Flesche the information before he went back East. The gutterman who has the robe will not give it up until he has looked the matter up. He told my friend that if the robe had been stolen he would give it up if he was reimbursed for the money he had paid for it. I then wrote to him and asked him how much he had paid for the robe but have yet received no answer. I suppose he is corresponding with some of the thieves at Warren. I have again written to him today and hope to hear from him soon. I have also written my friend and asked him to stir up the gutterman and see why he had not answered my letter. I hardly think there is, now, any doubt about our getting the robe but it may take a little time to get possession. After reading this you had better send it to Mr. La Flesche so he will know why I did not write him the second time.
Yours very truly,
E. J. DeBell

Little did he or Fletcher know that, in fact, the Robe's return would have to wait almost another century and that it would join the Sacred Pole in Nebraska rather than in the Peabody Museum. Finally, on September 25, 1899, DeBell wrote giving the "gutterman's" name: "I just got a letter from Mr. C. F. Gunther 212 State St. Chicago who has your White Buffalo and says that he is investigating the matter and will write me again soon. Have patience my friend. Everything comes to those who wait." On February 20, 1900, DeBell wrote Fletcher a long letter reporting on his negotiations with Mr. Gunther and suggesting that the only way to convince him to give up the Sacred Hide would be to obtain an affidavit from Mark Flowers admitting to the theft and one from Wakon'monthin declaring his original ownership on behalf of the tribe.

Chicago 2/20/1900
My Dear Miss Fletcher,

I just got your letter today from home. As soon as I received it I went right down and saw Mr. Chas. F. Gunther 212 State St. and had a talk about the white buffalo robe. He said he had the robe but that he would not give it up until he was convinced that it was your robe and not his. I asked him what would convince him that it was your robe. He said that there must be something official to show that it was yours. I think the best way you can do it is to write Mr. C. P. Mathewson, Agent at Winnebago, and get him to get hold of Mark Flowers who stole the robe from the Omahas (he can find out where Mark Flowers is from the Omahas and Winnebagos or at Sioux City or Dakota Co.) and scare him to make an affidavit setting forth the fact that he took the robe from an Omaha Indian and took it to Warren and sold it or gave it away or put it up as security (which ever way it was) and that he will not be prosecuted unless he refuses to make the affidavit &c.

DeBell concluded by advising Fletcher to have a lawyer present the papers to Mr. Gunther: "If you have to go to law about the matter I would not pay him a cent after that." Gunther must have been feeling some pressure after this visit from the straightforward DeBell. Sometime later that year he delivered his prize to the Chicago Academy of Sciences for display as a loan, where it was intentionally misidentified as "Skin of albino Buffalo (Bison americanus) worshipped by the Winnebago Indians as a god (Wakunta) and believed to be several hundred years old." The pipe was wrongly described as being made of pipe clay (letter from F. Williams to Alice Fletcher August 19, 1900).

Following DeBell's advice, La Flesche took several affidavits from Wakon'monthin describing the stolen objects and asserting his continued ownership of them. Despite cooperation from Agent Mathewson, it appears that Mark Flowers could not be persuaded to admit to the theft. The first of Wakon'monthin's affidavits was dated March 19, 1900. In it, the keeper stated:

> I sold the ritual connected with the sacred articles to Mr. Francis La Flesche, a member of the Omaha tribe, and that since said sale I had determined to let Mr. La Flesche take the Buffalo Hide and Pipe, to be deposited with other sacred articles of the Omaha tribe in the Peabody Museum of Harvard University, Cambridge, Mass., so that all the sacred articles which once belonged to the Omaha tribe might be kept together.

On June 11, 1900, Peabody director Putnam wrote Gunther a personal plea, reminding him that they had met at the recent world's fair and that Gunther had shown him his "interesting and valuable collection." He patiently explained that "the hide and pipe were stolen from their ancient keeper in the early spring of 1898, only two or three months before the ceremony of their transfer to this Museum was to take place." He informed Gunther that Fletcher and La Flesche were preparing to publish an account of Omaha sacred rituals, and he concluded that the Hide's loss:

> has been greatly lamented by the Omahas who regard it as a great disaster to the tribe, and they are unhappy until the objects are recovered and placed with their fellows. Of course, you will at once realize the great scientific importance of having all preserved together in order to illustrate the singular story of Indian life of which they are the material part.

I am confident, dear Mr. Gunther, that with this statement you will be willing to do your good part by making the hide and pipe over to this Museum, that all this past history of the Omahas may be brought out and the objects perpetually cared for here, in order as an old Omaha said, "that their children should be able in future times to see and understand the methods and thought of their fathers."

I personally beg of you to do this generous act that this material may be kept together; and I assure you that the Chicago Academy of Sciences shall not be the loser by the withdrawal of these objects from its cabinet.

With pleasant memories of the past,
I am, dear Sir,
Yours very truly,
F. W. Putnam

Five days later Mr. Gunther sent Putnam a terse rejection:

G. F. Gunther
Confectioner
212 State st. CHICAGO
June 16, 1900
Dear Sir,
In reply to yours would say that I do not care to part with the Sacred Hide at present. I am informed that the hide was *not stolen*, but traded with the Indians who had it, whiskey being one of the articles they took in trade. I no nothing of the pipe you mention, never saw it. I purchased the hide from an Editor at Warren, Ill., who got it from the man who traded with the Indians.
Yours truly,
G. F. Gunther

On August 30, 1900, the keeper gave another declaration asserting his ownership and describing the stolen artifacts:

Wa-komon-ne (James Robinson), a member of the Omaha tribe of Indians of Thurston County, Nebraska, being first duly sworn on oath and according to law, deposes and says: that he is eighty-five years old: that the Omaha indian tribe owned and kept a number of years ago a white buffalo skin and a pipe known as the "Sacred Buffalo Skin and Sacred Pipe" of the Omahas: that said articles were used by the tribe in the performance of its sacred ceremonies and ritualistic rites: that said Sacred Buffalo Skin was a complete hide of a buffalo, white in color, with shell disks fastened along its back from between its ears to the tail,

223

and that to each of the four legs of said skin was fastened a woven belt, such as is worn by the men of the Omaha tribe as belts or head dresses, and that the entire hoofs were left fastened to the said buffalo skin: that the Sacred pipe was peculiar and extraordinary in shape and form, being round like a disk, with a hole in the center for a bowl, and that for ornamentation the picture of the hoof or track of the buffalo was marked with lines, the hole for the bowl being in the center of the hoof, and that said pipe was unlike any other pipe used by the tribe.

And affiant further says that while the above described Sacred Buffalo Skin and Sacred Pipe were in the property of the Omaha tribe of Indians for about thirty-three years prior to about 1870, the affiant was duly elected and authorized keeper and custodian of said Sacred Buffalo Skin and Sacred Pipe and that during the time that said property was in affiants care and custody as above stated, and about 1870, the performances of the sacred ceremonies and rite by members of the Omaha tribe were discontinued and permanently abandoned: that at that time and while affiant was still in undisputed possession of said property the entire right, title, interest and ownership of said Sacred Buffalo Skin and Sacred Pipe were transferred and conveyed to affiant and that since that time affiant has been recognized by the members of the Omaha tribe as the owner of said sacred property and entitled to the entire use and possession thereof: and that at no time has affiant voluntarily relinquished his title or right to the possession of said Sacred Buffalo Skin and Pipe.

Affiant further says that after he had acquired title to said sacred property and while the same were in his possession as above set forth, the said Sacred Buffalo Skin and Sacred Pipe were by some person or persons, unknown to him, taken, stolen and carried away without his consent and he was thereby deprived of the possession thereof.

Affiant further says that said Sacred Buffalo Skin and Sacred Pipe are his property at the present time.

And further affiant saith not.

Signed Wa-kamon-ne + his mark James Robinson

in the presence of

Joseph J. Eukin

Susan La Flesche Picotte

Subscribed in my presence and sworn to before me this 30 day of August, A.D. 1900. Harry L. Keefe, Notary Public

In June 1901 a member of the tribe, R. Dorsey Stabler, wrote Putnam asking for information about the Sacred Hide. Putnam replied on July 3, 1901:

I wrote some time ago to Mr. Gunther asking him to make it over to the Peabody Museum; but up to this time he has not felt inclined to do so, claiming that he bought the hide and other objects with it in good faith and they belong to him. I regard it, however, that he is simply the recipient of stolen property. But of course if he is not inclined to give them up, a legal process would be necessary, and that I should not wish to enter into.

With the Peabody unwilling to bring legal action against Gunther, Fletcher and La Flesche were at a loss to find a way of reuniting the Hide with the Sacred Pole. Then, in 1904, a Mr. Walter C. Wyman wrote Fletcher expressing his desire to assist her in recovering the stolen items.

Union League Club
Chicago
Sept. 1st '04
My dear Miss Fletcher,

I am happy to be able to report that in a visit with Mr. Gunther this morning I have started him in your direction, and believe if you will write him immediately, referring to my having discussed this subject you will be Rewarded by the shipment of the prized skin. Mr. Gunther said if he would be given full credit as the donor he would be more disposed to contribute the specimen than to accept pay for it and I would suggest to you to proceed with profuse assurances of the acknowledgments that will be made to him for securing and giving this valuable object to the cause of science etc. in such a permanent and dignified institution as "Peabody" and I would go farther and mention that a notification to the tribe of Omahas will also be made of his generosity in restoring to the Pole and such other emblems his portion of the rituals and arrange if you can some recognition from their Chief to Gunther of the sort—all this will tickle his pride and win for the central object I am quite sure. He does not seem to remember having the pipe tho you spoke as if it was with the hide so that we had better refer to it. I can assure you of my pleasure in applying the process of asking and trying to impress upon him the proper thing to do after hearing of strong expression of regret at the separation of the objects. The delightful evening we passed in Washington will linger in my memory. With best wishes and regards.
Sincerely yours,
Walter C. Wyman

In another letter, dated only "Tuesday," Wyman gives Fletcher instructions about meeting Gunther in person at an anthropological congress in Saint Louis.

> My dear Miss Fletcher,
> Your kind acknowledgments of my efforts with Mr. G to secure the "Robe" were duly read and make me feel the more anxious for my words to have their full effect. I am trying to get away for the rest of the week from the city. Am yet uncertain of leaving other work. I wanted to write you however the information that Mr. Gunther is in St. Louis now but you may not have seen him. Would suggest your trying to find him and make a personal appeal to him now that I have broken the ice. I have no clue to his stopping place but am sure he will be found at the meeting, around the congress, or about the anthropological Bldg. where someone will identify him—a dapper man of about 60 with white hair, mustache, imperial and ruddy face. I'm sure he is in a state to act upon your appeal but you must pin him down with a card giving shipping directions &c. very explicitly or if I were you I should offer to come here and get it and thus you will be sure as he is in many ways a forgetful man with a multitude of matters occupying his mind constantly. With best wishes and kindest regards,
> Sincerely yours,
> Walter C. Wyman

There is no record of whether Fletcher ever met Gunther in person. Wyman, however, seems to have been acting in bad faith and actually wanted the objects for his own collection. Gunther did not send the Hide to Fletcher. The search for a solution came to a halt. Putnam refused to take legal action and no other recourse presented itself. Documents that came to light much later revealed that in 1928, Mr. George G. Heye, founder of the Heye Museum of the American Indian in New York, purchased the following items from the estate of Walter C. Wyman:

Items # 25   1 white buffalo robe, old, tattered, poor condition Plains
        ["Plains" scratched out and "Omaha" handwritten in]
    # 33   1 platform pipe, catlinite, goes with Item 25

It is unclear whether George Heye ever discovered the true identity of his new acquisitions, although at some point, curator Gary Galante of the Heye Museum knew enough to identify the Hide as "sacred" rather than simply "old, tattered, poor condition" and to catalog it with reference to the relevant pages in *The Omaha Tribe*. In the 1970s the Peabody Museum initiated further correspondence with the Chicago Academy of Science but was unable to learn anything more about what had happened. The Heye did not seem inclined to let the Peabody know that it had acquired the long-lost sacred object.

So matters rested until 1982, when Dennis Hastings wrote the Heye Museum asking for a list of its Omaha holdings. To his great surprise, among items such as leggings, flutes, bags, rattles, dried squash, and buffalo meat, were items 179687, "Sacred Albino Buffalo Skin," and 179688, "Catlinite Pipe." Also listed were medicine bundles and tattooing implements. Dennis suspected that the Peabody would claim the sacred objects if it learned of their true identity and he surmised that curators at the Heye knew what they had but also chose to keep the information to themselves. Accordingly, Dennis decided not to make his discovery public until he felt that the tribe was in a position to assert a claim that would take priority over that of the Peabody.

Significant changes in the relationship between museums and Native Americans were taking place at about the time the Omahas were negotiating for the return of the Sacred Pole. In 1990 Congress passed NAGPRA, the Native American Graves Protection and Repatriation Act. The Smithsonian Institution was also developing a plan to establish a National Museum of the American Indian. The core collections for the new flagship museum would come from their acquisition of the Heye. The time now seemed right for the tribe to act upon the discovery Dennis had made in 1982. Doran and a delegation of Omahas were planning to visit New York to introduce "The Return of the Sacred Pole" at a Native American film festival in April 1991. Accordingly, Doran phoned Heye Museum Assistant Curator Gary Galante in March and then wrote him as follows:

March 12, 1991
Dear Sir:
It was indeed a great pleasure speaking with you on the telephone this day, talking with you about one of the great concerns of our tribe, the White Buffalo Hide. The other sacred properties have come home, the Buffalo Hide would complete the most sacred circle in the culture of our people.

The good "Lord" certainly must be looking at our tribe, for all of these good things to come about. It still amazes me that our "Sacred Pole" was sent back to us without any problem.

Your forthright attitude concerning our White Buffalo Hide is greatly appreciated by myself and on behalf of the Omaha Tribe we thank you.

We are aware of Federal Law, but we would ignore it for the purpose of sitting down face to face and in good faith work out all the details of those "objects" that would be returned.

We have your list of properties of our tribe and we would expect them to be put on the table along with the "Sacred Pole."

I will be in New York City on the following dates, April 19, 20, and 21, 1991. I would appreciate it very much if a meeting could be set up so that we can come to an early conclusion on our matter. In conclusion, let me once again thank you very much for your concern.

Respectfully Yours,

Doran L. Morris, Sr.

Chairman

Omaha Tribe of Nebraska

Gary Galante took immediate action in a report to his curatorial council, dated March 27, 1991. After a summary of the Hide's significance to the tribe, he wrote:

In 1928, the Sacred White Buffalo Hide of the Omaha Tribe was acquired by George G. Heye from the estate of Walter C. Wyman. It is now part of the collections of the NMAI [National Museum of the American Indian], (catalog number 17/9687). Because this object is sacred; constitutes communal property; and must be regarded as stolen property, it is imperative that its return to the Omaha be effected without delay.

The visit of Omaha elders and tribal leaders to New York was emotional for them. For the first time since Mark Flowers had taken the Hide from Wakon'monthin's tent in 1898, Omahas once again looked upon Tethon'ha, and her Holy Pipe. The sudden appearance of these sacred objects must have seemed as miraculous to them as it had when Wakon'monthin sang the first of the Holy Pipe's nineteen songs in ceremony more than a century before:

The Holy Pipe!
Holy, I say.
Now it appears before you.
The Holy Pipe, behold ye!

Following the visit, Doran wrote to Richard West, director of the National Museum of the American Indian:

April 29, 1991

Dear Mr. West:

Recently, a couple members of the Omaha Tribal Council and I had the good fortune to meet face to face with our heritage in the form of our White Buffalo Hide, one of our sacred pipes, and a full-length eagle feather head-dress. This meeting was historic in that we were the first Omahas, in over 100 years, to come in actual physical contact with our past. Needless to say, the event elicited much emotion and great empathy with our heritage.

In our discussion with Mr. Gary Galante, Assistant Curator of the National Museum of the American Indian, we informed him that we, the Omaha Tribe, would like to reclaim what is rightfully ours. Mr. Galante has referred us to you. It is our understanding that there is to be policy development for the repatriation of Indian tribal artifacts with those respective Tribes. However, we also understand that this will probably occur over a period of three to four years. The Omaha Tribe does not want to wait that long.

The Omaha Tribe has been most successful in its repatriation efforts. Within the last two years we were able to have our Sacred Pole returned to us from the Peabody Museum in Boston. Currently, we have an arrangement with the University of Nebraska Museum for safekeeping our national heritage items until we complete construction of our own museum.

We are therefore requesting that the above three items be returned to the Omaha Tribe of Nebraska as soon as possible in addition to those listed on the enclosed inventory. We say as soon as possible because it does take time in which to accomplish a major task such as this. Your cooperation and support would be greatly appreciated and we look forward to working with you on this matter. We are also making plans for the receipt with the University of Nebraska and can therefore assure you that we are taking all the necessary precautions to protect and preserve the historical artifacts of our past. We ask this in good faith and we hope you will also receive this request in that same manner.

We look forward to hearing from you and working with you on this matter of great concern to the people of the Omaha Tribe of Nebraska.

The National Museum of the American Indian was swift to reply. Following an exchange of letters, museum director Richard West agreed to the immediate return of the objects that had been stolen from Wakon'monthin. On August 3, 1991, Director West, Deputy Director Dave Warren, staff person Duane King, and curator Gary Galante flew with the White Buffalo Hide and its pipe to Eppley Airfield in Omaha. The following day they drove to Macy with an Omaha tribal police escort. At 3:00 P.M. on August 4, they presented the sacred objects to the tribe. I was privileged to witness this powerful moment in the life of the tribe. As I sat in the tribal police cruiser, listening to officer Ben Cline on the radio making final arrangements for the Hide's entry into the pow-wow arena, I could not help thinking how happy La Flesche would have been had he known the story of how this sacred object returned to his people. He would have particularly appreciated the intelligence, vision, and determination which Dennis Hastings brought to his role as tribal historian, and he would have been happy to hear Doran Morris as he spoke to the assembled people:

> To the visitors that are here today, I want to thank you for being here, witnessing part of the Omaha tribe's culture. It was about two years ago that we brought the Sacred Pole that belongs to the Omaha tribe back. History tells us that the Sacred White Buffalo Hide and the Sacred Pole were once together amongst our people. Back in history these items were the central part of the Omaha tribe's lives, and the Omaha tribe considered these items sacred. And a lot of people think about and say that sacred is what we cannot see touched, but sacred means that we can see and touch and practice the religion that we have.

> These items back in history were amongst our people, and our people did touch and see the Sacred White Buffalo Hide and the Sacred Pole. Like I said, these items were a central part of our people. If the tribe went on the buffalo hunt, they approached these items and prayed through them to the Almighty for a good buffalo hunt. They moved their camp from one place to another; they did these things, prayed through these items. And today, I feel happy and glad that these items are back together again. It will be placed at the University of Nebraska Museum. As soon as they get through here, the Sacred White Buffalo Hide will be going back to Lincoln, Nebraska.

> A question always asked of me, what significance the Sacred White Buffalo Hide plays amongst the Omaha tribe today. I tell them that there is a big gap in our history and these items were taken from here. They were not taken appropriately. They were stolen from the Omaha tribe. So that gives me a mixed feeling. It sort of makes me disappointed in how these items left this reservation. Once again, we have these items back again amongst us, and I feel proud of that fact. The Omaha tribe today is working on getting a museum that we can store these specific items for the children that we have on the reservation today; also the children that are not here. This is the purpose we're doing this. That our tribe would be one people, one unit, like we used to be, back in history. We hope that can happen again.

> Today we have a gentleman from the Smithsonian Institution in Washington DC who has accompanied the Sacred White Buffalo Hide to the Omaha reservation. I'd like to introduce Mr. Dave Warren, who will briefly make a statement. He's the deputy director of the Museum of the American Indian, Smithsonian Institution.

Mr. Warren then spoke on behalf of himself and of the museum director, Richard West:

> Thank you. I'd like to introduce two of my colleagues who have accompanied me in bringing home the White Sacred Buffalo Hide. I'd like to introduce Gary Galante, who's been the curator in charge and a key person in terms of our staff in helping the trustees of the National Museum of the American Indian with the documentation on this item. I'd like to also introduce Dr. Duane King, who's the assistant director, the director of the National Museum of the American Indian, George Gustav Heye Center, which is in New York City. As many of you know, the National Museum of the American Indian is the latest or the newest member of the Smithsonian Institution, becoming part of a large complex of museums and galleries which literally stretch throughout this world. It is, however, the first national museum in the federal government which is solely dedicated to the history, the culture, and to the support of the contemporary Indian people.

Deputy Director Warren then read a statement by Richard West, who was unable to present it in person:

> I must begin by apologizing for not being with you on this most important of days for the Omaha people. I unfortunately had a previous long-standing obligation that had to be honored when we recently began to work with the Omaha tribe to select a date for the return of the Sacred White Buffalo Robe and Pipe. I can assure you, however, that although absent physically, I feel very much with you in spirit today. I also want to take this opportunity to pay tribute to a member of our staff who has played an extremely central and constructive role in the events leading up to this occasion. Gary Galante, a member of the curatorial staff of the National Museum of the American Indian, conducted the vital historical research that was necessary to enable the board of trustees of the museum to reach the determination that today brings these incomparable objects home. I am grateful to him for the sensitive and conscientious role that he played in this matter, and I am sure that you are too.
>
> As I thought about the return of these cultural materials that are so central to the religious and ceremonial life of the Omaha people, my mind turned to a stunning and indeed horrifying quotation that is attributed to Captain R. H. Pratt, the first superintendent of the Carlisle Indian Boarding School in Carlisle, Pennsylvania. This was his statement:

A great general has said that the only good Indian is a dead one. I agree with that, but only in this; that all the Indian there is in the race should be dead. Kill the Indian, save the man.

That quotation always has had a special meaning for me because my grandmother, Rena Flying Coyote, the daughter of Thunder Bull, a chief of the Southern Cheyenne, was sent to Carlisle in the 1890s to cease being an Indian and to be trained as a domestic in one of the great houses near Philadelphia. I always have been personally grateful that Captain Pratt's intended cultural destruction was a dismal failure in the case of my grandmother, who remained a fiercely Cheyenne woman all of her life.

Today the National Museum of the American Indian corrects another wrong that grew out of the tragically misguided notions of Captain Pratt and others like him. In the late nineteenth century when the overriding purpose of federal Indian policy was to ensure that all the Indian there was in the race should be dead, the Sacred White Buffalo Robe and the pipe were taken from the Omaha people, quite literally stolen, according to our research and investigation of the record.

We now complete a simple act of justice by returning property that is not ours. In so doing, however, we affirm much more in my view. We affirm that the Indian in us is not dead. We affirm that our culture, notwithstanding the tremendous adversity, continues to live and to sustain all of us into the future, as it has through the millennia. We affirm the place in our lives of materials such as those that are being returned to the Omaha people today. And that, in the end, is a precious and vital aspect of the very vision that drives the National Museum of the American Indian.

Mr. Chairman, members of the tribal council, the Omaha tribe, friends and visitors, we wish to speak on behalf of the trustees of the National Museum of the American Indian and to bring to a conclusion our part of a journey that began one hundred years ago. We bring this home to you in hopes that it will restore the peace and the happiness that, we read from the record, was taken at the time of its disappearance. With this, we officially withdraw our role in the handling and in the care of this robe, and return it to its owners. Thank you.

Director West's remarks bring to mind the first of the Holy Pipe's nineteen songs:

The Holy Pipe!
Holy, I say.
Now it appears before you.
The Holy Pipe, behold ye!

The Holy Pipe!
Holy, I say.
Now it appears before you.
The Holy Pipe, behold ye!

The Holy Pipe!
Holy, I say.
Now it appears before you.
The Holy Pipe, behold ye!

The Holy Pipe!
Holy, I say.
Now it appears before you.
The Holy Pipe, behold ye!

Epilogue

A BLESSING
Indian stories do not begin and end like the lines of words that make up a book. Rather, they start and stop at meaningful points within a circle. The return of Umon'hon'ti and Tethon'ha and the reburial of the people from Ton'wontonga mark important points in the circle of Omaha tribal history. Later generations may look on these events as important beginnings rather than as endings. The sacred objects are together, for the time being, at the University of Nebraska State Museum in Lincoln. As Richard West said, the reunion of these sacred emblems promises to restore the peace and happiness that was taken from the tribe during the last two decades of the nineteenth century.

As time passes and people slowly reacquaint themselves with the ceremonial traditions that were suppressed more than a century ago, the idea of having the sacred objects permanently housed on the reservation is beginning to take hold of peoples' imagination. Plans are now underway to develop a tribal interpretive and cultural center on a beautiful wooded site overlooking the Missouri River. The blessing these objects bring comes from a long time back and extends for a long time into the future. Umon'hon'ti is a venerable man. He has been patient through centuries of tribal history. That shared history is ongoing. The Omahas have survived as a people. Now that he has returned to Omaha hands, his life and the life of the tribe are gradually coming together once again. Dennis and I hope that this book, *Blessing for a Long Time*, will live up to its name and turn the thoughts of contemporary Omahas and their descendants toward the rich heritage that was kept so carefully by the ones who went before.

I hope that contemporary Omahas will continue to revere their Sacred Pole and come to respect the work of their own tribal member, Francis La Flesche. His dedication to the integrity and beauty of Omaha ceremonial language during the darkest days of oppression has, more than anything else, made this renewal of contact with the past possible. La Flesche knew that the ancient ceremonies had to be performed in perfect order. He knew that it would not be possible or appropriate for the tribe to attempt to reproduce them exactly. Rather, he hoped to provide knowledge of the past that would serve to inform future generations about tribal identity. In this, I believe, he succeeded.

HE MADE THE SONG TO HOLD THE WORDS

I completed the manuscript for this book in June 1996 and, following positive responses from academic readers Regna Darnell and Larry Zimmerman, returned to Nebraska in early October to meet with Dennis and sign a contract with the University of Nebraska Press. We agreed that his share of whatever royalties the book might generate should go to support the Omaha Tribal Historical Project. Then Dennis produced a bombshell in the form of a letter from Francis La Flesche to F. W. Putnam regarding an Omaha skeleton Francis had proposed to obtain for the Peabody Museum in 1890. Dennis had found the letter in a collection of Peabody Museum papers that Joan Mark made available to him some time ago. He told me he had known about it since before the Sacred Pole's return, but kept it to himself so that I could write about Francis strictly on the basis of his work as a writer and interpreter of Omaha tradition. I reported my finding to Gary Dunham, Native American studies editor for the University of Nebraska Press:

> The bombshell was this. In a letter from 1890, Francis wrote Putnam promising to obtain an Omaha skeleton for him. Dennis told me he has known about this letter since before the Sacred Pole came home and has been tormented by it. He said he didn't show it to me until now so that I could write up the story based on the record of what Francis accomplished. Now, he says, it should be added to that record.
>
> What I would like to do is report on it in the context of how Dennis brought it to my attention. I think that is an important part of the story. La Flesche was his role model for many years and discovering how deeply he had bought into the anthropology of his day was a personal shock and disappointment. Tribal people who have learned of the letter tend to react by condemning everything La Flesche wrote, which I think is an overreaction. I will mull this all over when I get home and work it into the book.

This is the letter Francis wrote Putnam:

> Washington D.C.
> Sept. 21, 1890
> My dear Mr. Putnam,
>   I have written to Miss Fletcher about an Omaha skeleton which I want to try and get for the Museum and have asked her to get some in-

formation from you as to how long it takes for bones to decay and crumble. The skeleton I am thinking of is of a man who was struck by lightning in 1876 or 77. There was no mound raised over his grave and I thought for that reason the moisture of the ground has reached the remains and rotted it so that it might be worthless. If you think it worth while to examine the skeleton I could have it taken up.

It would be very interesting to have the bones of that man with the first set of sacred articles you got from us as he was closely connected and in fact was in direct line of the hereditary keepers of these sacred articles. His brother was killed by lightning also and it is said that they were both killed in that manner for having slighted those things.

I write you this because it takes a long time for letters to reach Miss Fletcher from here and if you want that skeleton it had better be taken before the ground is frozen. I thought best to write direct to you so as to get the information sooner.

There is a field over the grave now so there will be no risk of giving offense to any who may be interested, if we take the bones up. Answer soon.

Yours sincerely,

F. La Flesche

(Peabody Museum Papers)

Besides being quite a shock, the letter is extraordinarily interesting. The bones Francis proposed to exhume were not simply those of a distant ancestor, like the ones from the people of Tonwon'tonga. They belonged to a particular individual, someone Francis had known personally. He was a member of Francis's own We'zhinshte (Elk) clan, a relative of Mon'hinthinge, the last keeper of the Tent of War, and a person who was said to have been struck by lightning "for having slighted these things." Francis wrote the letter just two years after his own father had died, following Yellow Smoke's telling of the story belonging to the Sacred Pole. As he wrote to Putnam immediately after his father's death, "The people are yet in the shackles of superstition and it will be hard to make them believe that my father's death was in no way the result of the taking away of the pole."

Francis had an obvious interest in denying the widespread belief that he had contributed to his father's death by removing the Sacred Pole and transforming it into an ethnographic specimen. He wanted to prove, at least to himself and to Putnam, that such beliefs reflected only "the shackles of superstition." Taking the bones of a man once responsible for the Tent of War mirrored his taking the Sacred Pole. In both cases, he transformed an Omaha person into an ethnographic specimen. In both cases, he removed something sacred from an Omaha context and gave it up to the secular context of Western science. In both cases, he rejected "superstition" in favor of "science." In both cases, what he did went to the heart of his personal conflict about being both an Indian and an ethnographer.

Why did Francis think it would be interesting to bring the bones together with the sacred objects from the Tent of War? There could have been no scientific reason for bringing these particular bones and sacred objects together, even in the context of a nineteenth-century physical anthropology devoted to racial taxonomy. The connection seems to have been entirely his own. Exhuming the bones somehow reinforced his belief that the culture was dying and could be preserved only as an ethnological specimen. Did Francis actually take the bones? A letter to Putnam dated October 5, 1890, indicates that he went so far as to engage someone "to go to work and find the skeleton I wrote you about" (Peabody Museum papers). It is up to the tribe to deal with the consequences of this information. Should the Peabody be holding these bones, it would be obliged under federal NAGPRA legislation to return them.

How does this information effect a reading of Francis and his work? The work remains, whatever else Francis may have done in the service of anthropology. Like a moment of experience within the story of a person's life, a story in the life of an Indian people is constantly taking on new meanings, as the context within which you understand it widens. Dennis wanted me to write about Francis in the context of his splendid documentation of Omaha poetics. I have done so, while pointing out that Francis worked in the shadow of an oppressive government whose aims were furthered by the anthropology of the day. You, the reader, must make sense of the information Dennis and I have made available to you. If Francis were alive today he might repeat the words of the Wathon' who led the buffalo hunt; "Pity me who belong to you."

Something that may assist you in understanding Francis is a story he wrote around 1895 called, "The Song of Flying Crow." It describes his experience during a summer when he set up a tipi on the reservation. One evening "we filled a huge pipe which we passed around and smoked. A fire was lighted so that we could see each others' faces, and being in a reminiscent mood we began tales of our own adventures and those of men in other days." Following the stories, a friend suggested, "Let's sing some of the old songs that used to stir the warlike feelings of the men who lived and died long ago." Francis went on to describe how "a little old man" began to sing:

> In a clear and musical voice the little old man gave the first bar of a song familiar to us all and we took it up and made the hills around echo with the sounds of the song. Of the thousands of songs in the tribe I knew a

few, some five or six hundred, so I did my part of the singing and enjoyed the thrill of the rhythm.

As Francis and his companions sang from the repertory of He'lushka songs, the Tent of War and the lightning-struck man who might have kept it cannot have been far from his mind. He was compelled, however, to remain silent regarding what he had experienced. There was no one with whom he could share the story. Taking the bones for anthropology had broken the circle of reciprocity. In "The Song of Flying Crow," Francis went on to describe hearing a song that he did not know:

Many other songs were sung and the story of each repeated just as I had heard it years ago. The little old man complimented my memory for songs, then said, "Let us see if you know this one." He started it and sang with a precision that denoted thorough knowledge of the song. I knew the class to which it belonged, from the vocables used and the terminating notes, but I could not follow, for the song was new to me. "It must be an old one just recalled by some old man." "It is a new song," said the little old man, "made and given to us by your friend Flying Crow just before he died not very long ago."

"How did he come to make the song?" I asked. "He knew he was near death," replied the little old man, "and before he died he wanted to say to his friends some words that would not be forgotten the moment he spoke them, so he made the song to hold the words. He lay in his tent one day, all silent, but thinking of the many, many people who came into this life, endured its hardships, and enjoyed its pleasures for a little space of time, then passed to the land of mystery, the land of spirits. Then he thought of the countless numbers that are to open their eyes to the light of the sun and pass on in the same way. He thought of the lives of the birds, the animals, and the little creatures that crawl and burrow in the earth, how their time, as well as that of men, was measured out long before they were brought to the earth. He had no fear of death but he thought of these things as being full of mystery. Struck with the realization that the duration of life at the longest was but brief he desired his friends to strive to make each other happy so that they may enter the next world without fear and with a joyous spirit. Although the words in the song are few they at once bring to our minds all these thoughts—and the memory of our friend."

"Let's sing it again," I said. "I like it and I must learn it."

We sang it again and again and now it is so fixed in my memory that I shall never forget it even if I should live to be a hundred years old.

It was past the hour of midnight when my friends took leave of me to go to their homes among the hills. I could hear their voices in the still night until they gradually died away in the distance, then I took to thinking of the song I had just learned and its maker, Flying Crow. We were boys together and went to the same school that was maintained by the missionaries on our reservation for the education of Indian youth. I remember he used to run away quite often and finally he stayed away altogether. He inherited the beliefs of his fathers who for generations had been the keepers of the sacred rites of the tribe. He learned very little of the instructions given in the schoolroom and much less of those given in the chapel which meant nothing to his untutored mind. Born a pagan he died a pagan, with the song of a pagan upon his lips. (Ramsey 1994, 187)

La Flesche took pride in being a knowledgeable performer of Omaha songs. He also took pride in his western education and his role as an anthropologist. While he chose not to acknowledge the places where these two identities were in conflict, he could not avoid conflict altogether. Perhaps he envied his friend Flying Crow for being able "to make a song to hold the words" and for being able to die "with the song of a pagan upon his lips." Like Flying Crow, Francis sometimes ran away from the mission school, but unlike his friend, he was always brought back to the white world the school represented. When he died in 1932 at the age of seventy-five, he was given both a traditional feast and masonic rites.

Because La Flesche took action in the 1880s, Omahas today have been able to renew contact with their most sacred traditions. Umon'hon'ti and Tethon'ha have come home. The story he could not tell has finally come into view, to be seen by all the people. The people of Ton'wontonga have been returned to Omaha land. Ethnological specimens are once again being revered as sacred emblems of tribal identity. As Lawrence Gilpin said, the tribe has "an undivided interest" in Umon'hon'ti and Tethon'ha. With proper care and respect, these sacred objects will continue to bless the Omaha tribe for a long time to come.

It has been an immense privilege to be witness to the story of Umon'hon'ti's return. When I first saw him in a glass case in 1962, I did not think that, a quarter of a century later, I would be addressing him directly in the Omaha tribal arena. Umon'hon'ti spans the life of many generations. Through him, Omahas today may come to know about the elders who cared for him in the nineteenth-century. Through him, they may rediscover a common center. Through him, they may carry a blessing forward to their children and grandchildren. As Lawrence Gilpin said in prayer:

Umon'hon'ti, they make him holy.
From way back in our camp he was the center,
Lived in the center of the people.
And whatever they did, how they lived,
They did it with him, through Wakon'da.
Wakon'da made life in that tree from the earth.
Dadeho, Wakon'da Xube
From God's power he gave that tree.
Father, you made that tree, you gave it life.
You gave it life from the earth.
And that was through your goodness,
Your power from the earth.
Dadeho, Wakon'da Xube

I will leave this place in the circle of stories with the greeting I gave upon entering it:

Aho Inshta'thunda, Hon'gashenu ti agathon kahon.
Ho Inshta'thunda, Sky people; Hon'gashenu, Earth people,
I greet you as both sides of a single house joined here
Together as one people.

All my relations.

Bibliography

Alexander, Hartley B.
1933 Francis La Flesche [obituary]. *American Anthropologist* n.s. 35:328–31.
Bailey, Garrick A., ed.
1995 *The Osage and the Invisible World: From the Work of Francis La Flesche*. Norman: University of Oklahoma Press.
Barnes, R. H.
1984 *Two Crows Denies It: A History of Controversy in Omaha Sociology*. Lincoln: University of Nebraska Press.
Barreis, David A.
1963 Foreword to *The Middle Five*. Madison: University of Wisconsin Press.
Conrad, Lawrence A.
1989 The Southeastern Ceremonial Complex on the Northern Middle Mississippian Frontier: Late Prehistoric Politico-religious Systems in the Central Illinois Valley. In *The Southeastern Ceremonial Complex: Artifacts and Analysis*, ed. by Patricia Galloway. Lincoln: University of Nebraska Press.
Dippie, Brian W.
1982 *The Vanishing American: White Attitudes and U.S. Indian Policy*. Lawrence: University Press of Kansas.
Dorsey, James Owen
1884 *Omaha Sociology*. BAE Third Annual Report. Washington DC: Government Printing Office.
1890 *The Cegiha Language*. Contributions to North American Ethnology, vol. 6. Washington DC: U.S. Geographical and Geological Survey of the Rocky Mountain Region.
1894 *A Study of Siouan Cults*. BAE Eleventh Annual Report. Washington DC: Smithsonian Institution.
Fletcher, Alice Cunningham
n.d. Life History of Joseph La Flesche. Washington DC: National Anthropological Archives 4558, Box 20, item 69, no. 1.
n.d. The Omaha Tribe With Special Reference to the Position, Work and Influ-

ence of Women. Washington DC: National Anthropological Archives 4558, Box 19, item 65, no. 3.

1885 Lands in Severalty to Indians: Illustrated by Experiences with the Omaha Tribe. *Proceedings of the American Association for the Advancement of Science* 33:654–55.

1888 Glimpses of Child-life among the Omaha Tribe of Indians. *Journal of American Folk-Lore* 2:115–23.

1888 The Legends of the Sacred Pole. Washington DC: National Anthropological Archives 4558, Box 19, item 67, no. 9.

1892 Hae-Thu-Ska Society of the Omaha Tribe. *Journal of American Folk-Lore* 5:135–44.

1893 A Study of Omaha Indian Music. Archaeological and Ethnological Papers of the Peabody Museum 1 (5). Reprint, Lincoln: University of Nebraska Press, 1994.

1894 Love Songs among the Omaha Indians. *Memoirs of the International Congress of Anthropology*, ed. by Staniland Wake, 153–57. Chicago: The Schulte Publishing Company.

n.d. Glimpses of Omaha Life [lecture notes]. Washington DC: National Anthropological Archives 4558, Box 19, item 65, no. 2.

n.d. The Omaha Tribe with Special Reference to the Position, Work and Influence of Indian Women [lecture notes]. Washington DC: National Anthropological Archives 4558, Box 19, item 65, no. 3.

Fletcher, Alice C., and Francis La Flesche

1911 *The Omaha Tribe*. Washington DC: BAE Twenty-seventh Annual Report. Washington DC: Smithsonian Institution. Reprint (2 vols.), Lincoln: University of Nebraska Press, 1992.

n.d. Fletcher—La Flesche Papers. Washington DC: National Anthropological Archives 4558, Box 20, item 69, no. 1.

Fortune, Reo F.

1932 *Omaha Secret Societies*. New York: Columbia University Press.

Garrett, Philip C.

1886 Indian Citizenship. *Proceedings of the Fourth Annual Lake Mohonk Conference*, 8–11. In Prucha 1973, 57–65.

Gates, Merrill E.

1885 Land and Law as Agents in Educating Indians. Seventeenth Annual Report of the Board of Indian Commissioners, 17–19, 26–35. In Prucha 1973, 45–56.

Green, Norma Kidd

1969 *Iron Eye's Family: The Children of Joseph La Flesche*. Lincoln: Johnson Publishing Co.

Howard, James H., in collaboration with Peter Le Claire, tribal historian and other members of the tribe

1965 *The Ponca Tribe*. Washington DC: Bureau of American Ethnology Bulletin 195.

James, Edwin
1823 Account of an Expedition from Pittsburgh to the Rocky Mountains, performed in the years 1819 and '20 . . . under the command of Major Stephen H Long. In *Early Western Travels*, vols. 14–17, ed. by Reuben G. Thwaites. Cleveland: Arthur H. Clark, Co., 1905. (Reprinted 1966, University Microfilms, Inc., Ann Arbor.)

La Flesche, Francis
1895 Notes taken in a talk with Wa-ke-de. Washington DC: National Anthropological Archives.
1963 *The Middle Five: Indian Schoolboys of the Omaha Tribe*. Madison: The University of Wisconsin Press.

Lee, Dorothy Sara, and Maria La Vigna
1985 Omaha Indian Music: Historical Recordings from the Fletcher/La Flesche Collection. Washington DC: American Folklife Center, Library of Congress.

Liberty, Margot
1976 Native American "Informants": The Contribution of Francis La Flesche. In *American Anthropology: The Early Years*, ed. by John V. Murra. St. Paul MN: West Publishing, 99–110.
1978 Francis La Flesche, Omaha, 1857–1932. In *American Indian Intellectuals*, ed. by Margot Liberty. St. Paul MN: West Publishing, 45–60.

Lurie, Nancy Oestreich
1966 Women in Early American Anthropology. In *Pioneers of American Anthropology: The Uses of Biography*, ed. by June Helm. Seattle: University of Washington Press, 29–82.

Mark, Joan
1980 *Four Anthropologists: An American Science in its Early Years*. New York: Science History Publications.
1982 Francis La Flesche: The American Indian as Anthropologist. *Isis* 73(269):497–510.
1988 *A Stranger in her Native Land: Alice Fletcher and the American Indians*. Lincoln: University of Nebraska Press.

Mead, Margaret
1932 *The Changing Culture of an Indian Tribe*. New York: Columbia University Press.
1965 Consequences of Racial Guilt. Introduction to 2d ed. of *The Changing Culture of an Indian Tribe*.

Merrill, William L., Edmund J. Ladd, and T. J. Ferguson
1993 The Return of the Ahayu:da: Lessons for Repatriation from Zuni Pueblo and the Smithsonian Institution. *Current Anthropology* 34(5):523–67.

Morgan, Thomas J.

1892 *Indian Courts*. U.S. House. 52nd Congress, 2nd sess. H. Doc. 3088, 28–32. In Prucha 1973, 300–5.

Moulton, Gary E., ed.

1986—*The Journals of the Lewis & Clark Expedition*, vol. 10 to date. Lincoln: University of Nebraska Press.

Myers, Thomas P.

1992 *Birth and Rebirth of the Omaha*. Lincoln: University of Nebraska Museum.

Nasatir, A. P., ed.

1952 *Before Lewis and Clark: Documents Illustrating the History of the Missouri 1785–1804*, vols. 1 and 2, Reprint (vol. 2), St. Louis: St. Louis Historical documents Foundation. Lincoln: University of Nebraska Press, 1990.

National Museum of the American Indian

n.d. Papers Relating to the Sacred White Buffalo Hide of the Omaha Tribe. Washington DC: Smithsonian Institution.

Olson, Paul A., ed.

1979 *The Book of the Omaha: Literature of the Omaha People*. Lincoln: Nebraska Curriculum Development Center.

O'Shea, John M., and John Ludwickson

1992 *Archaeology and Ethnohistory of the Omaha Indians: The Big Village Site*. Lincoln: University of Nebraska Press.

Pairns, James W., and Daniel F. Littlefield Jr., eds.

1995 *Ke-ma-ha: The Omaha Stories of Francis La Flesche*. Lincoln: University of Nebraska Press.

Peabody Museum Papers

n.d. Letters between Alice C. Fletcher, Francis La Flesche, and F. W. Putnam. Cambridge MA: Peabody Museum, Harvard University.

Pratt, Richard Henry

1964 *Battlefield and Classroom: Four Decades with the American Indian, 1876–1904*. Robert M. Utley, ed. New Haven CT: Yale University Press.

Prucha, F. P.

1973 *Americanizing the American Indians: Writings of the "Friends of the Indian" 1880–1900*. Cambridge MA: Harvard University Press.

1976 *American Indian Policy in Crisis: Christian Reformers and the Indian, 1865–1900*. Norman: University of Oklahoma Press.

1984 *The Great Father: The United States Government and the American Indians*. Lincoln: University of Nebraska Press.

Ramsey, Jarold

1994 Francis La Flesche's "The Song of Flying Crow" and the Limits of Ethnography. In *American Indian Persistence and Resurgence*, ed. by Karl Kroeber. Durham NC: Duke University Press, 181–96.

Reinhard, Karl J.
1994 Untitled report on Omaha skeletal remains. Department of Anthropology, University of Nebraska–Lincoln.

Ridington, Robin
n.d. Mottled As by Shadows: A Sacred Symbol of the Omaha Tribe. Unpublished paper.
1987 Omaha Survival: A Vanishing Indian Tribe That Would Not Vanish. *American Indian Quarterly* 11(1):37–51.
1988 Images of Cosmic Union: Omaha Ceremonies of Renewal. *History of Religions* 28(2):135–50.
1992 A Tree that Stands Burning: Reclaiming A Point of View as From the Center. In *Anthropology and Literature*, ed. by Paul Benson. Champaign: University of Illinois Press, 48–72.
1992 A Sacred Object as Text: Reclaiming the Sacred Pole of the Omaha Tribe. *American Indian Quarterly* 17(1):83–99.
1997 All the Old Spirits Have Come Back to Greet Him: Realizing the Sacred Pole of the Omaha Tribe. In *Present is Past: Some Uses of Tradition in Native Societies*, ed. by Marie Mauze. Lanham MD: University Press of America.

Robinson, Victor V.
1982 *The Hu'thuga*. Macy, Nebraska: privately published by Victor V. Robinson.

Tate, Michael L.
1991 *The Upstream People: An Annotated Research Bibliography of the Omaha Tribe*. Metuchen NJ: The Scarecrow Press.

Tibbles, Thomas Henry
1957 *Buckskin and Blanket Days*. Garden City NJ: Doubleday.

Tyler, S. Lyman
1973 *A History of Indian Policy*. Washington DC: United States Department of the Interior.

Welsch, Roger L.
1981 *Omaha Tribal Myths and Trickster Tales*. Chicago: Sage Books.

Wilson, Dorothy C.
1974 *Bright Eyes: The Story of Susette La Flesche, an Omaha Indian*. New York: McGraw-Hill.

Index

Wakon'monthin (*cont.*)
  223–24; reacts to theft of hide, 219;
    records songs of Sacred Pole, 83–84
Walker, Helen Grant, xiii, 167
Wandering Omahas (Poncas), 53
wanon'ce (buffalo surround), 118, 128
Warren, Dave, 200, 229, 231
Warren Academy of Beloit College, 220
Warren Leader, 220
washa'be (feathered staff), 128; and rela-
  tion to Sacred Pole, 71. *See also* buffalo
  hunt
Washa'begle (Shadowed One,
  Umon'hon'ti). *See* Sacred Pole
Washa'be itazhi (subdivision of the
  Tha'tada clan; Bear clan): role of, in
  serving keepers of sacred objects, xi,
  xv, xxvii, 38
Washabe'ton subclan. *See under* Hon'ga
Watha'wa (feast of the count). *See* Wat-
  hin'ethe
Wathi'gizhe subclan of the Inke'sabe, 119
Wathin'ethe (Count of the Hundred);
  and relation to Mark of Honor, 23;
  and relation to the Night Blessed Society, 57, 157–58; and seven grades of
  initiation, 56
Wathon'. *See under* buffalo hunt
Wa'wan (intertribal peace ceremony or
  hako), 7, 66, 99, 103, 107
Waxthe'xe (Mottled as by Shadows). *See*
  Cedar Pole; Sacred Pole of the Omaha
  tribe
Waxthe'xeton (subclan). *See* Hon'ga
Waxthe'xe xigithe (renewal ceremony): attempt to continue, using cattle, 139–
  41; description of, 144–56; description of, in "A Boy Memory," 78–80,
  86; and Holy Tent constructed around

Sacred Tents of the Hon'ga, 77, 85–
  86, 92; last held in 1875, 85, 141; and
  ritual order of songs, 148–53; and
  role of keeper in ceremony, 78–79,
  148–53; and role of keeper's wife, 79–
  86, 139, 153–56; songs of, recorded
  by Wakon'monthin, 82–84; and use
  of seven divinatory arrows, 79, 85,
  139, 153–55, 170. *See also* Sacred Pole
  of the Omaha tribe
Welsch, Roger, xiv, 206
West, Richard, 16, 228, 235; makes
  speech to tribe on return of Tethon'ha,
  231–32
We'bashna (to cut the hair), 115–16
Wejinste gens. *See* We'zhinshte
We'zhinshte (Elk clan), xix, xxiii, 10;
  keeper of Sacred Tent of War always a
  member of, 117, 237; meaning of
  name, 117; responsible for Thunder
  ceremonies, 116–17
White Buffalo Hide. *See* Tethon'ha
Williams, Stephen, 26, 30–31
Wolfe, Cary Alice (Pakason), 184
Wolfe, Clifford, Jr., xiii, 218
Wolfe, Clifford, Sr., xiii, 190; blessing re-
  turned artifacts, 194, 200; interview
  with, in 1985, v, 20–21
Wolfe, Robert, 183
Woods, Silas, 167
Woodworker (Zhongaxe), xix. *See also* La
  Flesche, Francis
Wunder, John, xiv; support for repatria-
  tion project, 206–10
Wyman, Walter C., 225–26

Xthexe (Blue Spot). *See* Mark of Honor
Xu'ka, 38, 114, 147